Kant on Emotions

New Studies in the History and Historiography of Philosophy

Edited by
Gerald Hartung and Sebastian Luft

Volume 8

Kant on Emotions

Critical Essays in the Contemporary Context

Edited by
Mariannina Failla and Nuria Sánchez Madrid

DE GRUYTER

ISBN 978-3-11-126602-2
e-ISBN (PDF) 978-3-11-072073-0
e-ISBN (EPUB) 978-3-11-072074-7
ISSN 2364-3161

Library of Congress Control Number: 2021938842

Bibliographic information published by the Deutsche Nationalbibliothek
The Deutsche Nationalbibliothek lists this publication in the Deutsche Nationalbibliografie;
detailed bibliographic data are available on the internet at http://dnb.dnb.de.

Table of Contents

Section 3: Kant's Emotions and Contemporary Philosophy of Mind

List of abbreviations

Works by Immanuel Kant cited with pagination of *Kants Gesammelte Schriften*.
Königlich Preussischen Akademie der Wissenschaften (Ed.). Berlin: De Gruyter.

Anth	Anthropologie in pragmatischer Hinsicht
BDG	Der eizig mögliche Beweisgrund zu einer Demonstration des Daseins Gottes
Di	Mediationum quarundam de igne succincta delienatio
EEKU	Erste Einleitung in die Kritik der Urteilskraft
FBZE	Fortgesetzte Betrachtung der seit einiger Zeit wahrgenommenen Erderschütterungen
GMS	Grundlegung zur Metaphysik der Sitten
GSE	Beobachtungen über das Gefühl des Schönen und Erhabenen
IaG	Idee zu einer allgemeinen Geschichte in weltbürgerlicher Absicht
KpV	Kritik der praktischen Vernunft
KrV	Kritik der reinen Vernunft
KU	Kritik der Urteilskraft
Log	Logik
MAM	Mutmaßlicher Anfang der Menschengeschichte
MS (RL/TL)	Die Metaphysik der Sitten
MSI	De mundi sensibilis atque intelligibilis forma et principiis
Op	Opus Postumum
PG	Physische Geographie
PND	Principiorum primorum cognitionis metaphysicae nova dilucidatio
Refl	Reflexion
RGV	Die Religion innerhalb der Grenzen der reinen Vernunft
TG	Träume eines Geistersehers, erläutert durch die Träume der Metaphysik
VAZef	Vorarbeiten zu Zum ewigen Frieden
V-Anth/Mron	Vorlesungen Wintersemester 1784/1785 Mrongovius
V-Met-K3/Arnoldt	Vorlesungen Wintersemester 1794/1795 Metaphysik Arnoldt (K 3)
V-Met/Dohna	Vorlesungen Wintersemester 1792/1793 Metaphysik Dohna
V-Met/Mron	Volresungen Wintersemester 1782/1783 Metaphysik Mrongovius
V-Met-L1/Pölitz	Kant Metaphysik L 1 (Pölitz) (Mitte 1770er)
V-Met-L2/Pölitz	Kant Metaphysik L2 (Pölitz, Original) (1790/91?)
V-Mo/Collins	Vorlesungen Wintersemester 1784/1785 Moralphilosophie Collins
V-Mo/Mron	Moral Mrongovius (Grundl.: 1774/75 bzw. 76/77)
V-MS/Vigil	Vorlesungen Wintersemester 1793/1794 Die Metaphysik der Sitten Vigilantius
V-PP/Herder	Praktische Philosophie Herder (1763/64 bzw. 64/65)
VNAEF	Verkündigung des nahen Abschlüsses eines Tractats zum ewigen Frieden in der Philosophie
VUE	Von den Ursachen der Erderschütterungen bei Gelegenheit des Unglücks, welches die westliche Länder in Europa gegen das Ende des vorigen Jahres betroffen hat.

https://doi.org/10.1515/9783110720730-001

Nuria Sánchez Madrid
Introduction

Tuning the Human Mind: The Contemporaneity of Kant's Account of Emotions

Kant's long-neglected account of emotions has only recently begun to receive the attention it deserves, in view of the light it sheds on the manifold features of transcendental philosophy. This volume aims to furnish a contemporary over-view of the Kantian treatment of emotions, yielding a systematic analysis of the capacity of affective phenomena to guide the critical enquiry of reason and the process that Kant calls the "hell of self-cognition" (MS 6: 441). In this vein, all of the chapters in this volume deal with the issues raised by Kant's well-known remark in "What Does it Mean to Orient Oneself in Thinking?", where he asserts that reason itself does not feel, but rather that it produces feelings through inner drives as a "subjective need" [*Bedürfnis*] (WDO 08: 139–140). Using this text as a common jumping off point, the various authors in this volume address how reason itself encourages the human being to feel or eliminate emotions, needs and passions that either enhance or hinder the purposes of the different faculties of the mind. Thus, the following chapters focus not only on the role that emotions play in the faculty of desire, but also address their function within the critique of the faculties of knowledge and judgment. The editors of this volume have tried to balance classical critical readings of Kant's account of emotions (Sánchez Madrid, González, Falcato, Failla, Borges) with approaches that engage Kant's philosophy in a dialogue with contemporary phenomenology and aesthetics (Cvejic, Feloj, Angelucci), as well as with novel lines of research related to philosophy of mind and neuroscience (Teruel, Mendonça, Ros). In assembling this diverse group of appraisals, the editors aim to provide those interested in developing Kantian approaches to rationality with a broad perspective on the attention that Kant devotes to the affective components of the human mind. This volume aims to argue for the contemporaneity of Kant's account of emotions, a goal that explains the chapters' focus on the support that emotions furnish to moral agency and also on its further contemporary reception and development in both continental and analytical lines of research. Thus, the volume attempts to overcome the usual gap between both of these philosophical traditions, insofar as they show a deep debt to Kant's approach to emotion and feeling.

Nuria Sánchez Madrid, Univ. Complutense of Madrid, Spain

https://doi.org/10.1515/9783110720730-002

The volume represents a collection of contributions by both established and emerging European researchers from five countries—Brazil, Italy, Serbia, Portugal and Spain—who have previously discussed papers in international workshops[1] and collaborated on publications,[2] as the frequent cross-references appearing in most of the chapters confirm. The group of contributors chosen reflects a strong commitment to gender equality and aims to foster academic acknowledgement and increased visibility of women philosophers in global scholarship of Kant. All of the authors have demonstrated expertise in Kant and the history of the European Enlightenment, and are specialized in classical European philosophy. As shown in the table of contents, the volume is divided in three main sections—*Mind, Moral Agency and Emotional Normativity, Critical Emotions: On Kant's Aftermath*, and *Kant's Emotions and Contemporary Philosophy of Mind* —which are intended to furnish a comprehensive overview of Kant's account of affective states.

Taken as a whole, the volume claims the existence of an emotional normativity in Kant's philosophy and argues that this model of rationality shows that, in Kant's view, the human being will be able to meet the ends of reason only with the support of the emotions. As previously stated, while historical appraisal is a chief concern of all the chapters, most address the capacity of Kant's philosophy to inspire contemporary research on moral agency and human emotions. The principal topics examined in the collected essays relate to the obstacles and tasks that human nature encounters in Kant's philosophy as it attempts to 1) make sense of worldly phenomena, 2) abide by moral law, 3) experience beauty and natural purposiveness, and 4) find orientation in pragmatic life. In all of these endeavours, emotions do not represent hindrances to the pursuit of truth, beauty and virtue. On the contrary, these values appear clearly embedded into a specific normativity, which enlarges the understanding of the subjective dynamics of reason.

---

1 We might mention, for instance, the Vth Congress of the Brazilian Kant Society (SKB), held at the UFSC (Florianópolis, Brazil) in May 2013, the workshops *Emotional Culture and Identity* and *Feelings and Reflexivity*, organized by the Project CEMID and held in March and November 2015 at the Institute Culture and Society of the University of Navarra (Spain) with Ana Marta González and Alejandro Vigo as convenors, the workshop *Leggere la* Kritik der Urteilskraft *di I. Kant*, held from 10 to 12 April 2017 at the Department of Philosophy, Communication and Spectacle of Roma Tre University (Italy), and the workshop *Rules, Normativity and Values. Revisiting the Kantian Perspective and Its Critics*, held on 14 May 2018 at the Faculty of Philosophy of the New University of Lisbon (Portugal).

2 See Faggion et al. (2016) and Krasnoff et al. (2018).

The first section—*Mind, Moral Agency and Emotional Normativity*—begins with an overview of the image of human epistemic and practical agency within the context of Kant's reflexions on reason, aesthetics, and morals, referencing certain outstanding studies representative of the "emotional turn" that Kantian studies have undergone in recent decades. In "Kant's Emotional Normativity and the Embodiment of Reason: Interests, Reflection and Moral Feelings", Nuria Sánchez Madrid (University Complutense of Madrid, Spain) argues that the interests of reason guide the subject to adopt feelings that do not guarantee the achievement of his own happiness, but rather the accomplishment of theoretical goals which are the product of epistemology. Moreover, Sánchez Madrid highlights that the reflexion on the power of judgment makes the subject acquainted with an emotional state that helps her disavow her own egoistic inclinations and consequently attune her views and reasoning with a universal epistemic pattern. This chapter also examines the fact that, in accordance with Kant's practical philosophy, certain feelings should be cultivated as a way of attaining moral strength and control over one's affective states, and in this way combat human frailty of will.

In "Unpacking Moral Feeling: Kantian Clues to a Map of the Moral World", Ana Marta González (University of. Navarra, Spain) focuses on the analogy between practical reason and moral feeling outlined by Kant. González seeks to unravel texts such as the following excerpt from *What Does it Mean to Orient Oneself in Thinking?*, in which Kant claims that moral feeling "does not cause any moral law, for this arises wholly from reason; rather, it is caused or effected by moral laws, hence by reason, because the active yet free will needs determinate grounds" (WDO 8: 139 – 140). This chapter aims to unpack this text and show the pivotal role of moral feeling as a helpful means of strengthening the *principium executionis* of moral law.

Mariannina Failla (Roma Tre University, Italy), in "Edenic Animality, Self-Sustenance, Loving and Dying: Corporeal Biological Needs and Emotions in Kant", takes a genealogical approach to Kant's account of emotions, with a particular focus on his reflection regarding the beginning of history. By addressing the scope of conjecture and the epistemic value it fulfils in the genesis of history, Failla analyses the close ties between instincts, emotions (*Rührungen*), sentiments (*Gefühle*) and human moral action. She argues that Kant's anthropological interpretation of the Holy Scriptures displays a psycho-corporeal genealogy of human moral agency. In fact, as Kant depicts the progressive emancipation from Edenic instinct, affective states—loss, love, fear, hope—appear as essential steps for giving shape to moral conscience.

The contribution by Ana Cristina Falcato (IFILNOVA/UNL, Portugal)—"Kant and the 'True Shame Instinct': Notes on the Future of the Human Species"—

shares a genealogical approach to Kant's writings on shame, taking issue with claims endorsed by contemporary moral philosophers. Falcato bases her claims on previously ignored textual sources, particularly on remarks from Kant's *Lectures on Anthropology* from the 1760s, which anticipate future critical developments regarding the potentially positive consequences of the so-called shame-instinct. This chapter criticizes the traditional appraisal of Kantian ethics by Anglo-American philosophy, while also addressing some entangled paradoxes in Kant's reasoning about the topic of shame.

The section ends with a contribution by Maria Borges (Federal University of Santa Caterina, Brazil)―"Passions and Evil in Kant's Philosophy"―which focuses on the links between passions and evil in Kant's philosophy. The chapter begins by explaining the difference between affects and passions in *Anthropology from a Pragmatic Point of View*, in which Kant argues that both are illnesses of the mind, given that both threaten the sovereignty of reason. Borges claims that, in Kant's view, passions are much more dangerous to morality than emotions, due to the fact that, from a moral point of view, passions distort the reflective judgment of the subject, thus thwarting any moral agency. The author also examines affects and passions with regard to their varying degrees of propensity to evil in the *Religionschrift*, analysing the ethical community as a necessary device to overcome evil, beyond the scope attained by any of the political and anthropological solutions proposed by Kant.

The second section of the volume―*Critical Emotions: On Kant's Aftermath*―focuses on studies of Kant's emotional treatment from the point of view of contemporary accounts of intentionality and aesthetic normativity. In this vein, in "Intentionality *Sui Generis* of Pleasure in Mere Reflection", Igor Cvejić (University of Belgrade, Serbia) claims that feelings in Kant's philosophy, particularly pleasure in mere reflection, ought to be understood as intentional states, positing, moreover, a feeling-intentionality *sui generis*. This chapter examines Kant's understanding of feelings and engages critically with some conclusions of the readings of the intentionality of affective states by Paul Guyer and Rachel Zuckert. The author argues that outlining a feeling-intentionality *sui generis* may help solve some paradoxes of the interpretation of this issue of Kant's aesthetics.

In "Exemplary Emotions: A Discussion of Normativity in Kant's Aesthetic Judgment", Serena Feloj (University of Pavia, Italy) claims that the sentimentalist elements of Kant's account necessitate a new interpretation of subjective universalism―specifically an appraisal developed from the standpoint of regulativity. As, according to Kant's aesthetical judgment, no value is attributed to an object, rather it is a feeling that is expressed, Feloj ponders whether and under which conditions a feeling can be normative, while also addressing Kant's arguments for assuming a normativity without rules, norms and standards. The chapter mainly aims to discuss the normative character of aesthetic emotions in Kant's *Critique of the Power of Judgment* by taking into account contemporary theories of aesthetics and focusing on notions such as regulativity and exemplarity.

The final chapter of this section aims to show how Kantian thought, and in particular the concept of the sublime, reappears in Deleuze's works on cinema— not so much in the first volume (*The Movement-Image*), where it is explicitly mentioned—but rather as a sort of antecedent of the appearance of time itself, the key topic of the second volume (*The Time-Image*). In "'An Emotion That Seems to Be No Play': Deleuze on Kantian Sublime", Daniela Angelucci (Roma Tre University, Italy) claims that Kant might be considered a precursor of the crystal-image, that is, the genetic moment of the time-image according to Deleuze, one of the most powerful concepts spawned by this thinker.

The third section—*Kant's Emotions and Contemporary Philosophy of Mind*— concentrates on approaches to Kant's account of emotions drawn from contemporary lines of research in philosophy of mind and neuroscience. In "The Ambiguity of Kantian Emotions: Philosophical, Biological and Neuroscientific Implications", Pedro Jesús Teruel (University of Valencia, Spain) suggests exploring the function of emotions through the German notion of *Erregung*, its German-Latin counterpart *Motion*, and its semantic field. Teruel argues that there is a link between the embodied aspect of emotions and the classical treatment of *pathos*, especially regarding the entwined moral phenomenon of *akrasia* and the state of *ataraxia* in Stoic thought, one of the main sources of Kant's moral theory. The author also draws neuroscientific implications from Kant's approach to affective phenomena by arguing that weakness of will can be understood within the Kantian frame of rationality with the help of a naturalized model of causation.

A further exploration of Kantian influence in contemporary philosophy of mind can be found in "Calibration Hypothesis: Rethinking Kant's Place for Emotion and the Brain's Resting State". In this chapter, Dina Mendonça (IFILNOVA/ UNL, Portugal) addresses how the predictive mind hypothesis can be seen as rooted in Kant's model of rationality. This chapter also conducts a renewed examination of the role of emotions in Kantian ethics, and claims that Kantian emotional imagery displays a mediate control over emotional states by integrating the experiences of the subject and calibrating her general emotional structure to better deal with future experiences.

In "Kantian *Lange Weile* Within the Contemporary Psychology of Boredom", Josefa Ros (Harvard University/University Complutense of Madrid, Spain) focuses on both the ancient and modern phenomenon of boredom by engaging Kant's account of this emotional state in a fruitful dialogue with contemporary psychologists and psychiatrists, cognitive neuroscientists, and experts in fMRI technology. With this approach, the author gives an account of the study of boredom within the contemporary psychological and psychiatric mainstream, and compares this with the Kantian anthropological treatment of boredom. Ros argues that Kant's views of boredom disavow understanding this affective phenomenon as a mental pathology, and rather, encourages analysing it within the framework of the socio-economic structures of modernity.

This book has been conceived as an assemblage of ground-breaking European research in the field of Kantian Studies, focusing on an aspect of Kant's philosophy of particular relevance to both contemporary neuronal and social sciences. We hope to have assembled a diverse collection of studies, which analyse important issues while providing formulas for revaluating neglected features of the Kantian model of human rationality. The editors especially thank Victoria Mallorga Hernández and Marshall Weiss for proofreading the volume.

Bibliography

Faggion, Andrea, Pinzani, Alessandro and Sánchez Madrid, Nuria (Eds.) (2016): *Kant and Social Policies*. London: Palgrave Macmillan.
Krasnoff, Larry, Sánchez Madrid, Nuria and Satne, Paula (Eds.) (2018): *Kant's Doctrine of Right in the 21st Century*. Cardiff: University of Wales Press.

Section 1: **Mind, Moral Agency and Emotional Normativity**

Nuria Sánchez Madrid

Kant's Emotional Normativity and the Embodiment of Reason: Interests, Reflection and Feelings

Abstract: This contribution aims to provide an overview of the image of human epistemic and practical agency drawn by reason, aesthetic reflection, and moral feeling, especially within the context of the "emotional turn" that research on Kant's philosophy has undergone in recent decades. This chapter will first point out that reason does not lead the subject to adopt feelings that foster their own happiness, but rather, motivates the individual to seek a theoretical grounding in epistemology. Second, I shall highlight that the reflexion on judgment acquaints the subject with an emotional state that allows her to disregard her own egoistic inclinations and attune her views and judgments with those of others. Finally, I will analyze the fact that, in Kant's view, certain feelings should be cultivated as a way of attaining moral strength and thus becoming better able to both control temporary mental disorders while also progressively overcoming human frailty of will.

Keywords: emotional normativity, interest, reflection, feeling, desire, inclination

This chapter focuses on an issue still somewhat neglected within Kantian scholarship: the emotional features of the transcendental model of reason. The main goal of my account shall be to cast some light on the way that Kant's map of the faculties shows human beings as inhabited by egoistic interests, while also drawing some conclusions about the notion of humanity that results from this view. Even if Kant systematically despises the image of human dignity drawn from

Acknowledgement: This article has been written with the support of the following granted research projects: *Precariedad laboral, cuerpo y vida dañada. Una investigación de filosofía social* (PID2019–105803GB-I0), funded by the Spanish Ministery of Research and Innovation, *Filosofía y pobreza. Una historia cultural de la exclusión social* (PR87/19–22633), funded by the UCM-Banco Santander, and the UCM 2017 Innovative Teaching Project n.º178 *Precarity, Exclusion and Disability. Logics and Subjective Effects of Contemporary Social Suffering*, funded by the University Complutense of Madrid. This chapter was also supported by the Community of Madrid and the European Social Fund, through grant number H2019/HUM-5699 (ON TRUST-CM): *Research Program on Culture of Lawfulness*.

Nuria Sánchez Madrid, Univ. Complutense of Madrid, Spain

https://doi.org/10.1515/9783110720730-003

human inclinations and instincts, he also holds that the purpose of every theoretical endeavour is to apply the rigorous tenets of pure practical reason to even the thorniest edges of the human agent (this can be seen, for example, in a well-known excerpt from *The Metaphysics of Morals*).[1] My chapter will thus mainly tackle Kant's commitment to categorising the order of emotions as a way of guaranteeing an enduring dominance of reason over desires and inclinations,[2] which in turn requires an unbiased inquiry into the affective drives of the human mind. Naturally, Kant was not acquainted with the findings of the psychoanalytical approaches to the human mind of the twentieth century. Yet the Kantian account of emotions displays a keen awareness of the fact that most human emotions belong to the realm of unconscious representations and states of mind, thus clearing a promising path for a dialogue between Kant's philosophy and contemporary research in neuroscience and philosophy of mind—both fields of study that are the focus of some chapters in this volume.

My reading will furnish an overview of the image of human epistemic and practical agency drawn by reason, aesthetic reflection and moral feeling, especially within the context of the "emotional turn" that research on Kant's philosophy has undergone in recent decades. According to Kant's usual critical method, any attempt to analyze the emotional aspects of reason should first acknowledge the difficulty of merely establishing the meaning of the term 'emotion', whose precise definition is fuzzy at best. As Alix Cohen has stated, "Kant's conception of the emotions encompasses a wide array of affective states, including desires, inclinations, affects, and passions, which differ from each other in a number of important ways" (Cohen 2014, p. 4). For this reason, according to Kant, the scholar of emotions should accurately rank, insofar as is possible, the entire range of affective states by their respective motivations and goals. My account is aware of the need to rank this "whole set of affective states", while also going beyond the mere recognition of the existence of a manifold

---

1 See MS 6: 217: "The counterpart of the metaphysics of morals, the other member of the division of practical philosophy as a whole, would be moral anthropology, which, however, would deal only with the subjective conditions that hinder men or help them in *fulfilling* the laws of a metaphysics of morals. It would deal with the development, spreading, and strengthening of moral principles (in education in schools and in popular instruction), and with other similar teachings and precepts based on experience. It cannot be dispensed with, but it must not precede a metaphysics of morals or be mixed with it". All translations of Kant's texts are from the volumes of *The Cambridge Edition of the Works of Immanuel Kant* mentioned in the bibliography of this chapter.

2 See MS 6: 408: "Since virtue is biased on inner freedom it contains a positive command to a human being, namely to bring all his capacities and inclinations under his reason's control and so to rule over himself".

map of emotions in Kant's practical thought, so as to illuminate the fact that they do not display the same traits, given that emotions may ensue from the interests of reason, the reflection of judgment, or the affective moral supports of the subject. It is a curious feature of Kant's appraisal of emotions and changes in emotional states, that he proposes three cases in which these changes may be the effects of drives that the subject is not always consciously aware of. Put differently, in Kant's philosophy, emotional states are often the result of dynamics of the mind that do not entirely overlap with the conscious agency of the subject. Even if the human being and agent remains the unique receiver of the emergence of an emotion in Kant's anthropological approach, not every emotion is a result of a human activity, at least if we understand this as purposeful activity. In this sense, we can see that, in Kant's view, emotions are not seen as simple human reactions to worldly phenomena, but on the contrary, are used to support higher faculties of mind in their ability to improve and fully develop the moral performance of the human agent.

In recent years, the explosion of papers regarding Kant's "impure ethics"—to borrow this felicitous expression from Robert B. Louden—have emphasized the function fulfilled by different sorts of feelings, but focused on these emotions as responses to reason. Here, instead, I first suggest that the interests of reason lead the subject to adopt feelings not as a means toward achieving happiness, but rather aimed at reaching firm epistemological ground. Second, I shall highlight the fact that the reflexion on judgment acquaints the subject with an emotional state that allows her to forget her own egoistic inclinations and to attune her views and judgments with those of others. Finally, I will analyze the fact that, according to Kant, certain feelings should be cultivated as a way of attaining moral strength, and thus improving one's ability to control temporary mental disorder and progressively overcome human frailty of will.

1 Expanded Horizons: Emotional Aspects of Reason

As is well known, Kant grants a heuristic value to the ideas of reason, and thus sets the goal of scientific enquiry as the greatest possible unity of reason (KrV A 679). To this end, the two sections of the "Appendix to the Transcendental Dialectic" of the first *Critique* provide guidance to theoretical reason in its pursuit of the continuous progress of knowledge, which Kant illustrates through the use of a hypothetical object that meets the demands of rational ends. Kant points out at various points within this section of the KrV, that under the requirement of systematicity, reason neither discovers any new noumenal object nor goes beyond the boundaries of experience of this epistemic ideal focus. Under the influence of the drive to unity and wholeness, this aim instead embodies the "conative character of reason", as formulated by P. Kleingeld (1998), yielding maxims, i.e. subjective principles stemming from "reason's feeling of its own need [*Bedürfnis*]" (WDO 8: 136; Kant 1996b, p. 136). Most commentators assume this sentimental life of reason was a metaphorical approach intended to help the reader better grasp the inner dynamics of this faculty, whose aims go far beyond the empirical epistemic purpose of the human understanding. Thus, as the demands of reason surpass the human capacity to obey them in practice, the first *Critique* suggests that an ideal world where rational purposes appear as completely fulfilled would encourage human understanding to overcome every possible material hindrance or subjective misgiving and lead to an all-encompassing hegemony of reason throughout the "land of truth" (KrV B 294). Yet, in a recent paper, the aforementioned scholar A. Cohen seeks to challenge this notion, as she proposes an understanding of rational feelings "in the full non-metaphorical sense of the term" (Cohen 2018, p. 12), that is, as drives guiding the transcendental agency of the epistemic subject. In my view, the key point in a correct assessment of Kant's view of reason as arising in the human mind should disregard the debate between the metaphorical or nonmetaphorical scope of these states of mind. Instead, I claim that the feelings produced by satisfying the interests of reason draw an ideal portrait of a human being that is fully congruent with rational demands and needs. Thus, this emotional dynamic triggered by reason has a normative effect, insofar as it improves the epistemic performance of the understanding and gives the subject a specific confidence for attaining her goals in the field of knowledge. Furthermore, the epistemic improvement of the rational ideas of the subject does not result from any empirical emotion or affect, but rather from the subject's receptivity to the guidance provided by reason, which every rational being cannot help but feel committed to. In this context, Kant chooses vocabulary that highlights the subjective need that the subject wishes to see met by objective reality and by the progress of his main faculty of knowledge, i.e. the understanding. Thus, as occurs in the field of geometrical enquiry, the understanding requires corollaries and postulates to obtain a fully determined picture of its purposes, which can also be expected to have an immensely positive impact on the epistemic performance of each subject. An excerpt from "What Does it Mean to Orient Oneself in Thinking?" hints at the way that reason's maxim of achieving the most systematic knowledge by considering all possible epistemic outcomes of the human species serves as an ideal focus for the human understanding:

> This guiding thread [i.e. the principle of systematicity] is not an objective principle of reason, a principle of insight, but a merely subjective one of the only use of reason allowed by its limits – a corollary of its need. (WDO 8: 140; Kant 1996b, p. 140)

Both the "Appendix to the Transcendental Dialectic" in the KrV as well as "What Does it Mean to Orient Oneself in Thinking?" display an array of textual evidence for the role of emotions as providing subjective support to reason in Kant's transcendental account of this faculty. In fact, as previously mentioned, reason does not require any support, given that it is able to encourage the accomplishment of its own goals. This support, and its emotional features, only become a necessary element as Kant focuses on the shortcomings that the human understanding might face when confronting the impossibly overwhelming goal of the creation of a system of all possible knowledge. Put differently, Kant exhibits a pronounced concern for the negative effects that these frustrating situations might cause for the seeker of knowledge, while also claiming that useful ideals may help the human understanding delude itself and thus overcome its lack of confidence in its own agency. This text establishes a serious tone, to the point that Kant depicts a landscape where human emotions such as fear and laziness—vices disavowed by the claims of Enlightenment—are banned, freeing up space for more hopeful and assertive feelings better able to assist the understanding in the completion of its purposes. It is important to highlight Kant's confidence in ideal rational objects, and the improvement of the resilience of the understanding, as opposed to concern about the hypothetical delusions regarding its own cognitive potential that may stem from a feeling of its own necessity brought about by reason. Kant seems to adopt this more optimistic position as he views reason as destined to take into account both human frailty and the epistemic flaws derived from the inescapable condition of human finitude. The way that reason heeds the boundaries of understanding offers an interesting point that I wish to highlight in this account of the interaction of faculties in Kant's philosophy and its emotional overtones. A central question arises here: is Kant interested in giving a "human face" to reason, insofar as this faculty is able to rescue a frail understanding from the anxiety of failure? Furthermore, assuming the validity of this contention, is there not then a reversal of emotional status between reason and the understanding, such that an emotion like courage, for example, could shift from the space of reason to the one of contingent epistemic agency? The following account shall suggest an answer to both queries.

The previous remarks allow us to draw the preliminary conclusion that the epistemic guidance offered by rational principles sets a clear distinction between the needs of inclination versus the needs of pure reason. Only the latter display the normativity of reason and allow the human mind to meet its own demands by providing a mechanism for overcoming the effects of emotions that can cloud true epistemology. Kant's treatment of aesthetic normativity allows us to further our account of the epistemic value of rational emotions, as the ties between epistemic progress and a distinctive feeling of pleasure confirm that the attainment of the goals set by reason regarding the knowledge of nature coincides with an innate yearning of human nature. As the published "Introduction" of KU points out,

> we are also delighted (strictly speaking, relieved of a need) when we encounter such a systematic unity among merely empirical laws, just as if it were a happy accident which happened to favour our aim, even though we necessarily had to assume that there is such a unity, yet without having been able to gain insight into it and to prove it. (KU 5: 184; Kant 2000, p. 184)

I consider that no other excerpt of Kant is so effective in illustrating the subtle ties between epistemic progress and the emotional reflex that allow for the unhindered subordination of worldly material diversity under common logical laws. Yet my point in this context is not to highlight, for instance, the differences between a rational feeling such as moral respect and the pleasure that the subject experiences upon accomplishing her epistemic goals. Even if the human mind shows receptivity to the systematic horizons of reason, Kant distinguishes between routine, mundane sources of pleasure, and the higher pleasure generated by the cognitive activity of human understanding. In the first case, our inclinations determine the positive feelings we experience, while in the second, reason itself acts as a transcendental guardian of human knowledge. Thus, emotional normativity also appears within the boundaries of theoretical knowledge as a necessary supplement for helping the human being overcome his cognitive flaws. As the subject and his cognitive agency may rely on the guidance furnished by rational ideas, he also receives external inputs that confirm that reason is no longer a source of a real cognitive content, but—as Alix Cohen puts it—a faculty that "enable[s] cognitive activity" (Cohen 2018, p. 23). In my view, this picture of cooperation between human cognitive resources and reason provides a clearer image of human understanding. In a nutshell, reason allows us to grasp a wider logical horizon, and thus enlarges and enriches the image we have of our own epistemic capabilities.

At this point, it is clear that the logical horizon that accompanies all our empirical concepts does not proceed from emotional needs and desires, but rather that it is the effect of higher needs rooted in reason, which, enigmatically, harbour a genuine comprehension for the flaws that the human mind might have. However, it will be useful to recall, in this context, a celebrated statement of

WDO, i.e.: "Reason does not feel; it has insight into its lack and through the *drive for cognition* it effects the feeling of a need [*Bedürfnis*]" (WDO 8: 139 n.; Kant, 1996b, p. 139n). This quote allows me to return to the two questions I have thus far left unanswered. In my view, reason's drive for cognition radically transforms human cognitive agency, insofar as it provides it with a kind of echo, which steadily reminds the subject of the existence of a gap between the logical demands of reason and the empirical outcomes that the human understanding is able to deliver. According to Kant it is not possible to breach this chasm. Yet emotions that only reason could bring about are intended to sustain progress and to guarantee the cohesion of human cognition, thus protecting the human mind from its own epistemic fears. Cohen has suggested an immanent view of the epistemic guidance that rational maxims provide for the subject:

> [B]y relying on reason's regulative function on the basis of the feeling of reason's need, what we are committed to is neither the presupposition of nature's systematic unity nor the duty to seek this unity; rather, we are committed to the activity of cognizing, and ultimately, to rational agency and the improvement of its condition. (Cohen 2018, p. 23)

I wholeheartedly agree with this immanent assumption of the regulative value of rational ideas, as it is the only way to reconcile these with Kant's theoretical normativity. Yet my account aims to shed light on the fact that this immanent use of rational ideas fulfils its purpose as the subject feels the demands raised by a non-human, rational faculty. This voice of reason seems to renounce a complete display of the exhaustive systematicity of knowledge, and thus serves to unfailingly inspire the epistemic labour that the human understanding must execute.

2 Pleasures of Reflexion, Pleasures of Community?

In this section I shall discuss the fact that, according to Kant, the feelings universally conveyed by the judgment of taste blur the boundaries between subjective, egoistic claims, and those that can be applied universally among human beings. Put slightly differently, the phenomenon of beauty, as well as the duties implied by the *sensus communis*, do not contribute to the isolation of the subject, but rather encourage her to seek out the point of view of others. Therefore, by broadening the power of judgment according to the aesthetic rules of taste, Kant upholds that human beings will become more sensitive to social intercourse and also have more opportunities to cultivate their humanity as they become more acquainted with a universal standpoint. Through this training that

acquaints the subject with the conditions of community, Kant promotes a transformation of the human being into a rational and sensible agent able to meet the
challenges of living together with others under a shared normativity. As Angelica
Nuzzo has pointed out, reflective judgment helps us "tune into the resonance of
the universal voice and speak on its behalf" (Nuzzo 2014, p. 99), putting the subject in contact with a specific emotion that attunes her to her maximum potential
as a human. Thus, the standpoint we adopt when making a judgment of taste
sharpens the human capacity to discern the universal under which a particular
case might be inscribed. In this way—as Schiller saw later with acuity—the aesthetic contemplation of the world and of human artistic creations deeply transforms our mind, insofar as it makes us better able to come to ideal agreements
with other subjects without neglecting our constitutive contingency. In fact, the
phenomenon of taste is intended to prepare the subject to suitably react to social
reality without betraying her duties as a moral being. Another remark of Nuzzo's
will be helpful in shedding more light on this point:

> Aesthetic experience is the experience of contingency. Such experience and the search for
> meaningfulness that constitutes it is the cipher of our humanity. [...] Our emotional re-
> sponse to contingency is the subjective alternative to the controlled act of legislation where-
> by understanding and reason institute the objective necessity of their laws. Transcendental-
> ly, the emotions are subjective ways of lending sense to contingency; reflectively, they are
> ways of voicing the awareness of our own contingency. (Nuzzo 2014, p. 102)

I agree with the overview provided by this excerpt regarding the role of emotions
in Kant's philosophy and especially with the principal consequence that Nuzzo
draws from it, i.e. the fact that an understanding of the contingent bonds that
link us with the forms of the world is closely related to our ability to attune
our emotional states to the pleasures considered characteristic of humanity. Indeed, the pleasure derived from taste expands the human capacity to cultivate a
sense of respect and justice with regard to his fellow human beings, which otherwise may remain concealed by the passions characteristic of the social sphere.
At this point we arrive at a question analogous to our earlier investigation regarding the ideas of reason: does the aesthetic duty to achieve a state of *Ein-* and *Zu-
sammenstimmung* with other individual judgments correspond to the natural
psychology of the human mind, or does it rather hint at an elevated, ideal
image of the subject? Does this goal represent the fulfilment of a duty, or is it
more related to social custom? The § 22 of the *Critique of the Power of Judgment*
focuses on precisely this point:

> This indeterminate norm of a common sense is really presupposed by us: our presumption
> in making judgments of taste proves that. Whether there is in fact such a common sense, as

a constitutive principle of the possibility of experience, or whether a yet higher principle of reason only makes it into a regulative principle for us first to produce a common sense in ourselves for higher ends, thus whether taste is an original and natural faculty, or only the idea of one that is yet to be acquired and is artificial, so that a judgment of taste, with its expectation of a universal assent, is in fact only a demand of reason to produce such a unanimity in the manner of sensing, and whether the "should", i.e., the objective necessity of the confluence of the feeling of everyone with that of each, signifies only the possibility of coming to agreement about this, and the judgment of taste only provides an example of the application of this principle – this we would not and cannot yet investigate here; for now we have only to resolve the faculty of taste into its elements and to unite them ultimately in the idea of a common sense. (KU 5: 240; Kant 2000, p. 124)

As in the case of the heuristic support that rational ideas provide to the subject of knowledge, in Kant's third Critique, aesthetic normativity implies a notion of humanity that relies on the success of education, which, at the same time, holds the promise of the future advancement of the species. Moreover, the promise of a social contract as a consequence of aesthetic agreement orients the construction of a community yet to come for humanity, as can be seen in the previous excerpt. In fact, the *sensus communis* hints at a common purpose to be constructed through the communicative efforts of the human species that will render clashes motivated by religious, cultural and class differences a thing of the past. One may ask: is this feature of community inspired by our social life? The answer lies in the fact that Kant's aesthetic community originates as a normative demand that aims to meet the higher moral requirements ordained by practical reason. It confirms that, for Kant, the community of taste is not something that exists for its own sake, but rather mirrors the emergence of a possible moral community. In my view, this relation of dependence of the aesthetic community on the moral community sheds some light on the function that emotions fulfil within the realm of taste. Just as the emotional component of reason highlighted in section 1 embodied impersonal traits which encouraged the subject of cognition to accomplish higher epistemic actions, aesthetic feelings as the pleasure that *sensus communis* yields are viewed as "the effect of the free play of our cognitive powers" (KU 5: 238; Kant 2000, p. 122) and allow one to put "oneself into the position of everyone else" (KU 5: 294; Kant 2000, p. 174). This, in turn, triggers a shift that transforms the human tendency towards egoism by enlarging the field in which the subject is able to feel the pleasures of reflection. Rather than prioritise the wit or *ingenium* of an individual subject, aesthetic experience provides an opportunity to affirm the shared conditions that give support to the knowledge able to be produced by the community of human subjects. Kant repeatedly holds that when one utters a judgment of taste, "everyone should agree with it" (KU 5: 239; Kant 2000, p. 123), i.e. everybody is expected to give their assent to the claim contained in the judgment.

Kant's claim is explicit about the fact that the aesthetic demand for constructing an aesthetic community is a task to be fulfilled in order to comply with the requirements and duties entailed by the conception of humans as a moral species. Yet no aesthetic pleasure could possibly be schematized or categorized in Kant's view (as in the case of moral objects and goals), given that the former relies on freely attuning a wide variety of different judgments and diverse voices that ought to inspire the construction of the modern republican state. Furthermore, in this case, an element external to the subject intervenes to bring out the foremost human capacities—the same capacities often endangered in the social sphere. This confirms that there must be mediation between the interests of the theoretical and practical use of reason, able to deploy a bridge between these two rational spheres.[3] Thus, to hold our judgments "up to human reason as a whole" (KU 5: 294; Kant 2000, p. 173) exemplifies the collective efforts that humanity is able to undertake, even if the human empirical subject may be led astray by their own self-interest. In this way, the emotional features of taste, in Kant's account, convey to the subject her potential to fulfil the purposes of both domains of reason, almost as if she should fake the accomplishment of epistemic and moral duties until she will be able to effectively perform them.[4] Ultimately, though, the most enigmatic point of the function of taste is the fact that aesthetic training helps the subject renounce his egoistic inclinations and desires and improve his capacity to abide by moral duties, and thus to construct a moral community governed by reason.

---

3 On this issue see Sweet (2018, p. 146): "The pleasure we take in the beautiful [...] is homologous with the theoretical sphere insofar as it announces a general agreement of our faculties with things in the world. It is homologous with the practical sphere insofar as it announces the community of all human beings. While cognition and moral goodness both legislate and thus accomplish something – the determination of a representation, the bringing about of a community – the pleasure in the judgment of taste, in its homology with each domain, suggests the possibility of success in each domain. And, insofar as it is homologous with each domain, it can allow for space in which they are joined together, though not unified". See the account of Borges (2019, pp. 139–151), which concerns the contributions of the *Anthropology* in refining the propaedeutic to morals in Kant's philosophy.

4 Cohen (2015) has focused on this effect of Kant's appraisal of the acquisition of virtue.

3 An Emotional Basis of Morality?

As we saw above, the role of taste in encouraging the transition of humanity towards a moral community sheds new light on the function that transcendental philosophy assigns to the emotions—that is, as helping tools to ease the transformation of the human being into a rational moral being. In my view, the conception of moral feelings as supports to moral progress can be understood within the overall impact of affective states on the moral development of the subject. In this vein, Kant's Lectures on Anthropology and Ethics yield many examples of emotions that can be expected to increase moral strength, and thus improve the capacity of the subject to look beyond her own particular self-interest and think in terms of the higher value of the common good. Kantian scholars have often highlighted the fact that Kant's practical philosophy extolls the classical stoic virtue of *apathy*, viewed as a tool for resisting the power of feelings and inclinations over the human mind and for cultivating self-mastery. In the *Doctrine of Virtue* Kant claims that

> virtue necessarily presupposes apathy; it forbid[s] him to let himself be governed by his feelings and inclinations (the duty of apathy); for unless reason hold the reins of government in its own hands, his feelings and inclinations play the master over him. (MS 6: 408)

Despite the admiration that Kant shows for emotions such as stoic apathy, my account will instead focus on Kant's attempts to prove, in his moral and anthropological writings, that human feelings can be transformed through a complex training process guided by practical reason. While stoic apathy can be seen as a useful tool for controlling human affects and breaking the hold of the passions, this virtue is too rigid to be of true value within Kant's view of the development of a firm moral character. I would like to highlight, at this point, that progress and continuous transformation are the terms most often used by Kant to describe the human effort to achieve true morality:

> Virtue is always in progress and yet always starts *from the beginning*. It is always in progress because, considered objectively, while yet in constant approximation to it is a duty. That it always starts from the beginning has a subjective basis in human nature, which is affected by inclinations because of which virtue can never settle down in peace and quiet with its maxims adopted once and for all but, if it is not rising, is unavoidably sinking. (MS 6: 409)

The previously cited excerpt from the *Doctrine of Virtue* depicts human progress in the realm of virtue as an emotional experience of inner transformation. This makes the agent more confident in the consequences of his own behaviour, while also enabling them to avoid falling prey to the arrogance that threatens to spoil the character of the subject and generate a "dishonesty" that Kant calls the "foul stain of our species" (RGV 6: 38). Thus, Kant considers that self-examination of the emotions that contribute to the moral struggle of a rational human agent between her moral duty and her own subjective, egoistic inclinations can help lay a solid foundation for achieving the moral destiny of humanity. The *Doctrine of Virtue* also urges the agent to adopt similar approaches to achieve moral progress within herself:

> Moral cognition of oneself, which seeks to penetrate into the depths (the abyss) of one's heart which are quite difficult to fathom, is the beginning of all human wisdom, which consists in harmony of a human being's will with its final end, requires him first to remove the obstacle within (can evil actually present in him) and then to develop the original predisposition to a good will with him, which can never be lost. (Only the descent into the hell of self-cognition can pave the way to godliness). (MS 6: 441)

Kant depicts, in this text, the task of moral self-cognition as a process capable of sparking an emotional transformation of the human being as a whole, enabling him to better attune his internal predisposition with a morally good will. Pablo Muchnik has claimed that the search for the *Gesinnung* rooted in human choices and actions that Kant encourages in his writings on morality overlaps, on many important points, with the task of cultivating good character, which is intended to mitigate the human propensity towards evil and consequently to ground a "heart" that shall shelter the "inner citadel" from external and internal threats. I agree with this account, as it places the emotional development of the agent at the centre of moral agency:

> The "heart" dissolves the tension between Kant's apparently contradictory commitments to the universality of the propensity and the freedom of the individual. It does so by mediating, at the level of individual morality, between the *a priori* principles that constitute an agent's character and their phenomenal expression in typical moral emotions – a mediation that in turn makes those emotions susceptible to anthropological generalization. If this reading is correct, the "heart" is the linchpin of Kant's moral anthropology – it is essential to understand his views in Religion about radical evil and moral regeneration, for the heart is the epicentre of an agent's moral struggle. (Muchnik 2014, p. 241)

As Muchnik correctly points out, in my view, Kant identifies the moral effort undertaken by the rational human agent with the construction of a good "heart", which plays the role of an inner guardian protecting the human subject in their never-ending struggle for true morality. Because aging can weaken human faculties and capacities, Kant suggests that the agent must cultivate his own morality by investing great effort and perseverance throughout his entire life.

In keeping with this project to redeem the emotional order of the human mind, it might be useful to enlarge the scope of our account so as to shed light on some circumstances that urge the use of emotions as embodied supports that improve human moral virtue. As expected, Kant rejects that an ordering or categorization of the emotions can provide the key to the attainment of virtue. On the contrary, his approach to ethics clearly disavows that a combination of human feelings and mechanical skills could lead to virtue, as virtue rather refines the sources of pleasure and acts as a check on the emotions that arise in the mind.[5] A passage from the *Doctrine of Virtue* neatly highlights this gap between the essential moral good and contingent human emotions:

> Considered in its complete perfection, virtue is therefore represented not as if a human being possesses him; for in the former case it would look as if he still had a choice (for which he would need yet another virtue in order to select virtue before any of the other wares on offer). (MS 6: 406)

According to this text, practical reason is expected to change the whole scale of emotions that human beings are able to feel, inculcating the subject with a firm willingness to constantly struggle against their base inclinations, which ultimately results in the development of moral character.[6] In this context, cultivating love and sympathy towards vulnerable people,[7] or love of honour as a means to self-

---

5 Precisely because Kant does not consider that virtue might be reduced to the acquisition of a skill, I cannot agree with the reading that Merritt proposes, see Merritt (2018, p. 203): "The strength of virtue is acquired through effort, and this is continually engaged. On my view, Kant says that the holy will should have the same strength because this strength is essentially cognitive: it is the readiness of one's commitment to morality, and the content of this commitment can be spelled put through the moral law. So, there is a sense, again, in which the content of the commitment is the same if it is regarded simply objectively, according to its internal principle. But a holy will does not gradually acquire a skill; a holy does not – it seems – have to learn". In my view, Merritt sheds light on the acquisition process of virtue as if which may also explain its human embodiment. Yet I consider that the process of embodiment of moral rules also impacts the assumption of the moral law by the human will.

6 N. Sherman was one of the first Kant scholars who openly focused on the dependence that Kant's foundation of morality had with regard to emotions. See Sherman (2014, p. 30): "The regulative procedure given by the moral law in the pure metaphysics of morals cannot itself suffice to set obligatory ends without the addition of empirical facts".

7 See MS 6: 457: "But while it is not in itself a duty to share the sufferings (as well the joys) of others, it is a duty to sympathize actively in their fate; and to this end it is therefore an indirect duty to cultivate the compassionate natural (aesthetic) feeling in us, and to make use of them as so many means to sympathy based on moral principles and the feeling appropriate to them. It is therefore a duty not to avoid the places where the poor who lack the most basic necessities are to be found but rather to seek them out, and not to shun sickrooms or debtors' prisons and so forth

esteem, are mentioned by Kant as examples of reliable, concrete guides towards moral duty. Thus, training our mind to overcome complex feelings such as sadness and joy exemplifies the mature development of the subject, in contrast to the common reactions to pleasure and pain as immediate reactions to the external environment. Therefore, Kant extolls the effort to keep affective states under control as a key dimension in the education of human nature, given that emotions are the main information upon which the rational agent makes her decisions. In fact, human inclinations such as love of honour convey that an agent considers herself a moral being, disposed to abide by a moral duty grounded in the respect of one's own person.[8] The *Doctrine of Virtue* points out that the feeling of self-esteem corresponds to the features of "the human being's feeling for his sublime vocation" (MS 6: 437), which involves a kind of pride for the dignity of humanity as well as a fear of behaving in a way inconsistent with respect for humanity. As we read in the Lectures on Ethics *Vigilantius:*

> A lover of honour finds in himself no need to be known [...] he does not require to be highly esteemed by others, yet his moral conduct is such, that if it were to be known, he would be acknowledged as one who is worthy of the [good opinion] of others. (V-Mo/Vigil 27: 665)

As this text confirms, Kant's treatment of affects and emotions is a rigorous analysis of the effect of the values of ethical consistency, integrity, and dignity on human behaviour. In Kant's view, moral dispositions such as love of honour can be considered as embodiments of virtue that help contribute to the achievement of moral virtue. Yet embodied virtue does not have to do with the impact that fickle emotions may possess on moral judgment, but rather at the influence that an internally rooted morality ought to show over our affective states. Thus, virtue is expected to shape the feelings and desires of the human being, deeply transforming the sources of pleasure and displeasure and encouraging the practical self-determination to guide one's actions based on the promise of a more moral future. As Kant claims in Reflection 7199 (Refl 19: 272): "The first and most important observation that a human being makes about himself is that, determined through nature, he is to be the author of his happiness and even of his

---

in order to avoid sharing painful feelings one may not be able to resist. For this is still one of the impulses that nature has implanted in us to do what the representation of duty alone might not accomplish". On the role that *Mitleid* fulfils in Kant doctrine of virtue, see Wehofsits (2017).
8 See L. Denis in Cohen (2014, p. 199): "Love of honour constitutes a moral aptitude for the fulfilment of a crucial subset of duties to oneself: those that concern one's maxims' consistency with one's prerogative as a moral being, one's inner freedom, which is an essential condition of character. Love of honour coheres with a fundamental commitment to morality. It is part of the moral perfection of a human being".

own inclinations and aptitudes, which makes this happiness possible". In a nut-shell, for Kant, moral progress entails a self-elaboration of affective states, which in turn represents one of the most inspiring of all human capabilities, invoking outright astonishment in the subject of this internal transformation.

4 Conclusion

My account of the role of emotions within the larger scope of Kant's philosophy has focused on the claim that Kant does not consider affective states as a matter of fact, or as the enemy of theoretical and moral philosophy. On the contrary, fol-lowing in the teachings of ancient classical doctrines of virtue, Kant views human emotion as a highly useful foundation in the struggle for moral self-transformation. The possibility of improving the human species by intervening in the emotions that rational human agents are able to feel acts as a key compo-nent of Kant's moral theory.[9] Kant does not seem to consider emotions as simply an immediate expression of raw human instincts and inclinations, but rather as an index of the power that moral values gain over an uncontrolled pursuit of happiness, orienting it according to the respect for human dignity within us. Thus, affective states are not intended to be an inescapable flaw of human be-ings, but rather appear as helpful guides that make the laborious path of epis-temic and moral progress more bearable.

Bibliography

Borges, Maria Lourdes (2019): *Emotions, Reason and Action in Kant*. London, New York: Bloomsbury.

Cohen Alix (Ed.) (2014): *Kant on Emotion and Value*. Hampshire: Palgrave McMillan.

Cohen, Alix (2015): "From Faking It to Making It: The Feeling of Love of Honor as an Aid to Morality". In: Robert Clewis (Ed.): *Reading Kant's Lectures*. Boston, Berlin: De Gruyter, pp. 243–256.

Cohen, Alix (2018): "Rational Feelings". In: Kristi Sorensen and Diane Williamson (Eds.): *Kant and the Faculty of Feeling*. Cambridge: Cambridge University Press, pp. 9–24.

---

9 Deimling has also suggested a reading of Kant's treatment of emotions which I partially agree with. He proposes a more pragmatic based account of affective states in Kant's philosophy which I find quite valuable, but in my view he also substantially modifies the centrality of mor-ality in this author. See Deimling (2014, p. 122): "Affective states that track complex values and that we can influence through mediate control are especially relevant for our decisions about how to act".

Deimling, Wiebke (2014): "Kant's Pragmatic Concept of Emotions". In: Alix Cohen (Ed.): *Kant on Emotion and Value*. Hampshire: Palgrave McMillan, pp. 108–125.

Denis, Lara (2014): "Love of Honor as a Kantian Virtue". In: Alix Cohen (Ed.): *Kant on Emotion and Value*. Hampshire: Palgrave McMillan, pp. 191–209.

Kant, Immanuel (1996a): *The Cambridge Edition of the Works of Immanuel Kant: Practical Philosophy*. Mary J. Gregor (Ed.) (Trans.). Cambridge: Cambridge University Press.

Kant, Immanuel (1996b): "What Does it Mean to Orient Oneself in Thinking?" In: *Religion and Rational Theology*. Allen W. Wood and George di Giovanni (Ed.) (Trans.). Cambridge: Cambridge University Press.

Kant, Immanuel (2000): *The Cambridge Edition of the Works of Immanuel Kant: Critique of the Power of Judgment*. Paul Guyer and Eric Mathews (Ed.) (Trans.). Cambridge: Cambridge University Press.

Kant, Immanuel (1900): *Kants Gesammelte Schriften*. Königlich Preussischen Akademie der Wissenschaften (Ed.). Berlin: De Gruyter.

Kleingeld, Pauline (1998): "The Conative Character of Reason in Kant's Philosophy". In: *Journal of the History of Philosophy* 36. No.1, pp. 77–97.

Merritt, Melissa (2018): *Kant on Reflection and Virtue*. Cambridge: Cambridge University Press.

Muchnik, Pablo (2014): "The Heart as Locus of Moral Struggle in the *Religion*". In: Alix Cohen (Ed.): *Kant on Emotion and Value*. Hampshire: Palgrave McMillan, pp. 224–244.

Nuzzo, Angelica (2014): "The Place of Emotions in Kant's Transcendental Philosophy". In: Alix Cohen (Ed.): *Kant on Emotion and Value*. Hampshire: Palgrave McMillan, pp. 88–107.

Sherman, Nancy (2014): "The Place of Emotions in Kantian Morality". In: Alix Cohen (Ed.): *Kant on Emotion and Value*. Hampshire: Palgrave McMillan, pp. 11–32.

Sweet, Kristi E. (2018): "Between Cognition and Morality: Pleasure as 'Transition' in Kant's Critical System". In: Kristi E. Sorensen and Diane Williamson (Eds.): *Kant and the Faculty of Feeling*. Cambridge: Cambridge University Press, pp. 130–146.

Wehofsits, Anna (2016): *Anthropologie und Moral. Affekte, Leidenschaften und Mitgefühl in Kants Ethik*. Berlin, Boston: De Gruyter.

Ana Marta González
Unpacking Moral Feeling: Kantian Clues to a Map of the Moral World

Abstract: In a brief footnote from "What Does it Mean to Orient Oneself in Thinking?", Kant says that, "Reason does not feel", yet he immediately adds that, "it has insight into its lack and through the drive for cognition it effects the feeling of a need". He then draws an analogy with moral feeling, "which does not cause any moral law, for this arises wholly from reason; rather, it is caused or effected by moral laws, hence by reason, because the active yet free will needs determinate grounds" (WDO 8: 139–140). This chapter aims to unpack this text, thereby showing the pivotal role of moral feeling in articulating the moral realm.

Keywords: moral feeling, interests of reason, moral receptivity, judgment

1 An Intriguing Footnote

In his short essay "What Does it Mean to Orient Oneself in Thinking?", written to counteract Jacobi's critique of Mendelssohn on his stance about Lessing's alleged Spinozism, Kant departs from the experience of geographical orientation to explore the idea of orientation in thinking—a different experience from that of knowing (KrV Bxxxvi). In Kant's own terminology, the contrast between both experiences points to the difference between regulatory and constitutive principles, between reflective and determining judgment; yet, on this occasion, Kant's effort is directed to make sense of Mendelssohn's resort to "common human reason" or "healthy reason", in contrast to Jacobi's resort to mere feeling (Wood 1996, pp. 3–6). Accordingly, Kant acknowledges that "healthy reason" remains within the realm of reason, even if Mendelssohn himself does not go as far as distinguishing clearly between thinking and knowing in Kant's own terms (WDO 8: 140), being more concerned with making sense of objective knowledge than with knowledge itself. Given that the human being is a limited and situated subject who needs to place knowledge within a broader context articulated around his own subjective position, only this broader context provides the background for meaningful thinking. Herein, Kant's point in analysing the metaphor of orientation is understood against the background of stressing the need for a subjective principle in order to make sense of objective data:

Ana Marta González, Univ. Navarra, Spain

https://doi.org/10.1515/9783110720730-004

> In the proper meaning of the word, to *orient* oneself means to use a given direction (when we divide the horizon into four of them) in order to find the others—literally, to find the sunrise. Now if I see the sun in the sky and know it is now midday, then I know how to find south, west, north, and east. For this, however, I also need the feeling of a difference in my own subject, namely, the difference between my right and left hands (WDO 8: 134).

As Chiara Fabrizzi (2008, pp. 86–87) has argued, the connection between space and body has a long history in Kant's pre-critical writings. The point Kant is interested in here, however, is quite simple: unless there is a subjective principle—"a feeling of a difference"—that helps us make sense of objective data, the latter do not tell us anything relevant about the world; indeed, there would be no experience at all. This is the basic idea behind transcendental philosophy: there is no experience without a subject. Yet, Kant's purpose here is not so much to use this idea to account for the experience of knowledge—as he does in the first *Critique*—as it is to account for the experience of searching for knowledge. In this context, the experience of geographical orientation is relevant not only because it makes explicit the need for a subjective principle, but also because it describes this principle as a feeling, although of a peculiar kind.

Indeed, as we know, Kant reserves the notion of "feeling" to designate "what is merely subjective in the relation of our representation and contains no relation at all to an object for possible cognition of it (or even cognition of our condition)" (MS 6: 211–212). By "merely subjective" he means the receptivity to pleasure or displeasure that follows certain representations. Nevertheless, in the "Orientation" essay, Kant could be seen as speaking about feeling in a slightly different way—not so much as receptivity to pleasure or displeasure—although this is obviously not excluded—but rather as an inner sense able to make us aware of our position in the world. Thus, he writes,

> I call this a feeling because these two sides outwardly display no designatable difference in intuition. If I did not have this faculty of distinguishing, without the need of any difference in the objects, between moving from left to right and right to left and moving in the opposite direction and thereby determining a priori a difference in the position of the objects, then in describing a circle I would not know whether west was right or left of the southern-most point of the horizon, or whether I should complete the circle by moving north and east and thus back to south. Thus even with all the objective data of the sky, I orient myself geographically only through a subjective ground of differentiation. (WDO 8: 135)

Such ground is not a sensation, an intuition; Kant calls it a "feeling", meaning that it involves an inner sense—which should be distinguished from interior sense (Fabrizzi 2009, p. 115). According to Kant, "inner sense is not pure apperception, a consciousness of what the human being does, since this belongs to the faculty of thinking. Rather, it is a consciousness of what he undergoes, in so far as he is affected by the play of his own thoughts" (Anth 07: 161). We could say that inner sense is the source of sensible self-awareness; it thus entails a peculiar sort of (sensible) reflexivity whereby I perceive myself as a physical living subject, who, through my own life, makes a difference in the world.

Kant describes this feeling as "a faculty implanted by nature but made habitual through frequent practice" (WDO 8: 135). Both aspects are important: (1) it is a natural endowment, whereby human beings, as living beings, become aware of their own roots in the physical world. The reference to nature, in this context, could be taken as a way of referring to the faculty of desire as well as to life, because Kant defines life as "the faculty of a being to act in accordance with its representations", and desire as "the faculty to be by means of one's representations the cause of the objects of these representations" (MS 06: 211). However, (2) the fact that such natural endowment can develop through practice into something habitual, that is, something at hand and ready to use, is also important, because this is one of the few places in which Kant explicitly refers to "habit" as a behavioural quality resulting from the interaction between nature (desire) and practice. Overall, the idea is that, with self-awareness as a condition for orientating ourselves in the external world, the ability to orientate oneself in it improves with practice.

Now, the analogy with orientation in thinking runs as follows: just as we can dare to explore new, unknown territory, based on the feeling that provides us with sensible orientation, we can also dare to think about things that exceed strict knowledge, based on a peculiar feeling derived from our own reason:

> By analogy, one can easily guess that it will be a concern of pure reason to guide its use when it wants to leave familiar objects (of experience) behind, extending itself beyond all the bounds of experience and finding no object of intuition at all, but merely space for intuition; for then it is no longer in a position to bring its judgments under a determinate maxim according to objective grounds of cognition, but solely to bring its judgments under a determinate maxim according to a subjective ground of differentiation in the determination of its own faculty of judgment. This subjective means still remaining is nothing other than reason's feeling of its own need. (WDO 8: 136)

In the preceding paragraph, the contrast between determining and reflective judgment is already implicit. While determining judgment is possible only when we can apply understanding to phenomena, reflective judgment operates either when our reason is in search of knowledge, or moves itself beyond the bounds of experience, guided by its own desire/need for knowledge. In this context, I shall focus on Kant's reference to "reason's feeling of its own need" as the subjective ground to orientate oneself in thinking, a topic that according to Birgit Recki (2006, pp. 92–110) has been little explored. Specifically, I am interested in analysing what kind of feeling "reason's feeling" can be understood to be. Kant himself takes up this question a few lines later in a footnote:

> Reason does not feel; it has insight into its lack and *through the drive for cognition* it effects the feeling of a need. It is the same way with moral feeling, which does not cause any moral law, for this arises wholly from reason; rather, it is caused or effected by moral laws, hence by reason, because the active yet free will needs determinate grounds (WDO 8: 139–140)

Kant is explicit in saying that reason does not feel; yet, it is an active and reflective power, which not only searches actively for knowledge, but is also reflectively aware of whether it has achieved its objective or failed in its attempt. This awareness, or consciousness, produces a feeling, which Kant compares with the way reason produces moral feeling. This should encourage us to take the latter as a model to understand the peculiar nature of "reason's feelings". Meanwhile, however, we should note that there is a significant difference between the role reason's feelings play in the theoretical realm and the role they play in the practical realm. Indeed, in theoretical matters, feeling results from a natural desire or need for determining judgment, which cannot always be fully satisfied. Precisely at this point

> there enters the right of reason's need, as a subjective ground for presupposing and assuming something which reason may not presume to know through objective grounds; and consequently for orienting itself in thinking, solely through reason's own need, in that immeasurable space of the supersensible, which for us is filled with dark night. (WDO 8: 136–137)

In practical matters, however, feeling results from a determining judgment, which operates entirely *a priori* on the basis of what Kant calls "the Typic of judgment", which first provides us with a rational cartography of the moral world.

2 The Effect of an Active Yet Finite Reason

A basic way of approaching the issue of "reason's feeling of its own need" is simply to note that we want to know, and yet we know that we do not know as we would like to. The Socratic principle is at the basis of every quest for knowledge. This quest is witness to human reason's finitude. Reason is an active power, yet human reason is not an absolute power, but rather a dependent one: in order to achieve knowledge, it needs empirical data; it is thus interested in acquiring said data and, when they are lacking, reason feels its own need. Importantly, feeling results from the finite and interested nature of reason, and not the other way around. This is crucial for understanding the difference that, especially in practical contexts, Kant draws between inclination and interest:

> The dependence of the faculty of desire upon feelings is called inclination, and this accordingly always indicates a need. The dependence of a contingently determinable will on principles of reason, however, is called an interest. (GMS 4: 414)

In the *Anthropology* (Anth 7: 251) and in the *Metaphysics of Morals* (MS 6: 212), Kant characterises inclination as "habitual desire", and interest as "the connection of pleasure with the faculty of desire that the understanding judges to hold as a general rule (though only for the subject)". Accordingly, he distinguishes between "interest of inclination" and "interest of reason", depending on whether pleasure precedes a desire or rather it "follows upon an antecedent determination of the faculty of desire", in which case he speaks of "intellectual pleasure", based on a peculiar sort of "sense-free inclination (*propensio intellectualis*)" (MS 6: 213).[1]

While every sensible being endowed with a faculty of desire has inclinations, only a rational being has *interests*. As pointed out above, for Kant, human reason is not an inert principle; it has an intrinsic dynamism, which manifests itself in a number of interests. Thus, in the first *Critique*, he defines "interest" more generally as "a principle that contains the condition under which alone its exercise is promoted". Along these lines, he notes that, "reason, as the faculty of principles, determines the interest of all the power of the mind but itself determines its own" (KpV 5: 119). Indeed, reason does not merely entail the principle for advancing the operation of other powers; as a reflective power, it also entails the principle for its own progress, both in speculative as well as in practical matters:

> The interest of its speculative use consists in the cognition of the object up to the highest a priori principles; that of its practical use consists in the determination of the will with respect to the final and complete end. (KpV 5: 119–120)

A well-known passage from the first *Critique* resonates in these words: "All interest of my reason (the speculative as well as the practical) is united in the following three questions: 1. What can I know? 2. What should I do? 3. What may I hope?" (KrV A 804/B832).

---

1 "The subjective possibility of the emergence of a certain desire, which precedes the representation of its object, is propensity (*propensio*)" (Anth 7: 265).

Neither animals nor God have interests (GMS 4: 414); the notion of "interest" is characteristic of human beings, insofar as they have a finite reason (Schadow 2013, p. 115–116). From this perspective, it could be argued that Kant uses the notion of "interest" to define humanity. In any event, reason's interests, and specifically its interest in achieving sufficient ground for knowledge and action, are at the basis of the feelings it engenders in human beings. Reason's feelings can therefore be taken both as effects and signs of those interests, which constitute the proper subjective ground—Kant even speaks of the "right of reason"—to assume certain concepts as guiding threads for rational exploration (WDO 08: 136–137). In moral matters, the notion of interest is likewise of paramount importance, especially for understanding the articulation between Kant's theory of normativity and his theory of motivation.

Indeed, as we know, in order to act morally, we need not only to act in conformity with duty, but also from duty. Now, Kant often characterises acting from duty in contrast with acting from inclination or interest in terms of the contrast between the universalisability of actions performed from duty and the non-universalisability of actions performed from inclination and interest. Yet, we should keep in mind that motivation is always rooted in particular situations, and that this is an integral part of our being in the world. Accordingly, there should be a way to articulate the normative requirement for universalisability with the particularity required by motivation. In this context, Kant introduces the distinction between "having an interest" and "taking an interest", which is crucial in order to account for the possibility of acting from duty—hence morally—and yet being moved by particular situations. For Kant,

> The human will can take an interest in the action, without therefore acting from interest. The first signifies practical interest in the action, the second, pathological interest in the object of the action. The former indicates only dependence of the will upon principles of reason in themselves; the second, dependence upon principles of reason for the sake of inclination, namely where reason supplies only the practical rule as to how to remedy the need of inclination. In the first case the action interests me; in the second, the object of the action (insofar as it is agreeable to me)... In the case of an action from duty we must look not to interest in the object but merely to that in the action itself and its principle in reason (the law). (GMS 4: 414)

Kant's position is not substantially different from that of other thinkers who distinguish acting out of choice and acting out of passion (González 2016). According to Kant, when acting out of choice, the agent is following a maxim of reason, while when acting out of passion, he is merely driven by an inclination—herein lies the difference between *arbitrium liberum* and *arbitrium brutum* (MS 6: 213–214). Kant thus writes that, "on the concept of an interest is based that of a maxim. A maxim is [...] morally genuine only if it rests solely on the interest one takes in compliance with the law" (KpV 5: 79).

As finite beings, humans must be impelled to activity by some incentive (KpV 5: 79), yet there is a difference between being merely impelled by a sensible incentive and being impelled by reason, between "having an interest" and "taking an interest". That finite rational beings can take an interest in the moral law, however, follows from their mixed nature as rational and sensible beings: while as sensible beings they are influenced by inclinations, as rational beings they do not find those inclinations decisive in themselves. Negative freedom creates room for the thought of the law to have its peculiar effect on our sensible nature, inducing a peculiar kind of feeling, which, unlike other feelings, has its source in moral law itself and enables us to act to not just in conformity with the law, but also out of respect for the law (KpV 5: 81). While Kant acknowledges that before man arrives at the use of reason, nature can provide him with a sensible incentive for the good as a temporary surrogate for reason (Anth 7: 253), it is important to note the difference between this surrogate and moral feeling as such. Indeed, as we read in his *Lectures on Ethics*, "moral feeling is inner reverence for the law" (V-Mo/Mron II 29: 626). In the *Groundwork*, he speaks directly of respect:

> Though respect is a feeling, it is not one received by means of influence; it is, instead, a feeling self-wrought by means of a rational concept and therefore specifically different from all feelings of the first kind, which can be reduced to inclination or fear. What I cognize immediately as a law for me I cognize with respect, which signifies merely consciousness of the subordination of my will to a law without the mediation of other influences on my sense. Immediate determination of the will by means of the law and consciousness of this is called respect, so that this is regarded as the effect of the law on the subject, and not as the cause of the law. (GMS 4: 401)

As Kant observes, the feeling of respect shares features of both fear and inclination. However, respect is not based on inclinations, but rather on reason, or, more specifically, on the contrast between the universal requirements of reason and the particular requirements of acting in the sensible world. Hence, it is under the influence of other inclinations.

3 Moral Feeling as principium executionis

Kant dwells on the special nature of moral feeling in the KpV under the heading "the moral incentive". Therein, he speaks more at length about an issue that had occupied him since the pre-critical period, when he was confronted with Wolff's rationalism, on the one hand, and the moral sentimentalists, on the other (Schadow 2013).

By "incentive", which he identifies with the Latin expression *elater animi*, that is, "driving force" (Reath and Timmerman 2010, p. 93), he generally means "the subjective determining ground of the will of a being whose reason does not by its nature necessarily conform with the objective law". Now, as indicated above, this subjective determining ground is not merely feeling as such, which is simply an effect, but also the interest of reason, without which there would be no feeling at all. Accordingly, while

> no incentives at all can be attributed to the divine will [...] the incentive of the human will (and of the will of every created rational being) can never be anything other than the moral law; and thus that the objective determining ground must always and quite alone be also the subjectively sufficient determining ground of action. (KpV 5: 71)

In Kant's view, "how a law can be of itself and immediately a determining ground for the will (though this is what is essential in all morality)"—remains an insoluble problem for human reason "and identical with that of how a free will is possible" (KpV 5: 71). However, while we cannot explain how the law can become *of* itself a determining ground for the will, we can and actually should assume that this is the case. That is, we can and should assume that reason is in itself practical, such that, confronted with the law, it actually moves us to act in the sensible world thanks to the feeling it induces (Klemme 2006, p. 131–132). While this moral feeling is not infallible—because it may concur with other (sensible) incentives to act differently—it is necessary in order to counteract other feelings and their inclinations; yet, in contrast with pathological feelings, the source of moral feeling is entirely *a priori* and is found in our reason. True, Kant cannot show "the ground from which the moral law in itself supplies such an incentive" (KpV 5: 72), but he does not hesitate to describe the effect of such law on our mind as a *negative* feeling, following the contrast between the universality of the law and the particularity of inclination, which is always based on (other) feelings:

> The effect of the moral law as incentive is only negative, and as such this incentive can be cognized *a priori*. For, all inclination and every sensible impulse is based on feeling, and the negative effect on feeling (by the infringement upon the inclinations that takes place) is itself feeling. (KpV 5: 72)

In spite of not knowing why moral law can move our will, we do know something about the specific feeling accompanying that movement, given the fact that every impulse—hence also the impulse to act in a certain way—is based on feeling. Every particular impulse to act is bound to conflict with the universal requirements of the law, thereby producing another, different feeling, which, because of its rational origin, can be called moral feeling. Kant describes the origin of this feeling as a sort of pain:

> Hence we can see *a priori* that the moral law, as the determining ground of the will, must by thwarting all our inclinations produce a feeling that can be called pain; and here we have the first and perhaps the only case in which we can determine a priori from concepts the relation of a cognition (here the cognition of a pure practical reason) to the feeling of pleasure or displeasure. (KpV 5: 73)

He is specific about the origin of this pain: infringement upon self-love and the striking down of self-conceit. Kant distinguishes between self-love, which is "natural and active in us prior to the moral law", and what he designates as "rational self-love", resulting from subduing the former to the requirements of the law. For Kant natural self-love is not wrong in itself but rather is only antecedent to reason. However, this is not the case with "self-conceit", which he does consider negatively, due to the fact that it suggests we are worthy of something prior to the operation of reason. Indeed, while Kant acknowledges the existence of a certain inclination toward self-esteem, he thinks it completely groundless if not based on reason (KpV 5: 73). On the contrary, it is only receptivity to the moral law that allows us to recognise our dignity as rational beings, subject to the laws of freedom rather than the laws of nature. From this perspective, the pain implicit in moral feeling unveils its *positive* side—namely, the feeling of respect:

> Since this law is still something in itself positive – namely the form of an intellectual causality, that is, of freedom – it is at the same time an object of respect [...] and so too the ground of a positive feeling that is not of empirical origin and is cognized a priori. Consequently, respect for the moral law is a feeling that is produced by an intellectual ground, and this feeling is the only one that we can cognize completely a priori and the necessity of which we can have insight into. (KpV 5: 73)

Although Kant's insistence that this feeling is based on intellectual considerations may be found puzzling, his position makes sense as a phenomenology of moral experience. As Jeanine Grenberg (2013, p. 66) puts it, "whenever we find ourselves experiencing a conflict between the competing demands of happiness and morality, our affective state is best described by what Kant calls the moral feeling of respect". While we cannot categorically exclude the possibility of even more qualified moral feelings,[2] Kant underlines that this is the only feeling accessible to us *a priori*. Its importance definitively lies in providing human agents with a *principium executionis* of what has been previously judged to conform to reason. This stresses the fact that, as such—that is, independently of its rational principle—moral feeling is not a *principium iudicationis:*

> One might still grant the moral feeling, if it were a question of the mind's incentives to morality, but not as a principle for the judgment of moral action. It may be the receptivity of our will, to be moved by moral laws as incentives. The judgment of morality consists in objective principles, but the incentive is subjective; this makes the will practical. If reason itself can determine our will, then it has moral feeling. (V-Mo/Mron II 29: 625)

The will becomes practical, able to move us to act in a certain way, insofar as it judges a certain action as a right action in conformity with the law (Pollok 2006, p. 200). Whether Kant thereby defends an internalist or an externalist approach to agency (Klemme, Kühn and Schönecker 2006) remains undecided; while it is certain that no moral action deserves to be categorised as moral if it is not motivated by inner respect for the law, and, in this sense, by moral feeling, this does not necessarily equate knowledge—of the moral action—and the will. As Heiner Klemme points out, the need for moral feeling to recognise the moral principle in a practical way explains that we can decide either for or against moral action without thereby being entirely irrational (Klemme 2006, pp. 130 – 132). Indeed, according to Kant, "reason attends either to the interest of the inclinations, or to its own interest. In the first case it is subservient, but in the other, legislative" (V-Mo/Mron II 29: 625). Thus, it may be the case that, instead of taking an interest in the moral law (GMS 4: 401; KpV 5:79), we take an interest in the satisfaction of an inclination and construct our maxim accordingly. After all, as Schadow (2013, p. 202) notes, if human beings were to always and immediately act according to the law, they would be holy beings. Kant acknowledges that human beings do not always behave according to moral reasons. Yet, since this is only a matter of execution, it does not compromise the legislative power of reason:

> If reason determines the will through the moral law, it has the force of an incentive, and in that case has, not autonomy merely, but also autocracy. It then has both legislative and executive power. The autocracy of reason, to determine the will in accordance with moral laws, would then be the moral feeling. Man does really possess the force for this, if only he is taught to perceive the strength and necessity of virtue. He has within him the source for conquering everything. (V-Mo/Mron II 29: 625)

---

2 Chapter III of the KpV is entitled "On the incentives of pure practical reason", in the plural: "Von den Triebfedern der reinen praktischen Vernunft".

While autonomy refers to a property of rational beings who legislate for themselves, autocracy refers to the ability to make the law effective in practice (Baxley 2010). Thus, in the *Metaphysics of Virtue,* Kant establishes a link between autocracy and virtue. Relatedly, the passage above suggests a special connection between moral feeling and moral virtue based in the fact that both have to do with the executive rather than with the legislative or judiciary branch of moral agency:

> Moral feeling does not pertain to the giving of laws, but is the basis for their execution; a criterion for the good it cannot, however, be, for feeling is different in everyone, and one cannot contend about it, because nobody can communicate his feeling to another. The good, however, has to be universally valid. If someone says that he feels the truth, then the other can do nothing with him. It is a refuge of idiots to say that they feel it to be true. Morality must be based on a priori grounds. (V-Mo/Mron II 29: 625 – 626)

In the *Lectures,* Kant often distinguishes sharply between the *principium iudicationis* and *executionis* as a way to delineate the role of reason and sentiment in moral life. Yet, insofar as moral feeling has a rational ground, it makes sense to question whether, confronted with particular actions, moral feeling could work as a moral compass in charge of orientating oneself in the moral world. Interestingly, although in the second *Critique* Kant again stresses that moral feeling "does not serve for appraising actions" (KpV 5: 76), he analyses moral incentive right after explaining the "typic of judgment", that is, after explaining how the rational principle can be brought to bear on the particular actions that take place in the sensible world. This means that there is a direct connection between moral judgment and moral incentive—the latter being both a sign and an effect of the former. Accordingly, to the extent that the moral feeling relies on rational grounds, there is reason to think that it, too, represents a moral compass for our being in the world.

4 The Typic of Judgment: A Precondition for Moral Feeling

In the "Typic of Judgment", Kant deals with the problem of issuing practical judgments about the moral feasibility of a particular action; the role of judgment is to recognise the universal rule of reason in actions that can actually be performed in the sensible world (KpV 5: 66).[3] Thus, we exercise moral judgment whenever we "apply" a universal moral principle—the categorical imperative—to a particular action that is feasible in the sensible world, to see whether it passes the test. In the second *Critique*, Kant wonders how this is possible at all.

The problem of moral judgment is the problem of mediating between two worlds. Kant reminds us of how an analogous problem is solved in the theoretical realm, where the knowing subject applies pure concepts of understanding to the phenomena presented to the senses. In that case, at least in the A-edition of the first *Critique*, the solution was found in the schemata of the imagination, which apply to the manifold intuitions of the senses, thereby creating room for applying the categories of understanding and achieving knowledge (Freydberg 2013, p. 109 – 110). Yet, in the case of practical judgment, we cannot proceed in the same way: the problem of practical reason is how to apply a rational principle—a moral law—to actions that, found in the sensible world, are already subject to natural laws. The problem, therefore, is not to "organise" data coming from the senses, but rather to assess whether actions possible in the sensible world are also possible in a moral world. Solving this problem entails realising, first, that "subsumption of an action possible to me in the sensible world under a pure practical law does not concern the possibility of the action as an event in the sensible world", but only its moral feasibility. Now, this can only be done by resorting to the common feature of both laws, which is nothing other than the "schema" of the law itself, its universal form plus its causal power (KpV 5: 68 – 9). Indeed,

> [t]he moral law has no cognitive faculty other than the understanding (not the imagination) by means of which it can be applied to objects of nature, and what the understanding can put under an idea of reason is not a schema of sensibility but a law, such a law, however, as can be presented *in concreto* in objects of the senses and hence a law of nature, though only as to its form; this law is what the understanding can put under an idea of reason on behalf of judgment, and we can, accordingly, call it the type of the moral law. (KpV 5: 69)

As Freydberg notes, "the distinction between a schema and a type plays an important methodological role in Kant's practical philosophy [...] to say, as Kant does, that a type is a symbol and not a schema abrogates the connection to pure intuition" (Freydberg 2013, p. 114 – 115). This is not to say that the imagination plays no role in moral matters. It does, not only insofar as an act of imagination is included in every synthetic judgment, but also insofar as it expands

---

3 The reader will find a helpful guidance regarding the role that the "Typic" fulfills in Kant's practical rationality in Westra (2016).

the realm of thought (Costa-Mattos 2013; Freydberg 2013, p. 111) and makes room for reflective judgment to prepare the ground for deliberation and application of determining judgment (Makkreel 2013). Before I judge the moral feasibility of any action that is possible for me here and now, I must make sense of the context in which I plan to act, and this task is a matter of imagination and reflective judgment (González 2004). By contrast, moral judgment entails determination according to the rule of reason:

> The rule of judgment under laws of pure practical reason is this: ask yourself whether, if the action you propose were to take place by a law of the nature of which you were yourself a part, you could indeed regard it as possible through your will. (KpV 5: 69)

Kant states that, "everyone does, in fact, appraise actions as morally good or evil by this rule" (KpV 5: 69). Once it is "applied" to actions that we deem possible for us according to the laws of nature, these actions receive a new qualification according to the different "categories of freedom" (KpV 5: 66) introduced by Kant in the preceding section, after positing that freedom is regarded as a kind of causality. In this way, freedom can be articulated according to the categories that apply to the natural possibility of the actions it effects. Thus, according to the categories of quantity, Kant distinguishes between intentions, precepts and laws; of quality: practical rules of commission, omission, exceptions; of relation: to personality, to the condition of the person, reciprocally; and of modality: the permitted and the forbidden, duty and contrary to duty, perfect and imperfect duty (KpV 5: 67).

Yet, clarifying how those categories apply to the specific case of human beings, and defining types of actions that can be regarded as (morally) forbidden, permitted, prescribed, etc., involves taking into account the general and particular features of human existence, which cannot be known apart from experience, and hence apart from the imagination and the senses. As Rudolf Makkreel observes,

> Although Kant did not develop an orientational theory of the imagination, he does offer some suggestive ideas about orientation as such. To be oriented to the world is to define my relation to some horizon in terms of a capacity to locate my own place in it. Now I am no longer a disembodied mind that perceives representationally and am more than a recipient of what has been historically acquired. Orientation locates me in the world both perceptually and in terms of felt relations. (Makkreel 2013, p. 211)

The *Metaphysics of Morals* is supposed to provide us with an initial cartography of the moral world; it is an account of the general duties that accompany human existence, which should inform particular moral judgments. To the extent that moral feelings are indicators of moral judgments, there seems to be ground to understand those feelings as a moral compass that helps us to map out the human moral world.

Indeed, assuming that moral feeling presupposes moral judgment, and that this, in turn, brings the law to bear on an action that is possible for us in the sensible world, there is ground to say that moral feeling constitutes a gateway towards a moral anthropology. As Kant makes clear, such moral anthropology is needed for knowing how to apply the moral principle to human life rather than to ground it, which is an entirely a priori process.

5 Moral Cartography and Moral Compass

In the *Metaphysics of Morals*, Kant considers how to apply the moral principle to the material conditions of human existence, without thereby compromising the purity of moral determination (MS 6: 215); in this context he introduces the notion of "principles of application":

> Just as there must be principles in a metaphysics of nature for applying those highest universal principles of a nature in general to objects of experience, a metaphysics of morals cannot dispense with principles of application, and we shall often have to take as our object the particular nature of human beings, which is cognized only by experience, in order to show in it what can be inferred from universal moral principles. But this will in no way detract from the purity of these principles or cast doubt on their *a priori* source. This is to say, in effect, that a metaphysics of morals cannot be based upon anthropology but can still be applied to it. (MS 6: 216–217)

Along these lines, Kant introduces the idea of a "moral anthropology, which would deal only with the *subjective conditions* in human nature that hinder people or help them in fulfilling the laws of a metaphysics of morals" (MS 6: 216–217). Hence, he introduces the term to, first, mark a clear distinction between the metaphysical first principles of the doctrine of right and the doctrine of virtue and, second, highlight the subjective conditions that every individual needs to take into account in order to advance morality in his or her own life.

Accordingly, the Metaphysics of Morals deals with the metaphysical first principles of law and virtue, which represent specifications of the moral principle for its application to human beings, affected by a number of material and subjective conditions. But taking these latter subjective conditions directly into account pertains to moral anthropology; this pertains to the development, spreading, and strengthening of moral principles (in education in schools and in popular instruction), and with other similar teachings and precepts based on experience. It cannot be dispensed with, but it must not precede a metaphysics of morals or be mixed with it. (MS 6: 216–217)

Indeed, the moral cartography designed in the *Metaphysics of Morals* is not enough for human beings to orient themselves in the world; for this we need more than identifying action types amenable to determining moral judgment; we need appropriate subjective conditions to recognise those duties as duties and as something that concern us, that is, we need moral receptivity. Additionally, we need pragmatic knowledge of the world in which we live, and imagination to anticipate a horizon that is practically significant for our actions—a horizon that presents happiness in accordance with morality, i.e., a theory of hope. Focusing only on the first of these requirements, we should consider, with Kant, that

There are certain moral endowments such that anyone lacking them could have no duty to acquire them. – They are moral feeling, conscience, love of one's neighbour, and respect for oneself (self-esteem). There is no obligation to have these because they lie at the basis of morality, as subjective conditions of receptiveness to the concept of duty, not as objective conditions of morality. All of them are natural predispositions of the mind (*praedispositio*) for being affected by concepts of duty, antecedent predispositions on the side of feeling. To have these predispositions cannot be considered a duty; rather, every human being has them, and it is by virtue of them that he can be put under obligation. – Consciousness of them is not of empirical origin; it can, instead, only follow from consciousness of a moral law, as the effect this has on the mind. (MS 6: 399)

It is worth noting that, while Kant speaks of these conditions as "moral endowments", he also designates them as "natural predispositions of the mind". At any rate, they are "subjective conditions of receptiveness to the concept of duty". In other words, they are feelings that derive from our peculiar human nature, insofar as it partakes in reason and the senses. Thus, consciousness of these dispositions "is not of empirical origin; it can, instead, only follow from consciousness of a moral law, as the effect this has on the mind" (MS 6: 399).

Thus, here Kant characterises moral feeling as "the susceptibility to feel pleasure or displeasure merely from being aware that our actions are consistent with or contrary to the law of duty"; he then recalls the difference between pathological and practical feelings, and highlights the need for moral feeling in order to become aware of the thought of an obligation, or ultimately of the coercive presence of the law:

> Since any consciousness of obligation depends upon moral feeling to make us aware of the constraint present in the thought of duty, there can be no duty to have moral feeling or to acquire it; instead every human being (as a moral being) has it in him originally. (MS 6: 399)

For this reason, Kant cannot admit of humanity devoid of moral feeling, which would amount to being "morally dead" (MS 6: 399–400). In this excerpt, moral feeling is present once again, although it is considered not so much from the perspective of the law that impinges upon human nature, as from the perspective of human nature that receives the impact of the law. The point is that we must have a human nature in order to feel the coercion of the law, that is, in order to generate moral feeling.

Of course, speaking of "human nature" involves something more than considering an isolated human being with her psychological endowments, which are developed and activated in particular cases, and specifically in interaction with other human beings. For this reason, Kant also speaks of a duty to cultivate moral feeling and strengthen it (MS 6: 399–400). As suggested above, this belongs to the nature of human feelings: while human feelings are natural, they can also be perfected through practice, thus reinforcing their efficacy. By developing moral virtue we develop a moral character, which strengthens moral feeling and perfects autonomy with autocracy. Moral feeling fully incorporated into character represents a moral compass, insofar as it involves not just a "judgment sharpened by experience" (GMS 4: 389–390), i.e., trained in knowledge of the world, but above all a moral judgment, i.e., one that retains the difference between the world as it is and the world as it should be. While pragmatic knowledge, which Kant exhibits in the *Anthropology*, is supposed to provide us with the knowledge of the means necessary to advance the ends of virtue, it is morality that determines those ends: our own perfection and the happiness of others.

6 Concluding Remarks

This chapter set out to clarify Kant's thought on "reason's feelings". In order to do so, I first argued that reason is an active power, yet not an absolute power, because of the fact that it has needs, desires, and interests. Thus, reason's interests, and specifically its interest in achieving sufficient ground for knowledge and action, are the basis for the feelings it engenders, both in the theoretical and in the practical realm. A closer look at the Kantian account of moral feeling served to illustrate its genesis as the effect of contrasting the universal requirements of reason with the particular requirements of other inclinations. If moral feeling qualifies as a "feeling of reason", however, it is only because it primarily follows the activity of reason, and not the other way around.

Yet, in order to argue that moral feeling plays a key role in orientating ourselves in moral matters, a further step was required due to the fact that Kant explicitly states that moral feeling only represents a *principium executionis*, and is never a *principium iudicationis*. In my view, this third step is provided by the very structure of Kant's KpV, in which the section on moral judgment precedes the section on moral incentive, showing that moral feeling comes after moral judgment as an effect thereof, or, to put it in another way, that moral feeling incorporates moral judgment. Accordingly, defining the cartography of moral life around the logical requirements of the categorical imperative for human beings can be interpreted as an attempt to make explicit what is implicit in contextualised moral feeling; from an architectonic point of view, the result of this cartography is the *Metaphysics of Morals*.

Of course, it is one thing to have a map and another to use that map. From a practical point of view, the *Metaphysics of Morals* is not the last word on moral behaviour. In order to orientate ourselves in the world, we need something more than theoretically identifying action types amenable to determining moral judgment; we need moral receptivity, and the ability to anticipate a practically significant horizon for our actions, that is, a horizon that presents happiness in accordance with morality, as well as the pragmatic knowledge provided by the *Anthropology*.

Bibliography

Baxley, Anne Margaret (2010): *Kant's Theory of Virtue. The Value of Autocracy*. Cambridge: Cambridge University Press.

Costa Mattos, Fernando (2013): "The Postulates of Pure Practical Reason. A Possible Place for Imagination in Kant's Moral Philosophy?" In: Michael L. Thompson (Ed.): *Imagination in Kant's Critical Philosophy*. Berlin, Boston: De Gruyter, pp. 123–140.

Fabrizzi, Chiara (2008): *Mente e corpo in Kant*. Rome: Aracne.

Freydberg, Bernard (2013): "Functions of Imagination in Kant's Moral Philosophy". In: Michael L. Thompson (Ed.): *Imagination in Kant's Critical Philosophy*. Berlin, Boston: De Gruyter, pp. 105–121.

Gibbon, Sarah L. (1994): *Kant's Theory of the Imagination*. Oxford: Clarendon Press.

González, Ana Marta (2004): "Cultura y felicidad en Kant". In: *Teorema* 23. Nos. 1–3, pp. 215–232.

González, Ana Marta (2015): "Emoción, Sentimiento y Pasión en Kant". In *Trans-Form-Açao* 38. No. 3, pp. 75–98. DOI: http://dx.doi.org/10.1590/S0101–31732015000300006, accessed on 16 March, 2021.

González, Ana Marta (2016): "The Recovery of Action in Social Theory. Acting out of
   Sentiment, Acting out of Character, Acting out of Interest, Acting out of Will". In: Mark
   Alznauer and Jose María Torralba (Eds.): *Theories of Action and Morality. Perspectives
   from Philosophy and Social Theory*. Hildesheim, Zürich, New York: Georg Olms Verlag,
   pp. 79–111.
Grenberg, Jeanine (2013): *Kant's Defense of Common Moral Experience. A Phenomenological
   Account*. Cambridge: Cambridge University Press.
Kant, Immanuel (1996a): "What Does it Mean to Orient Oneself in Thinking?" In: Allen W.
   Wood and George di Giovanni (Eds.): *Immanuel Kant, Religion and Rational Theology*.
   Cambridge: Cambridge University Press, pp. 7–18.
Kant, Immanuel (1996b): *The Metaphysics of Morals*. Mary J. Gregor (Ed.). Cambridge:
   Cambridge University Press.
Kant, Immanuel (1997a): *Groundwork of the Metaphysics of Morals*. Mary J. Gregor (Ed.).
   Cambridge: Cambridge University Press.
Kant, Immanuel (1997b): *Critique of Practical Reason*. Mary J. Gregor (Ed.). Cambridge:
   Cambridge University Press.
Kant, Immanuel (1998): *Critique of Pure Reason*. Paul Guyer and Allen W. Wood (Eds.).
   Cambridge, New York: Cambridge University Press.
Kant, Immanuel (2001): "Morality According to Prof. Kant: Mongrovius' Second Set of Lecture
   Notes". In: Peter Heath and Jerome B. Schneewind (Eds.): *Lectures on Ethics*. Cambridge:
   Cambridge University Press.
Kant, Immanuel (2009): "Anthropology from a Pragmatic Point of View". In: Robert B. Louden
   and Gunther Zöller (Eds.): *Anthropology, History, and Education*. Cambridge, New York:
   Cambridge University Press.
Klemme, Heiner F., Kühn, Manfred and Schönecker, Dieter (Eds.) (2006): *Moralische
   Motivation. Kant und die Alternativen*. Hamburg: Felix Meiner Verlag.
Klemme, Heiner F. (2006): "Praktische Gründe und Moralische Motivation". In: Heiner F.
   Klemme, Manfred Kühn and Dieter Schönecker (Eds.): *Moralische Motivation. Kant und
   die Alternativen*. Hamburg: Felix Meiner Verlag, pp. 113–153.
Makkreel, Rudolf (2013): "Recontextualizing Kant's Theory of Imagination". In: Michael L.
   Thompson (Ed.): *Imagination in Kant's Critical Philosophy*. Berlin, Boston: De Gruyter,
   pp. 205–220.
Pollok, Konstantin (2006): "Kant und Habermas über das *principium executionis* moralischer
   Handlungen". In: Heiner F. Klemme, Manfred Kühn and Dieter Schönecker (Eds.):
   Moralische Motivation. Kant und die Alternativen. Hamburg: Felix Meiner Verlag,
   pp. 193–227.
Raedler, Sebastian (2015): *Kant and the Interests of Reason*. Berlin, Boston: De Gruyter.
Reath, Andrews and Timmerman, Jens (Eds.) (2010): *Kant's 'Critique of Practical Reason':
   A Critical Guide*. Cambridge: Cambridge University Press.
Recki, Birgit (2006): *Die Vernunft, ihre Natur, ihr Gefühl und der Fortschritt*. Paderborn:
   Mentis.
Schadow, Steffi (2013): *Achtung für das Gesetz. Moral und Motivation bei Kant*. Berlin,
   Boston: De Gruyter.
Thompson, Michael L. (Ed.) (2013): *Imagination in Kant's Critical Philosophy*. Berlin, Boston:
   De Gruyter.

Westra, Adam (2016): *The Typic in Kant's Critique of Practical Reason: Moral Judgment and Symbolic Representation*. Boston, Berlin: De Gruyter.

Wood, Allen (1996): "Introduction to 'What Does it Mean to Orient Oneself in Thinking?' In: Allen W. Wood and George di Giovanni (Eds.): Immanuel Kant, *Religion and Rational Theology*. Cambridge: Cambridge University Press, pp. 3–6.

Mariannina Failla
Edenic Animality, Self-Sustenance, Loving and Dying: Corporeal Biological Needs and Emotions in Kant

Abstract: The first part of the title (Edenic Animality) establishes a direct link to the Old Testament Creation narrative, the heart of the Book of Genesis, which Kant interpreted to develop a conjecture about the beginning of history. What is the meaning of conjecture and what is its relationship with the genesis of history? What does the first human being mean to Kant and what is its relationship with the impulses and instincts experienced in the Garden of Eden? Further still, what link is established between instincts, emotions (*Rührungen*), sentiments (*Gefühle*) and human moral action? This short text will seek to answer these questions by demonstrating how the anthropological interpretation of the Holy Scriptures offers a psycho-corporeal genealogy of moral behaviour. In describing the progressive emancipation from Edenic instinct, Kant considers emotional states (loss, love, fear, hope) as essential steps toward the formation of a moral conscience.

Keywords: instincts, emotions, sentiments, moral action, moral conscience

1 Conjecture and Genesis

Conjecture is a "non-serious" relationship between reason and imagination. It is a "pleasing" exercise of the imagination, accompanied by reason. These words immediately introduce us to the aesthetic realm of Kantian thinking. Yet we are unaccustomed to the manner in which they do so, or at least it would appear this way. In the *Critique of Judgment*, non-seriousness is associated with play; indeterminate and free from the faculties of the mind, it gives rise to the disinterested pleasure of beauty. This "non-serious", harmonious and spontaneous game involving our faculties does not, however, involve reason. With regards to our faculties, reason intervenes only in the sublime, disrupting the playful and free harmony that exists between imagination and intellect. Reason violates the imagination and obliges it—as Gilles Deleuze puts it—to accept its limits. Through this painful experience, the imagination ensures that the human

Mariannina Failla, Univ. Roma Tre, Italy

https://doi.org/10.1515/9783110720730-005

mind senses the seriousness of its own intelligible nature and entrusts itself to its sublimity.

In Kant's 1786 essay on the beginning of history, reason neither interrupts nor upsets the playfulness of the imagination; on the contrary, it guides and moderates the imagination and helps avoid any overenthusiasm (*Schwärmerei*, MAM 8: 110.7; Kant 2006a, p. 25) that would shift it away from experience. Through the interaction between reason and imagination, we are able to conceive of a beginning of history that, "[needs] not be fabricated, but rather can be derived from experience" (MAM 8: 109.12–13; Kant 2006a, p. 24). It is not reveries, but the guidance of healthy human reason that allows us to imagine a Beginning (*Der Anfang*) that is genesis, or, better yet, generation. The synonymy of genesis and generation, intended as the birth of the human race (an *alias* for its liberty) finds documentary proof in the Holy Scriptures, in particular in the first book of the Pentateuch, with the moment of a beginning: *Bereshit*. The "literal" meaning of the Holy Text is replaced by its philosophical meaning. Precisely this philosophical interpretation of the "Genesis" brings us back to the question: what is the meaning of genesis in Kant's philosophy?

While "genesis" is undoubtedly a rare word in Kant's vocabulary, it cannot be ignored. Its use responds to the need to distinguish the physiological or psychological, (the genetic dimension of knowledge), from the transcendental dimension, which is concerned with legitimising intuitive and even *a priori* categorial forms, as well as investigating their possible congruence and operativity.

Together with the word "real", which refers to the essential contents of the concept or idea in general, "genesis" appears in pre-critical writings, yet remains obscured by the "metaphysical exposition" in the *Critique of Pure Reason*. In *Kant's Inaugural Dissertation of 1770*, the term "genesis" directly refers to the metaphysical, and is used to qualify the use that the intellect makes of pure principles such as "real".

In truth, while Kant comes across as quite radical in the *Inaugural Dissertation*, he goes even further when he fuses method [the use of the intellect] and pure principles, understood as the real principles of reason. Objects (here we could say the "real" of pure thinking) and the axioms to be applied to these same objects constitute the nature of reason. Presenting the laws of reason, according to their correct use, inherently signifies genetically producing the rational contents of metaphysical thinking. What is important here is the close and reciprocal link between the *expositio* and the *genesis* of the essential contents of reason, that is, the relationship between *expositio* and the *rational real*. Presenting pure rational contents is the genesis of pure science, while the illustrative (expositive) procedure is in itself the constitution of pure thinking (MSI 2: 411.15–20; Kant 2014, [1894[1]], p. 34–35). At the end of the first part of the essay *The One Possible Basis for a Demonstration of the Existence of God* (written before 1770), Kant identifies *the genuinely genetic* with the derivation of the existence of God from what "really" constitutes His absolute necessity: "In this way the existence of the being is known from what *really* constitutes its absolute necessity and thus entirely *genetically*" (BDG 2: 91.7–11; Kant, 1994: 95, [emphasis added]). Thus, even here, genesis and the reality of pure thinking are strictly connected.

In the conjectures of 1786, the *expositio*, despite being an imaginative story, coincides with the original constitution of human nature. Imaginative conjecture aligns closely with the role played by *genesis* in thinking, yet it abandons the metaphysical and entrusts itself to the aesthetic plane. Indeed, the conjecture appears similar to the characteristic of the concept behind the genesis of the Kantian aesthetic, about which Gilles Deleuze writes in his essay (*L'idée de genèse dans l'esthétique de Kant*) holding together sensible matter and reason (Deleuze 1963, pp. 118–125).

"Imagining" the origin of the human being, through the use of reason, yet also experience, is to identify the essential components of "humanity". While during the pre-critical period, Kant established a link between the exposition of the genesis of the real contents of thinking and their constitution, during the empirical and historical period, sensible and imaginative delight, guided by reason, permitted a conjecture not of man's accidental characteristics, but of his "nature"—the essential components of his constitution as a historic being. In this way, we may posit that conjecture makes it possible to imagine the historic reality of man. Imagining the genesis is equivalent to exposing the essence of human nature,[1] which is the coincidence, the fusion, of the sensible real and reason.

2 Self-sustenance

We must now confront the question: who is the first man? In Kant's analysis, his differences with Rousseau are evident: the first man is not a noble savage, nor a nomad. Moreover, he does not lack lasting relationships, and his language is not limited to *le cri de la natur*. Rather, in Kant's view, the imaginative story does not begin with a single, asocial human being, but with the couple in the Garden of

---

1 The idea of a conjecture regarding the story of mankind induces a reflection on Kant's positions on natural history, and his attempt to propose a mediation between experimentalists (Buffon, Diderot) and the so-called "systematists" (Linnaeus). On this topic see (Failla 2012, pp. 61–63; Marcucci 2010, pp. 55–85).

Eden—the family, the first nucleus of society. To render this conjecture as plausible as possible, Kant recalls *homo erectus*—able to walk, capable of discussion and thinking, and already equipped with logos. This is a being with physical-motorial and linguistic-discursive abilities, acquired through experience. Kant writes: "These are all skills that the human being had to acquire on its own (for if they had been inborn, they would also be passed on, an assumption contradicted by experience). But I shall assume the human being as already in possession of these, simply in order to be able to consider the development of decency and morals in his activities, something which necessarily presupposes the above skills" (MAM 8: 110.31–111.3; Kant 2006a, p. 25).

Kant also uses this passage to delineate the scope of his conjecture: an explanation of man's moral development. Kant seeks a phenomenology of action, and more specifically, acting on oneself, so that one can achieve autonomy and understand his rational purpose. This is the true meaning of the Kantian story of the origins of the human race.

The Edenic couple originally survived by following the voice of instinct, which Kant identifies with "the voice of God" (MAM 8: 111.4; Kant 2006a, p. 26), (hinting at the potential influence of Homer on Kant's writings). God appears comparable to *tymos*, the voice that speaks to Homeric heroes and stimulates their vital, sentimental and instinctive forces.[2] Following "the voice of God, which all animals must obey" (MAM 8:111.18; Kant 2006a, p. 26), "the newcomer" could nurture and provide for himself, while others were prohibited from doing so (to paraphrase Genesis 3:2–3). Obeying his instincts, the first man, like all other animals in the Garden of Eden, used his sense of smell to distinguish foods that were permitted from those that were prohibited.

> Yet *reason* soon began to stir and sought, by comparing foods with what was presented to him as similar foods by a different sense than the one to which instinct was bound, say by the sense of sight, to extend his knowledge of foodstuffs beyond the confines of mere instinct (3: 6). (MAM 8: 111.19–24; Kant 2006a, p. 26)

Human reason was thus dormant in the animal nature of the Garden of Eden. Primed for self-emancipation, however, reason soon set limits on instinct, in other words, on the *voice of God*, entirely replacing the sense of smell with an-

---

2 Kant considers Homer to be a crasser cantor than Virgil, whose "eloquence" is due "merely to the lack of means for expressing their concepts" (Kant, Anth 07: 191.30–33, § 38; 2006b, p. 84, § 38). Precisely the consideration of Homer as a poet devoid of any conceptual sophistication and refined eloquence may make him the most suitable inspiration for describing man's infancy.

other sense: sight. Reason soon learned not only to limit, but to oppose the Edenic instinct that, through the sense of smell, rendered man akin to animals.

For Edenic man, deceiving the voice of nature by favouring choice over instinct, and the newfound ability to decide whether or not to eat certain foods through the use of sight, resulted in human's discovery of more than one way of life. Humans, no longer bound to one *ethos*, could now choose between a plurality of behaviours. It is precisely this element—the first leap beyond the bounds of instinct—that distinguishes the earliest form of emancipation from Edenic animalism.

> He discovered in himself a capacity to choose a way of life for himself and not, as other animals, to be bound to a single one. The momentary delight caused by his noticing this advantage must have been followed by anxiety and fear as to how he, having not yet known anything according to his hidden traits and remote effects, should proceed with his newly discovered ability. He stood at the edge of an abyss, as it were. For whereas instinct had hitherto directed him to individual objects of his desire, an infinity of such objects now opened itself up to him, from among which he did not yet know how to choose. Yet once he had had a taste of this state of freedom it was impossible for him to return to the taste of servitude (under the rule of instinct). (MAM 8: 112.14 – 26; Kant 2006a, p. 26 – 27)

While the domination of the instinct of self-sustenance represents the first manifestation of man's state of freedom, it remained an entirely fragile state, in which the bodily impulse to feed was strongly connected with powerful emotions of anxiety. In this early stage, the fear of one's ability to choose, and, ultimately, the fear of the unknown depths concealed within the human mind, was still in its infancy. But Edenic man was now, for the first time, facing the abyss of his still unexplored soul.

These reflections are undoubtedly of great relevance as they help us shed light on the body-mind relationship in a philosophy criticised repeatedly and by many for its formalistic and intellectualistic emptying of the self (Simmel 1904). In Kant's creation story, Edenic man, the prototype of the human being, discovers the articulate and sophisticated actions of his own psyche thanks to the transition from one sensorial-bodily activity to another: from smell to sight.[3] The interaction between psychical and bodily drives is irrefutable. It evokes Kant's temporary call to common sense in his pre-critical text *Dreams of a Spirit-seer illustrated by Dreams of Metaphysics*, where he affirmed: "I would, therefore, keep to common experience, and would say, provisionally, where I sense, there I am. I am just as immediately in the tips of my fingers,

---

3 On the organisation of the senses, the superiority of vision and the coarseness of the sense of smell, see (Anth 7: 153 – 160.10, §§ 15 – 22; Kant 2006b, pp. 45 – 51, §§ 15 – 22).

as in my head" (TG 02: 324.30–32; Kant 1900, p. 49). The psyche is to be found where the body senses and perceives.[4] We can now add that the psyche is found where the sensing body creates diverse emotional states: pleasure (delight), fear, and loss.[5] All the same, in his 1786 text, while retracing the history of a physiology of the psyche, or rather, the history of physiological anthropology,[6] Kant sought to change meaning and direction to apply them to pragmatic psychology (that is, man can and must act on his own).[7] We must not forget that the cognitive bodily element, expressed in and through the transition from the sense of smell to the sense of sight, is accompanied by a practical experience: that of choice. We must not ignore the fact that the onset of this practical ability creates lacerating emotional states that the first man must live through and overcome in order to become aware of his own freedom.

3 From Loving and Hoping to Purpose

Another form of domination, specifically domination of sexual instinct, would offer man a way to protect himself against an initial state of anxiety. In the Kantian treatment of sexuality, it is striking that the famous "fig leaf" from Genesis 3:7 is not a symbol of man's shame and guilt at having chosen to orient his instinct to feed against the voice of God, nor does it allude to the first symbolic myth of the birth of technique. After eating the forbidden fruit, and having dis-

---

4 For an interpretation that establishes a relationship between Kantian analyses and Freudian reflections on the body-mind relationship, see the interesting article by Carignani (2018, pp. 665–689).

5 Here it is as if we can hear the motifs prepared by the Leibnizian vision of the body-mind relationship, sketched out in a short and interesting fragment of uncertain dating. In this text, Leibniz argues in favour of a very close connection between sensory stimuli, sophisticated cerebral activities (the vital spirits of scholastic origin) and psychic representations. Leibniz's description also has the aim of revealing the intimate overlap between psychic perceptive-cognitive and practical activities (Leibniz 2003, pp. 4–23). He thus shows a closeness to the reflections of Aristotle, according to whom the faculty of practical intellect is not truly separate from theoretical intellect. In its activities, intellect sets objectives and regulates desires (*De Anima*, III 10, 433 a 13–16).

6 Brandt (1999, p. 50) claimed that the rationalist-Baumgartian conception of empirical psychology belonging to anthropology, to which Kant alludes, is already present in Otto Casmann and, in particular, in his *Psychologia Anthropologica* from 1594. In this work, anthropology is interpreted as a theory of man's experience as a psycho-corporeal being.

7 Kant (Anth 7: 119.11–14; Kant 2006b, p. 3): "Physiological knowledge of the human being concerns the investigation of what *nature* makes of the human being; pragmatic, the investigation of what *he* as a free-acting being makes of himself, or can and should make of himself".

covered himself nude, destitute, and fragile (in comparison with animals), man protects himself with nature (the leaf). For Kant, the "fig leaf" symbolises the acquisition of the capacity to defer sexual pleasure. Man, who has broken free of the voice of instinct, acquires the capacity to extend and prolong his sexual impulse—he discovers that he is able to sublimate his libido. More importantly, he now has the ability to substitute the fleeting and periodic impulse of the animal with a prolonged desire, whose intensity is heightened by the imagination.

> The human being soon discovered that the appeal of sex, which in animals is based on stimuli that are merely temporary and mostly periodic, could be extended and even augmented through his imagination, which compelled him, to be sure, with more moderation, but also in a more enduring and consistent manner the more the object is *withdrawn from the senses*. And in this way the human being did not tire of it as he would if a merely animal desire were satisfied. (MAM 8: 112. 31–113.1; Kant 2006a, p. 27)

The act of imagining, its capacity to prolong pleasure even in the absence of the object, elevates man to a taste for human and natural beauty, and introduces him to the customs of social life. Subtraction and renunciation are the artifice that leads man from instinctive stimuli to ideal stimuli, from animalesque instinct to sexual love that is experienced with and through the mediation of social customs.

It is this governance of sexual impulse, which implies the renunciation, deferral and sublimation of the immediacy of pleasure, that leads to the creation of the first societies.

> Hence the fig leaf (v. 7) was the product of a much greater expression of reason than it had shown during the first stage of its development. For to make an inclination more fervent and fasting by withdrawing its object from the senses already shows the awareness of some degree of mastery of reason over the instincts and not merely, as with the first step, an ability to serve the latter to a lesser or greater extent. *Refusal* was the feat by means of which stimuli that were merely sensual were converted to those that were dependent on ideas. Mere animal desire was gradually converted to love and, with this, the feeling of mere pleasure was converted to a taste for beauty, initially only in the human being, but then also in nature. *Decency*, an inclination to inspire the respect of others toward our person through good manners (the hiding of that which could arouse disdain), as the actual basis of all true sociability, was the first signal to the development of the human being as a moral creature. (MAM 8: 113.1–15; Kant 2006a, p. 27)

Thus, it could be said that Kant recognises a true and proper process of social integration in the sublimation of sexual instinct. Mediating between sexual instinct and customs is aesthetic taste, considered in the *Nachschrift Collins* and in the *Anthropology* as socially shared pleasure:

[T]aste is the faculty of the aesthetic power of judgment to choose with universal validity.'
Taste is, accordingly, a faculty of making *social* judgments of external objects within the
power of imagination. – Here the mind feels its freedom in the play of images (therefore
of sensibility); for sociability with other human beings presupposes freedom – and this
feeling is pleasure. (Anth 07: 241.4–10; Kant 2006a, p. 137–138)

Taste implies the capacity to feel pleasure and satisfaction together with others,
to feel social satisfaction. Through man's aspiration to please others, to be loved
or admired, taste becomes a path toward his integration within society, guided
by decency. We can thus state that the sublimating instinct—renouncing the immediacy and presence of the desired object through imaginative artifice—signifies initiating a process of social integration. This is a process that, for Kant,
has an important ethical significance: recognising the value of customs to edu-
cate man to respect others and virtues.[8]

To date, the biblical myth continues to fulfil its preordained role as a narrative crafted by human reason, in concert with the wings of the imagination, designed to identify the constituent elements of the human race. These include
processes of socialisation and integration, such as sublimation, as well as the
exercise of aesthetic taste and intense love, seen as ideal instincts and good
manners.[9]

The third consequence of reason, after its effect on man's primary needs of
self-sustenance and sexual instinct, was "the conscious anticipation of future"
(MAM 8: 113. 20–21; Kant 2006a, p. 27). Satiating himself on the fruits of the
tree of awareness (and, in doing so, disobeying the voice of God), humans not
only came to know the fatigue of toil (man) or the pains of labour (woman),
but also the experience of death. It is precisely these unavoidable experiences
of life that allow man, through the use of reason, to develop a feeling of hope
for the future: humans die hoping to provide a better future for their descendants. In that way, once again, it is the psychic experience of corporeality, of
his own end, of his dissolution, that produces an interior conflict that leads to
the birth of a new emotional state and feeling: hope in future generations.

---

8 Promoting morality in this way, that is, through the exercise of aesthetic taste, implies a role
for aesthetic taste similar to that of the illusion of the senses in the anthropological analysis of
the faculty of cognition: preparing and promoting social consensus, and guided by the idea of
moral legitimacy (Failla 2016, pp. 55–80).
9 Certainly, the allusion to love as an ideal that guarantees the duration of sexual impulse cannot but evoke various passages on love by St. Augustine, astutely interpreted by Hannah Arendt
as the source of the idea of the durability of the ego. The durable ego, beyond the restlessness of
desire, is the ego that loves (Arendt 1978, p. 419 and following).

> Both of them [the man and the woman] foresaw with fear, in the background of the picture, that which, to be sure, inevitably comes upon all animals, yet does not cause the latter any worry, namely death, after a life of toil. They seemed to rebuke and make into a crime the use of reason that caused all these ills to befall them. To live through their offspring, who would perhaps have it better, or who even as members of a family could ameliorate their woes, was perhaps the only consoling prospect that gave them heart (vv.16–20). (MAM 8: 113.32–114.2; Kant 2006a, p. 28)

Here, Kant demonstrates a subtle sensitivity for those expressions repeatedly present in the *Torah*, according to which a blessed death is one that restores man to his antecedents. The Jew is happy to survive vicariously through his progeny and happy to die old and wizened by the years. This idea is also seen in Cicero, according to whom man only truly dies when communities die, as a result of sin. Beyond the sympathies Kant may have harboured for Jewish religious culture, (which may perhaps be the source of the idea of immortality as a return to a bloodline, or of the sacredness of birth right) (Tafani 2008, pp. 33–58), in this context he appears to emphasise that reason affects anxiety regarding death by reminding us of the value of community, understood as a bloodline or family. It is not difficult to see the active role of emotions in these reflections: fear of death generates the hope to survive vicariously in the happiness and prosperity of successive generations. What is significant is that the Jewish religion, elsewhere considered reason for the theocratic foundation of political power, is viewed here as propaedeutic to the development of human morality. This imaginative interpretation of the Book of Genesis arrives, all the same, at the moral essence of the human race, with Kant's use of the word "finality". This is the moment when man becomes aware of himself as a purpose of nature. Indeed, for Kant, understanding that he is *Naturzweck* (the concept of a natural end), constitutes the true leap taken by man's Edenic instinct, which is, however, a leap he must continually make throughout the course of history and the succession of cultures. Understanding that he is the final purpose of nature means assuming his own moral purpose as his objective (*moralische Bestimmung*) (Höffe 2008, pp. 289–308). Kant's imaginative narrative shows us how man prepares for his moral destiny by passing through multiple emotional states: fear of choice, love of pleasure, anxiety regarding death, and finally, hope for the future. Only the progressive experience of these affective states prepares the human being to experience himself and others as ends in themselves.

Bibliography

Arendt, Hannah (1978): *The Life of the Mind*. New York, London: Harcourt Brace Jovanovich.

Brandt, Reinhard (1999): *Kommentar zu Kants Anthropologie*. Hamburg: Felix Meiner Verlag.

Carignani, Paolo (2018): "'Psyche is Extended': From Kant to Freud". In: *Journal of Psychoanalysis* 99. No. 3, pp. 665–689.

Deleuze, Gilles (1963): "L'idée de genèse dans l'esthétique de Kant". In: *Revue d'esthétique* 16, pp. 113–136.

Failla, Mariannina (2012): *Poter agire*. Pisa: ETS.

Failla, Mariannina (2016): "L'empirismo di Kant: illusione, menzogna e biasimo". In: *Con-texos-Kantianos* 3, pp. 55–80.

Höffe, Otfried (2008): "Der Mensch als Endzweck (§§ 82–84)". In: Otfried Höffe (Ed.): *Immanuel Kant. Kritik der Urteilskraft*. Berlin: Akademie Verlag, pp. 289–308.

Kant, Immanuel (1900): *Dreams of Spirit-seer Illustrated by Dreams of Metaphysik*. London: Swan Sonnenschein & Co.

Kant, Immanuel (1994): *The One Possible Basis for a Demonstration of the Existence of God*. Gordon Treash (Trans.). Lincoln, London: University of Nebraska Press.

Kant, Immanuel (2006a): "Conjectural Beginning of Human History". In: Pauline Kleingeld (Ed.): *Toward Perpetual Peace* and *Other Writings on Politics, Peace, and History*. New Haven, London: Yale University Press, pp. 24–36.

Kant, Immanuel (2006b): *Anthropology from a Pragmatic Point of View*. Robert B. Louden (Ed.) (Trans.). New York: Cambridge University Press.

Kant, Immanuel (2007): *Critique of Judgment*. James Creed Meredith (Trans.). Oxford: Oxford University Press.

Kant, Immanuel (2014, [1894[1]]): *Kant's Inaugural Dissertation of 1770. Dissertation on the Form and Principles of the Sensible and the Intelligible World*. New York: Columbia College.

Leibniz Gottfried Wilhelm (2003): "Das Leib-Seele Pentagon und die moralische Sphäre des Verstandes (1663)". In: Hubertus Busche (Ed.): *Frühe Schriften zum Naturrecht*. Hamburg: Felix Meiner Verlag, pp. 4–23.

Marcucci, Silvestro (2010): "Kant e Linneo. Un 'superamento' scientifico-filosofico di una visione 'descrittiva' della natura". In: C. Claudio La Rocca (Ed.): *Scritti su Kant. Scienza, teleologia, mondo*. Pisa: ETS, pp. 55–85.

Simmel, Georg (1904): *Kant. Sechzehn Vorlesungen Gehalten an der Berliner Universität*. Leipzig: Duncker & Humblot.

Tafani, Daniela (2008): "Religione e diritti civili: la questione ebraica in Kant". In: *Studi kantiani* 31, pp. 33–58.

Ana Cristina Falcato

Kant and the 'True Shame Instinct': Notes on the Future of the Human Species

'I am not ashamed of what I did then, but of the intention which I had' – And didn't the intention lie *also* in what I did? What justifies the shame? *The whole history of the incident.*[1]
Ludwig Wittgenstein, *Philosophical Investigations*, §644.

Abstract: Shame is usually taken to be an emotion far removed from Kant's practical philosophy broadly understood. Mostly for good reasons, Kantianism has been charged with neglecting the role that emotions play in practical deliberation and action. Whenever such a claim is explicitly endorsed by contemporary moral philosophers, however, textual sources are largely ignored, and a stricture between pre-critical and critical writings is assumed. In this essay, I rely on some highly relevant remarks Kant wrote in the 1760s, all of which anticipate future developments in Critical Philosophy whilst speculating about the role played by the so-called "shame-instinct" on the improvement of the human species over time. I thus address a gross misjudgment of Kantian ethics by Anglo-American philosophy, while also pointing out some seemingly unsolvable paradoxes in Kant's reasoning on the topic, which only become apparent once their premises have been made explicit.

Keywords: instinct of shame, shame, state of nature, anthropology

1 Introduction: An All-too-systematic View of Critical Philosophy

Contemporary moral philosophers keen on systematizing traditional moral outlooks without closely examining the evolution of their textual sources run the risk of mistakenly ascribing views of thinkers to traditions they never actually

Acknoweledgement: This work was supported by National Funds through FCT (Fundação para a Ciência e Tecnologia). The author is supported by FCT under the contractual programme in accordance with articles 4, 5, and 6 of the Law Decree no. 57/2016, of August 29, altered by Law no. 57/2017, July 19.

1 My italics.

Ana Cristina Falcato, IFILNOVA/UNL, Portugal

https://doi.org/10.1515/9783110720730-006

identified with. For all his genius, the English moral philosopher Bernard Williams is a good example of this habit. In an oft-quoted passage from *Shame and Necessity*,[2] Williams charges Kant with an utter dismissal of the role shame plays in human relations in general, and especially within a normative framework which stresses the universality of rational standards, as against individual character traits and personal choice.

The crucial passage in *Shame and Necessity* where such criticism is explicitly articulated is as follows:

> In the scheme of Kantian oppositions, shame is on the bad side of all the lines. This is well brought out in its notorious association with the notion of losing or saving face. 'Face' stands for appearance against reality and the outer versus the inner, so its values are superficial; I lose or save it only in the eyes of others, so the values are heteronomous; it is simply my face to save or lose, so they are egoistic. (Williams 1993, p. 77)

In this essay I reflect upon the more schematic features characteristic of this definition of shame; moreover, I turn to concrete sources in the Kantian corpus as a whole, where a very complex idea of an 'instinct of shame' is articulated and its moral value is stressed. In truth, Bernard Williams never quotes Kantian sources, nor does he even allude to possible passages from the *Nachlass* where the topic might have been raised and discussed. Throughout *Shame and Necessity*, there is no shred of textual evidence that Williams' conjectures reflect Kant's view on the issue.

In the following pages, I explore Kant's reflections regarding the role of shame in the evolution of the relationship between the sexes. Particular attention is paid to the historic and genetic development of a complex line of reasoning Kant seems to have first presented in his courses on Ethics, dating from the beginning of the 1760s.[3] I conduct my analysis of this problem in Kant's early texts through a comparison with a structural expansion of the same model applied to a justification of the ultimate purpose of the relationship between the sexes. I conclude with a note on some paradoxical conclusions my analysis may give rise to, when compared with contemporary views on shame understood as a moral emotion. Our first order of business, however, is to map out the problematic puzzle in which a discussion of the instinct of shame appears in Kant's early work, so as to better understand the paradoxical conclusions it leads to.

---

2 See Williams (1993, p. 77).
3 See V-PP/Herder 27: 48; Kant 1997, p. 22; V-PP/Herder 27: 53, Kant 1997, p. 24.

2 Continuities and Discontinuities in Kant's Critical Project

Reading Kant's early texts today, it is hard to avoid the impression that the very evolution of his thought anticipates concepts and patterns of reasoning that only the later work will fully develop. One such reasoning pattern, strikingly akin to the description of a teleological judgment, can be found in texts as early as the second section of the *Observations on the Feeling of the Beautiful and Sublime* (1764) as well as in some lecture notes on Moral Philosophy. Here, Kant traces a deep connection between one crucial end of nature—the propagation of the human species—and a sense of shame. He does not, however, provide an argument for this connection. One of this essay's main objectives, thus, is to establish an argument for this association.

I shall begin my analysis with a well-known set of lecture notes taken by Johann Gottfried Herder at the beginning of Kant's career as a teacher. Herder attended Kant's Lectures at Albertina University in Königsberg between 1762 and 1764. While in later years he would strongly dispute Kant's most important views regarding history and the role of rationality as the ultimate source of normativity, during his student days, Herder considered himself a fierce disciple of Kant.

From the many sets of notes known to us, we can, at the very least, infer that the young philosopher took part in Kant's courses on Ethics. The German scholar Paul Menzer first compiled the notes from the lectures on Ethics in 1924,[4] marking the occasion of the bicentennial of Kant's birth. And in spite of some discrepancies between the Menzer edition of *Eine Vorlesung Kants über Ethik* and the notes attributed to Herder, some of the topics discussed in both texts overlap. The range of problems discussed in what are now referred to as the 'Herder Lecture Notes' is impressive, among them the difference between physically and morally good actions, egoism versus the core of moral motivation, atheism in *sensu privationis* and *sensu contradictoriae*, and the natural evolution of the sexual impulse.[5]

While presenting a hypothesis for humanity's overcoming of the state of nature, which Kant relates to the maturation of our bodily functions and the evolution of the sexual impulse from a sheer drive for reproduction to the institution of marriage, Kant refers to a basic shame-instinct (a 'true shame instinct', as he

---

4 See. Menzer 1924.
5 See Menzer 1924, §§ 27, p. 48 ss.

calls it). This shame instinct would not only bridge the two phases of humanity's development, but would also justify this evolution and its perfectible teleology. Herder writes:

> The sexual impulse would not have developed so early, but once the powers of the body had matured, for it would not have been accelerated by instruction. The impulse satisfied itself merely by immediate pleasure, and there would probably not have been a permanent bond. But since, no doubt, the man would have felt that the impulse would recur, he would allow the woman to follow him into the forest; she became his companion, and both would have cared for the children. He would have had to help her while she was suckling them, and thus arouse monogamy, since there are as many women as men. The impulse would not have been so rampant then, since the fantasied pleasures of the civilized were lacking. Moreover, this impulse is covered with the veil of shame, which is also found among the majority of savages, and *is quite unlike any other form of shame and restrains the impulse* [my italics]. There is much truth in the objections of the cynic: we should be ashamed only of what is dishonourable; but for all that, there is a genuine shame instinct, which has indeed no rational cause, and is strange, but whose aims are: 1) *to restrain the untamed sexual impulse*; and 2) *to maintain the attraction of it by secrecy*. The male sex, which has more principles, possesses this shame in a lesser degree; for want of principles, the woman has a great deal of it, and it dominates her; and where this shame has already been uprooted in women, all virtue and respectability have lost their authority, and they go further in shamelessness than the most dissolute of men. Such shame, moreover, has an *analogon* with an act that is intrinsically dishonourable, and this has produced the stupid shame of monkishness. *It is not, however, in itself the mark of an unpermitted act, but the veil of an honourable one, which propagates mankind.*[6]

The course of Kant's reasoning is far from clear, and some reconstruction must take place if we are to get both a firm grasp of the inner logic of his position and a sense of some of its paradoxical consequences. One point that Kant is certainly trying to get across concerns the establishment of monogamy in civilized societies. Kant does this by sketching out a sort of metaphysical story recounting the first encounters of members of the two sexes, along with the persistence of the sexual impulse and the supposedly equal number of members of each sex. This story, however, is not the ultimate purpose of Kant's complex speculative account regarding the state of nature and its evolution towards a civil state; rather, it is only a contextualization for what Kant intends to claim about the relations between members of the opposite sex in a civilized society and the promise of species improvement across generations.

Kant's intricate story about the final purpose of the association between members of each sex takes monogamy as no more than a condition for the propagation of the human species itself and, as one can safely infer from many other

---

6 V-PP/Herder 27: 49; Kant 1997, p. 22.

texts in the Kantian *corpus* (aside from the *Vorlesungen*), its perfectibility over time.[7] Monogamy is but a condition of species improvement.

As a matter of fact, Herder's lengthy remark on the connection of shame with the maturation of the sexual impulse in the History of Man first introduces a pattern of reasoning which Kant will later fixate on as the principle enabling the achievement of the ultimate purpose of the encounter between the sexes.[8] A form of restraint, shame is said to operate in the background of intersexual relations as a means of disciplining the sexual drive, taming sensual excesses, and ensuring the human species not only survives but becomes stronger. When, in the *Observations on the Feeling of the Beautiful and the Sublime*, Kant selects the features most relevant to determining the relation between man and woman, a twofold model emerges from a very provocative description: first, Kant points out how behavioural norms come about, develop and become conventions for members of each sex; second, he attempts to determine the ultimate meaning and purpose of that behavioural pattern.

In section three of the *Observations* ("Of the Distinction of the Beautiful and Sublime in the Interrelations of the two Sexes"), published in Königsberg in 1764, Kant writes the following about the "sense of shame":

> The sense of shame is a secrecy of nature aimed at setting bounds to a most intractable inclination, and which, in so far as it has the call of nature on its side, always seems compatible with good, moral qualities, even if it is excessive. It is accordingly most necessary as a supplement to principles, for there is no case in which inclination so readily becomes a sophist cooking up complaisant principles as here. At the same time, it also serves to draw a secretive curtain before even the most appropriate and necessary ends of nature, so that too familiar an acquaintance with them will not occasion disgust or at least indifference with respect to the final aims of a drive on to which the finest and liveliest inclinations are grafted. (GSE 2: 234; Kant 2011, p. 41)

This is an extremely complex stretch of prose, and some reconstruction of its main argument is called for. Regardless, the attentive reader will understand that Kant is tackling a huge issue here, by relating the propagation of the species

---

7 See especially the *Observations on the Feeling of the Beautiful and the Sublime*, Third Section, GSE 2: 236; Kant 1997, p. 46: "This whole enchantment is at bottom spread over the sexual drive. Nature pursues its great aim, and all refinements that are associated with it, however remote from it they seem to be, are only veils, and in the end derive their charm from the very same source. [...] If this taste is not exactly fine, still it is not on that account to be despised. For the greatest part of humanity follows by its means the greatest order of nature in a very simple and certain manner. By this means most marriages are brought about, and indeed among the most industrious part of humanity [...]".

8 See Kant 2007, pp. 18–63.

with the natural-historic taming of the sexual drive. The most important point to be gleaned from this strange passage is this: the shame-instinct works as a natural bridge between the two purposes ultimately ascribed to the satisfaction of the sexual impulse that brings together human beings of the opposite sex. Kant seems to have been extraordinarily impressed by the fact that one such purpose is immediate and inconsequential, whilst the other is noble and world-historical. Furthermore, he seems to posit that it is *shame* that mediates between the two.[9]

Behind Kant's explicit reasoning relating sex with shame, we find the following associative mechanism: if one can conceive of a sexual pattern of attraction drawing men and women to each other, this means there is also a deeper motivation at work which transcends the demands of subjectivity and which one may term 'the drive of the species itself' to thrive and become stronger. It goes without saying that, to the extent that it helps explain and make sense of the very subsistence of the human species over time, such a supra-individual force for perfectibility must lay beyond the reach of empirical evidence, and its explanatory role can't but be inferred from other, observable phenomena—in the case at hand, behavioral patterns common to both sexes.

Precisely this added twist in Kant's genetic story regarding the maturation of the sexual drive begins to reveal a dual dynamic, whose external and internal features may lead to paradoxes. Reconstructing Kant's two long and convoluted remarks, we must first stress that it is the sexual impulse itself that Kant says is covered with the veil of shame. When one interprets this strange passage with a view to analysing its rationale, what is here described as 'a sense of shame' appears to work thus: by restraining the naturally ungovernable expression of the sexual drive, the so-called 'veil of shame' actually allows it to attain its ultimate

---

9 Kant derives the most important elements in this complex association from Rousseau's *Discourse on Inequality*. As usual, Rousseau's influence on Kant's moral ideas cannot be discounted, but the ultimate shape of their views on this issue is highly heterogeneous. Wishing to legitimate the freedom human beings experienced in a state of nature, Rousseau holds that, because in such a primordial state of development the cultural aspects of the fundamental human drives – including the sexual drive – have not yet had the chance to develop at all, the impulse was quickly satisfied and died away. Were it not for the fact that he is merely framing a counterfactual narrative about the birth of human societies, it would be hard to understand how, under such factual conditions, the species could have survived. In any case, Kant insists not only that the spontaneous meetings between men and women happen ever more often, but that somehow the performance of the species as a whole overcomes the limitations of its members and, through shame, the immediate satisfaction of the sexual impulse is both tamed and rationally linked with the continuation of humankind beyond the natural state (See Rousseau 2002 and Kant 1997).

goal, which is not immediate satisfaction, but rather the propagation of mankind [the so-called *Menschenpflanzung*]. One should, however, bear in mind that Kant believes this to be a sort of evolutionary inheritance, and thus this peculiar type of experience should map out both the way the sexual drive is felt by the uncivilized man and the way we experience it in a civilized state. Once this reasoning is analysed in detail, however, structural problems immediately arise.

I will here attempt to lay bare the intuitive flaws behind Kant's reasoning by deploying a reflective strategy of testing my interpretive proposal from different standpoints so as to illustrate exactly how the model flounders. One can reason as follows: from an internal, strictly subjective viewpoint, how can we reconcile the *curbing* of the sexual impulse—mostly experienced as one peculiar kind of social constraint—with the ultimate design of that drive, which is entirely rational and concerns the sustained propagation of the species? We can, of course, think about the continuation of the human species as one of the ends ultimately fulfilled by reproduction—even by sexual desire—and simultaneously experience the restriction of the sexual impulse as both a natural and a cultural necessity. But it hardly fits with our experience of a limited, organized, socially framed sexual expression that it be a function of a higher purpose which, above all, and being by nature expansive, precisely contradicts a restrained form of activity.

Any attempt to render an external perspective of this experience does not fare much better, though. When one reconstructs the fundamental moments in Kant's complicated argument, one can at least abstract away the following features: the original force of the sexual drive must be curbed, so that its ultimate purpose can be accomplished. Kant alleges that an effective sense of shame is what performs this dual role of i) keeping the impulse within bounds, and ii) 'maintaining its attraction by secrecy'. However, conceiving of the experience in its functional, dual-aspect role—as an inner feeling with a given external manifestation which should anticipate a teleological design stretching beyond mere experience—another question emerges: how is shame supposed to do this? How can a deeply individual, negative emotion like shame perform this ambitious role of reconciling the natural and the rational dimensions of one of our most primitive dispositions?

If one examines available theories of shame, which range from the descriptive approaches of the emotion produced by twentieth-century phenomenology,[10] to contractualist discussions of its impact upon an individual's self-esteem

---

10 See Sartre (1943), Scheler (1957 [1913]) or Rawls (1999).

(i.e. the Rawlsian model presented in Part III of *A Theory of Justice*),[11] to the fast-growing, specialized research done in moral philosophy, moral psychology or in the neurosciences, shame is almost unanimously characterized as an emotion which damages the core of the self and is thoroughly first-personal.[12] It is thus extremely difficult to reconcile the first, naturalized function that Kant (along with many anthropologists and moral philosophers) ascribes to the emotion, with its supposedly noble, teleological aim. Unless one can prove either that Kant is using the notion with a double connotation here—for example, objective and subjective, or external and internal—or that he is employing a most *sui generis* concept of 'shame', it is difficult to make a case for this interpretative model.

There may be something to gain, however, from insisting that this complex scenario admits of three separate descriptions. There is, first of all, the reflective exercise one must make in order to grasp the inner logic of Kant's association of an ungoverned sexual drive, which is dominated by shame, with the fulfilment of its ultimate end—an accomplishment only satisfied to the extent that shame is able to curb the instinct. In a way, this effort objectifies the content of Kant's ideas regarding the problem of shame. A second description focuses on the purely subjective experience of this supposed association between the two aims—say, one feels ashamed of one's sexual appetite and does what one can to get it under control, unaware that one is fulfilling some non-empirical end that the drive ultimately serves. Finally, this inner experience, or set of related experiences, is revealed through the behavior of the target of shame, which we can also describe, but hardly as shame-behavior, as long as one respects the two main features suggested by the first description. This is because, while one can observe someone in the grip of this strange kind of shame, one cannot trace the relationship between this shame behavior with its factors that had caused it.

Now, having unpacked the main elements structuring Kant's complex reasoning, I would like to specify the hermeneutic difficulties I have with this sketchy description of the moral phenomenon of shame. One can well conceive the

---

11 See (Rawls 1999, § 67, pp. 388–389): "We may characterize shame as the feeling that someone has when he experiences an injury to his self-respect or suffers a blow to his self-esteem. [...] Shame is the emotion evoked by shocks to our self-respect, a special kind of good. Now both regret and shame are self-regarding, but shame implies an especially intimate connection with persons and with those upon whom we depend to confirm the sense of our own worth". John Rawls discusses the problem of shame at a very peculiar point in his *opus magnum*. Having defined human virtues as excellences, i.e., personal character traits which increase interpersonal common good, Rawls further takes self-respect to be a basic sort of good, indispensable to the flourishing of any reasonable individual. To the extent that shame undermines self-respect, the key to personal integrity, it blocks the possibility of social cohesion.
12 See Taylor (1985), Sartre (1992), Thomason (2013).

sort of experience Kant describes as (i) restricting an untamed sexual impulse and (ii) maintaining the attraction of sex through its very prohibition. The latter could be described as shame-behavior, which, as a matter of fact, might well encompass the characteristic awkwardness with which human beings live out their sexuality in different social settings. At the same time, it is at least plausible that this be observed as one typical form of self-restraint, which is so characteristic of shame-feelings. What is, in any case, counter-intuitive, is the addition of the functional role Kant claims that this form of shyness is meant to perform—the higher goal of propagating and strengthening the species—while still retaining the necessary features that define the experience of shame.

If Kant's thought-experiment seems too grand, or my exposition thus far too abstract, consider the following, quite common, first-personal reflection. If one desires having offspring, some form of calculated planning might well encompass at least part of the ingenious line of reasoning Kant presents as being effective in fulfilling the 'great design of nature'. Individuals, couples, and states or corporations make, attend and foster birth-control programs, rely on fertility cycles, even shape entire aspects of work—and social life in accordance with the limited potential modern life allows for reproduction to actually take place—which may imply an effective channelling of sexual energy to the appropriate moments.

But it is hardly imaginable that any sort of prudential measures adopted in response to thoughts akin to those Kant expounds in both texts encompasses anything even remotely associated with a shame instinct. There may be self-imposed restrictions, and typical, primitive impressions of shame regarding sex acts may occur, but the very plan to have children will remain unaffected by both.

Well-known objections to this brief account of how the so-called 'shame-instinct' works within Kant's reasoning are bound to be raised, and I touched upon some of them earlier. One may think, for instance, that Kant is making use of a rather technical—or circumstantial—idea of 'shame' (more accurately: of a 'shame-instinct') here, and that applying it to the common forms that the emotion takes in our daily life is simply inadequate. The first part of this objection, at least, is accurate and was anticipated by Kant himself.[13]

Be it as it may, this semantic concern does not impede my reconstruction of Kant's argument, for two reasons. First, the objection is unsatisfactory because

---

13 Taking Herder's notes for a reliable historical document, it seems likely that Kant himself was aware of the peculiarities surrounding the experience of shame in relation to the sexual impulse. See V-PP/Herder 27: 99; Kant 1997, p. 22: "[...] there is a genuine shame-instinct, which has indeed no rational cause, and is strange..."

although Kant's idea of a primitive shame-instinct is indeed *sui generis*, and even somewhat parochial in terms of its application, its components are exactly those examined above, and in at least some concrete situations they can be taken to exemplify—as the example above bears proof—that their applicability matches extremely primitive shame-situations with which we are all familiar. Second, there are other mentions in the opus as a whole—for example, when relating shame to the privacy of prayer—[14] where Kant develops an idea of shame identical to the definition proposed by moral psychologists and classical phenomenologists. In this way, even when considering the problem in strictly conceptual terms, we have textual evidence that Kant was indeed familiar with the idea of shame commonly endorsed by modern moral theories, matching an extremely intuitive experience of the emotion under analysis.[15]

One may still try to raise an objection regarding different formal accounts of the same phenomenon: how can a process whose inner rationality is strictly dependent on our ability for reflective thinking make sense of how its own components hang together and for which, then, any appeal whatsoever to an empirical order is clearly insufficient? There are still problems with this attempted refutation, however, and they are twofold. On the one hand, even if what Kant is offering us is a kind of a-perspectival explanation of a complex natural, as well as historical, phenomenon, which only a fiction of human reason allows us to grasp, nothing bars the interpreter of these lecture notes from shaping their most abstract elements from different individual standpoints. Furthermore, when one considers Kant's modular description of the shame-instinct in terms of different singular perspectives, common features of one's personal and interpersonal acquaintance with it immediately become apparent. The structural articulation of its parts is, then, no mere rational fiction.

It seems plausible to think that, if there is something in Kant's reasoning—as presented both in the *Lectures on Ethics* and later in the *Observations*—working to obscure the full coherence of its elements when brought together under a unified description, it is the supra-individual justification of partial features of individual human experience. Thus, if Kant's fully rational overview of natural phenomena indeed fails, this comes from an unwarranted overlapping of

---

14 See *Moral Philosophy Collins:* "The more upright a man is, the more readily he is ashamed if surprised in an act of devotion. A hypocrite will not be ashamed, but on the contrary, will let himself be seen. For a man is ashamed if another thinks any ill of him, even though he has committed no fault" (V-Mo/Collins: 27: 337; Kant 1997, p. 119).

15 Amongst contemporary philosophical proposals, the more nuanced accounts of shame, considered from an intersubjective and a subjective point of view are, respectively, those of J. Rawls (1999) and G. Taylor (1985).

explanatory layers rather than the presumed partiality of singular points of view. As stressed above, Kant's full explanatory model for the inner dynamics of the most primitive manifestation of a shame-instinct is altogether general and supra-individual, but its constitutive parts can only make sense once they are conceived from personal standpoints.

Finally, on account of the reconstructive effort taken to explain how exactly one can make sense of Kant's explanation of a single natural and historical phenomenon, surveyed from different points of view and rationally recombined with the help of a third notion which makes sense of its partial features once these are fully depersonalized, any objection to the effect that Kant may be describing the so-called shame-instinct from subjective *vs* objective or internal *vs* external perspectives is ruled out. A thorough examination of the early writings has shown that Kant does indeed rely upon a fixed but undeveloped proposal to explain how an extremely primitive feeling of shame contributes to the improvement of the human species, but as soon as the details of this general framework are examined more closely, structural problems emerge. Not only is it extremely hard to experience limitations of the sexual impulse as a means of expanding and improving the human species *in totum*, but it is also counterintuitive to associate a pattern of behavior performed at the level of the species itself, and which bears a closer resemblance to pride than to any other intuitively portrayed human experience, with a negative moral emotion like shame.

Regardless of how complex and ultimately paradoxical Kant's account of the so-called shame-instinct ends up being, there is, in fact, a highly structured explanatory model lying behind a limited set of associations. A close examination of textual references provides us with a genuinely Kantian view on shame—that is, a view which is true to the letter and not just the spirit of what acting morally 'in the scheme of Kantian oppositions' ultimately implies. Perhaps only a more congenial reception of the Kantian *opus* as a whole by recent Anglo-American philosophy could have provided Bernard Williams with a truly informed view of what Kant had to say about this highly complex moral emotion.

3 Conclusion: The Way Beyond Language

The set of reflections collected in this essay would seem to allow for a rather bleak diagnosis of the consequences of the methodological split in contemporary philosophy. One hundred years since the so-called 'linguistic turn', it looks as if language has led even one of the most historically minded of all English philosophers of the last century to fall for an oversimplification of human experience as portrayed in a very simple proverbial phrase. In *Shame and Neces-*

sity, Bernard Williams charges an anonymized Kantian philosopher with neglecting the relevance of shame for moral deliberation and action due to the alleged superficiality of what is at stake for moral agents whenever an experience of shame supervenes. However, in making this claim, Williams relies on a simplistic and rather parochial definition of the emotion he seeks to characterize. In romance languages, for instance, the notion of 'losing or saving face' has no direct equivalent in ordinary speech, and thus it also has no association whatsoever with shame-feelings. The most analogous Portuguese term that comes to mind, for instance, bears a direct connotation with courage, even with bravery.

As a matter of fact, and taking into account the well-known complexity of Kant's prose, with which every philosophy undergraduate is already familiar, it would be doubtful that, having discussed shame at all, Kant would have done so in either simple linguistic terms, or with a view to simplify a philosophical account of its structural features. As I hope my discussion up to this point has made abundantly clear, the description of the inner mechanisms of a primitive shame-instinct stands at a crossroads of several problematic threads in Kant's philosophical development and has major implications for Kantian philosophy in general. In the first half of the 1760s—in academic writings as well as public lectures—Kant is seen struggling with Rousseau's political ideas, while simultaneously beginning to model some of his most distinguished ethical notions on a genetic account of the origin of human society. In fact, one could even claim that, without making it wholly explicit, here Kant is crafting a sort of existential aesthetics. The attentive reader can almost literally *see* how some of the central insights from critical philosophy emerge as Kant lectures for a public of young enthusiasts.

By this I do not mean that a conceptual niche is being deduced from overly abstract reasoning aiming to map the ultimate structures of reality, but that a purely phenomenal description of concrete events in human life is undertaken in such sketchy linguistic formulations that one must deploy highly structured reflective capabilities to extract implied meanings from explicit formulations. Furthermore, this heuristic method has a direct impact on an adequate grasp of the peculiarities of the phenomenon under analysis. Thus, regarding shame, Kant holds that the sheer observation of the natural attraction between men and women and the typical oddities of behavior related to the expression of sexual desire has more to it, even in purely phenomenal terms, than what any one of us, unreflectively, is in a position to claim. Moreover, at the level of something we might call 'anthropological time', shame fundamentally obscures more than it reveals. In the long run, then, the ultimate purpose of feelings of shame in relation to sex is said to become wholly intelligible—at the price, however, of utterly dismissing any empirical plausibility it could be shown to have. Regardless of how it may be read and reconstructed, however, the development of humanity lying behind the so-called 'shame-instinct' is central to Kantian philosophy, and thus so is shame, as the emotion enabling it.

Bibliography

Aramayo, Roberto R. (1988): "La cara oculta del formalismo ético". In: Immanuel Kant, *Lecciones de ética*. Barcelona: Crítica, pp. 7–34.

Kant, Immanuel (1900): *Kants Gesammelte Schriften*. Königlich Preussischen Akademie der Wissenschaften (Ed.). Berlin: De Gruyter.

Kant, Immanuel (1997): *Lectures on Ethics*. Peter Heath and Jerome B. Schneewind (Trans.). Cambridge: Cambridge University Press.

Lehmann, Gerhard (1967): "Kants Entwicklung im Spiegel der *Vorlesungen*". In: Heinz Heimsoeth, Dieter Henrich and Giorgio Tonelli (Eds.): *Studien zu Kants philosophischer Entwicklung*. Hildesheim: Olms Verlag.

Lehmann, Gerhard (1974): "Einleitung zur Kants *Vorlesungen über Moralphilosophie*". In: *Kants Gesammelte Schriften* 27. Königlich Preussischen Akademie der Wissenschaften (Ed.). Berlin: De Gruyter, p. 1036.

Menzer, Paul (Ed.) (1924): *Eine Vorlesung Kants über Ethik*. Berlin: Pan Verlag Rolf Heise.

Rawls, John (1999): *A Theory of Justice*. Cambridge: Harvard University Press.

Rousseau, Jean-Jacques (2002): *The Social Contract and the First and Second Discourses*. Susan Dunn (Ed.): New Haven, London: Yale University Press.

Sartre, Jean-Paul (1943): *L'Être et le Neant: Un essai de theorie phenomenologique*. Paris: Gallimard.

Scheler, Max (1957 [1913]): "Über Scham und Schamgefühl". In: *Schriften aus dem Nachlass*, Vol. I: Zur Ethik und Erkenntnislehre. Bern: Francke Verlag.

Taylor, Gabriele (1985): *Shame, Pride and Guilt*. Oxford: Clarendon Press.

Thomason, Krista K. (2013): "Shame and Contempt in Kant's Moral Theory". *Kantian Review* 18, pp. 221–240.

Vaihinger, Hans (1911): *Die Philosophie des Als Ob. System der theoretischen, praktischen und religiösen Fiktionen der Menschheit auf Grund eines idealistichen Positivismus*. Berlin: Reuther und Reichard.

Williams, Bernard (1973): "Morality and the Emotions". In: *Problems of the Self*. Cambridge: Cambridge University Press, pp. 207–229.

Williams, Bernard (1993): *Shame and Necessity*. Berkeley: University of California Press.

Williams, Bernard (2011): *Ethics and the Limits of Philosophy*. London, New York: Routledge Classics.

Williams, Howard (2003): *Kant's Critique of Hobbes: Sovereignty and Cosmopolitanism*. Cardiff: University of Wales Press.

Wittgenstein, Ludwig (2008): *Philosophical Investigations*. Oxford: Blackwell.

Maria Borges
Passions and Evil in Kant's Philosophy

Abstract: In this chapter, I aim to elucidate the relationship between passions and evil in Kant's philosophy. I begin by explaining the difference between affects and passions in the text *Anthropology from a Pragmatic Point of View*, in which Kant claims that both affects and passions are illnesses of the mind, because they hinder the sovereignty of reason. I argue that passions, however, represent a greater threat to pure reason than affects. Next, I relate affects and passions to the varying degrees of the propensity to evil in the *Religion*. Finally, I analyse the idea of an ethical community as a means of overcoming evil, which goes beyond the political and anthropological solutions offered by Kant.

Keywords: anthropology, passions, affects, evil, ethical community

1 Fickle and Uncontrolled Affects

According to Kant, feelings of pleasure or displeasure caused by an object can be sensible or intellectual—the former caused by sensation or imagination; the latter triggered by a concept or idea. (Anth 7: 230). Pleasure and displeasure as a consequence of sensibility alone are feelings of gratification and pain.

Kant defines affects as belonging "to the feeling of pleasure and displeasure", while passions belong "to the faculty of desire." (V-Anth/Mron 25.2: 1340). In the *Lectures on Metaphysics* of the 1770s, Kant explains that feeling relates to the way we are affected by an object, rather than to properties of said object: "If I speak of an object insofar as it is beautiful or ugly, agreeable or disagreeable, then I am acquainted not with the object in itself, as it is, but rather as it affects me" (V-Met- L1/Politz, 28: 245).

The difference between feelings related to affects and feelings related to the beautiful can be discerned in the *Anthropology* (Anth 7: 230), where sensuous pleasure is divided into pleasure derived from sensation and pleasure derived from the imagination. While the feeling of the beautiful is partly sensuous, partly intellectual, (depending upon the harmony between the cognitive faculties of the

Note: This chapter was previously published in *Manuscrito* 37. No. 2 (2014), 333–355.

Maria Borges, Federal Univ. of Santa Catarina, Brazil

https://doi.org/10.1515/9783110720730-007

understanding and the imagination), the feeling of pain (*Schmerz*) and gratification (*Vergnügen*) is related to the pleasure and displeasure of sensation alone.

Affects are feelings of pleasure or displeasure that hinder the reflection through which inclinations are to be submitted to rational maxims—affects are sudden and rash, making reflection impossible (TL 6: 408) (Kant offers such comparisons as water that breaks through a dam, or strokes of apoplexy (Anth 7: 252). They can even lead the agent to moral blindness in that they hinder deliberation—with the slight consolation that this emotional distraction easily disappears, allowing the subject to return to a state where reflection is possible again. Kant cites the example of a person who marries out of love, blind to the character flaws of her beloved, but regains her vision a week after marriage (Anth 7: 253). The paradigmatic Kantian example of affect is anger—a tempestuous feeling by nature, and fickle in the same way as love.

The fickleness of the emotion of love can be illustrated in Juliet's speech in the Shakespearean tragedy, Romeo and Juliet:

ROMEO:
Lady, by yonder blessed moon I vow,
That tips with silver all these fruit-tree tops–

JULIET:
O, swear not by the moon, th' inconstant moon,
That monthly changes in her circle orb,
Lest that thy love prove likewise variable.
ROMEO:
What shall I swear by?
[...]

JULIET:
Well, do not swear. Although I joy in thee,
I have no joy of this contract tonight.
It is too rash, too unadvised, too sudden;
Too like the lightning, which doth cease to be
Ere one can say it lightens. (Act 2, Scene II)

This passage ably illustrates the fickleness of affects: they are rash, sudden, and fleeting.

While explaining the essence of affects in the *Anthropology*, Kant references the Scottish doctor John Brown:

Affects are generally morbid occurrences (symptoms) and may be divided (according to analogy with Brown's system) into sthenic affects as to strength and asthenic affects as to weakness. Sthenic affects are of the exciting and frequently exhausting nature; asthenic affects are of a sedative nature, which often prepare for relaxation. (Anth 7: 256)

Many eighteenth-century medical writers had claimed that the causes of diseases were excesses or irregularities in human activity. Towards the end of the eighteenth century, John Brown, (1735–1788), posited that the same external forces of nature that produce life and health also produce sickness and death. He saw the decline of the organism in a quantifiable loss of excitability, which steadily decreased in all parts of the body from childhood to old age. Life is nothing but a state of force—if the forces of excitability diminish, death necessarily follows. Diseases are caused, then, by an increase or decrease in excitability. Sthenic diseases are caused by an excess of the forces of excitability, while asthenic diseases are brought on by a lack of the same.

Following Brown, Kant discusses affects as physiological states of excitement or release. Laughing with emotion (a sthenic affect) is an example of the former; weeping with emotion (an asthenic affect) of the latter. Furthermore, numerous other affects are related to bodily functions: anger and its expression is a way to aid digestion (Anth 7: 261), fear in battle is seen as related to acid indigestion, etc. (Anth 7: 256).

2 Maxims of Passion and Evil

Kant's realm of inclinations also includes passion, which is related to the faculty of desire and can be understood as a strong desire for something. Passion is also related to sensation, however, it is not linked to the way we are affected by an object, but rather to the way we desire it. The faculty of desire admits of four levels of intensity: the first is propensity (*Hang, propensio*)—a desire that precedes the representation of the object. In the *Lectures on Anthropology/Mrongovius* (V-Anth/Mron 25: 1340), Kant cites the Northern European habit of drinking strong drinks as an example of propensity. The second level of intensity is instinct (*Instinkt*), which consists of desire without prior knowledge of the object by which it is to be satisfied, e. g., a child's instinctual desire for milk, or an animal's instinct to protect his offspring (Anth 7: 265). The third level of desire is inclination (*Neigung, inclinatio*), [1] which is defined as a habitual desire, and exemplified by the desire to play games or drink. If an inclination is too strong, it becomes a passion (*Leidenschaft, passio animi*), which is the fourth and final degree of the faculty of desire. Inclination, Kant argues, is "a habitual sensuous desire", and passion is

---

[1] Although inclination is sometimes used to refer to all sensible incentives of human nature that is opposed to reason, in its specific definition, it refers to only one of the divisions of the faculty of desire.

the "inclination which can hardly, or not at all, be controlled by reason" (Anth 7: 251).

In light of his analysis of passions and affects, can we still agree with the Kantian claim regarding the reality of practical freedom as the independence of the will from the influence of inclinations? While affects and passions are said to be obstacles to moral deliberation, Kant also relies on a strong conception of freedom which does not allow for pathological compulsion. In the *Lectures on Ethics/Mrongovius*, we read:

> Can I really conceive of a pathological compulsion in man as well? Truly, I cannot, for freedom consists in this, that he can be without compulsion in the pathological sense; nor should he be compelled in that way. Even if a man is so constrained, he can nevertheless act otherwise. (V-Mo/Mron II 29: 618)

In other words, while we have strong emotions that can be difficult to control, we also have means of taming them so as to act out of personal choice. Virtue is one of these means. We are not responsible for our emotions, but can be held responsible for our actions, because even the strongest emotions cannot be equated with compulsion. Some philosophers have tried to establish a parallel between strong emotions and addiction (Elster 2000). Kant would reject this claim, however, because as strong as emotions can be, and as much of a problem for morality as they may represent, the very idea of practical reason presupposes that agents can decide how to act. The Kantian view is in alignment moral common sense that holds that a strong emotion can never completely excuse a heinous action. Agents may mention intense anger as a way of explaining or rationalizing their violent acts, yet not as a way of excusing them. People are held responsible for morally wrong actions, even those stemming from strong emotions, because it is presupposed that they could have acted otherwise.

If we disregard, for the moment, the difference in how they are related to objects, we find that both affects and passions are considered illnesses of the mind, because both hinder the sovereignty of reason. Affects, however, are seen as less harmful than passions, in Kant's view. This claim can be understood in a comparison of anger (affect) with hate (passion). Anger intensifies quickly and subsides in an equally instantaneous manner. Hatred, because it is a passion, does not allow for such control.

> Since the passions can exist concurrently with the calmest reflection, one can easily see that they must be neither rash, like the emotions, nor transitory; but rather they must take root gradually and even be able to coexist with reason. (Anth 7: 266)

Passions, then, are more closely related to the will; nevertheless, this does not imply that they can be brought under greater control by reason. In fact, they can be considered a perversion of reason, since they "take root" in reason and coexist with rational decision. Curiously, the irrational aspects of affects make them preferable to passions. Kant uses many medical metaphors to stress this very distinction: affect is an intoxicant that causes a headache, while passion is a poison that causes a permanent illness (Anth 7: 252), affect is a delirium (Anth 7: 266) or a "stroke of apoplexy" (Anth 7: 252), while passion "works like consumption or atrophy" (Anth 7: 252) or an illness that abhors all medication (Anth 7: 266). Furthermore, passions are "cancerous sores for pure practical reason" (Anth 7: 266) to which the physician of the soul could only prescribe palliative medicines (Anth 7: 252). These metaphors for the infirmity of emotions speaks to their degree of evil. Affect, however, seen as the least dangerous of the "illnesses of mind", is related to weakness, which can still coexist with a good will:

> Affects belong to feeling insofar as, preceding the reflection; it makes this impossible or more difficult. Hence, an affect is called precipitate or rash (*animus praeceps*), and reason says, through the concept of virtue, that one should get hold of oneself. Yet this weakness is the use of one's understanding coupled with the strength of one's affects, is only a lack of virtue and, as it were, something childish and weak, which can indeed coexist with the best will. (TL 6: 408)

Passions exhibit a contradictory nature. On the one hand, Kant says that they inhibit reason's ability to compare a specific inclination against the sum of all inclinations (Anth 7: 265). On the other hand, they do allow for some rational deliberation regarding the best way to obtain the agent's desire. One good example is found in the *Anthropology*, where Kant compares the inability of a man experiencing the affect of love to seduce someone, with the seductive skill of one in the throes of the passion of love. The former will be unsuccessful, while the latter can easily trap the helpless victim of their desire (Anth 7: 265). The difference is found in that the man moved by affect is experiencing a complete agitation of the mind, whereas the man guided by passion coolly plots the optimal way to obtain his desire.

While affects are outbursts of feelings, which can coexist with a good, albeit weak, heart, passions are persistent inclinations that can lead the agent to choose maxims that go against the moral law. Here, evil does not stem from frailty, but from the conscious choice of a maxim over the moral law. This can be illustrated by Lady Macbeth's speech in the play Macbeth, in which she calls upon evil spirits to make her follow the wicked maxim she has chosen:

Come, you spirits
That tend on mortal thoughts, unsex me here,
And fill me from the crown to the toe top-full
Of direst cruelty! make thick my blood;
Stop up the access and passage to remorse,
That no compunctious visitings of nature
Shake my fell purpose, nor keep peace between
The effect and it! Come to my woman's breasts,
And take my milk for gall, you murdering ministers,
Wherever in your sightless substances
You wait on nature's mischief! Come, thick night,
And pall thee in the dunnest smoke of hell,
That my keen knife see not the wound it makes,
Nor heaven peep through the blanket of the dark,
To cry 'Hold, hold!' (Act I, Scene V)

Passions do not operate in the same way as affects. An agent experiencing an uncontrollable affect may act against her own maxim, which may lead to irrational actions that go beyond what one may call rational agency. On the contrary, passions may themselves form maxims of action, which speaks to their evil disposition. Actions resulting from passions form part of the realm of rational agency; however, they are not motivated by prudential reasons. One example is the case of the ambitious man. If ambition is only an inclination, then ambition can ground maxims of action, which will the ambitious man to achieve what he desires. However, when ambition as a passion grounds maxims of action, it can lead to the opposite of what is desired, because passion is a mania (*Sucht*). To return to our example of Lady Macbeth, blind ambition, such as Lady Macbeth's lust for power, can lead to the opposite of what is desired—while Lady Macbeth madly wanted her husband to be king, she ultimately caused his death.

Passions are beyond adjectives like 'weak', or 'childish'—they are not just signs of weakness, but of true evil:

> A passion is a sensible desire that has become a lasting inclination (e. g., hatred, as opposed to anger). The calm with which one gives oneself up to it permits reflection and allows the mind to form principles upon it and so, if inclination lights upon something contrary to the law, to brood upon it, to get it rooted deeply, and so take up what is evil (as something premeditated) into its maxim. And this evil is then properly evil, that is, true vice. (TL 6: 408)

Unlike affects, which are temporary emotions, passion is characterised as a lasting inclination. Evil, then, is connected with reflection and with the will's formulation of maxims based on emotions. While an affect constitutes a subjective incentive that may run contrary to a maxim, passion may itself form principles for action. The passion of ambition, for instance, could lead someone to premeditate a murder. Of course, one could also murder someone upon experiencing a momentary uncontrolled affect, such as a fit of rage. Even if the morally wrong action is the same, however, the latter results from a discrepancy between the force of emotion and the will, while the former results from a will that has chosen to act according to a non-moral maxim. For this reason, Kant holds that passions are a greater threat to freedom than affects:

> One can also easily see that passions do the greatest harm to freedom; and if affect is a delirium, then passion is an illness which abhors all medication. Therefore, passion is by far worse than all the transitory affects which stir themselves at least to the good intention of improvement; instead, passion is an enchantment which also rejects improvement. (Anth 7: 266)

The evil character of passions stems from two main features. First, passion leads the agent to choose immoral maxims, which are decided upon reflection. It implies that these maxims present a kind of perversion of moral reasoning, inverting the priority of moral maxims and those based on self-love. Second, passions are never completely satisfied, for which reason they are labelled with the word mania (*Sucht*), meaning that they become an obsession regarding a forever unattainable object. For this reason, Kant claims that no physical love can count as a passion. Only the refusal of the object of love can turn an affect of love into a passion of love.

There are, of course, other feelings that can be either affects or transition into passions. Aside from love, Kant gives the example of ambition. An ambitious person, aside from their own goals, often wants to be loved by others; however, if he is passionately ambitious, he may be hated by others, and may even risk becoming poor, because he has been blinded by his passion. If ambition, however, remains an inclination, it will be compared with the other inclinations of the subject, and thus will not lead to the downfall of the ambitious man. This is the reason Kant declares that "inclination, which hinders the use of reason to compare, at a particular moment of choice, a specific inclination against the sum of all inclinations, is passion" (Anth 7: 265).

3 Social Passions

Kant classifies passions into the two categories of "natural" and "social". Natural passions are called "burning passions", such as the inclinations for freedom and sex; social passions are referred to as "cold passions" and can be seen in the examples of ambition (*Ehrsucht*), lust of power (*Herrschsucht*) and greed (*Habsucht*) (Anth 7: 272–275). The passion of freedom should not be understood as a rational desire to determine the will autonomously; rather, it is a desire not to depend on others: "whoever is able to be happy only at the option of another person, feels that he is unhappy" (Anth 7: 268). Freedom, thus, is a natural desire, a desire for isolation from others, and to live "as a wanderer in the wilderness". It is a desire to be free from dependence on others, characteristic of man in the "state of nature" before "public law protected him".

The most dangerous passions, however, are not innate, but acquired, and arise from culture. In the *Religion*, Kant states that the evil aspects of human nature are consequences of passions, "which wreak such great devastation in [the human being's] originally good disposition" (RGV 6: 93) (here Kant is referring mostly to the social passions of addiction to power, addiction to honour and greed). The danger of the passions consists in their having characteristics shared with reason: "passion appears to imitate the idea of a faculty which is closely linked with freedom, by which alone those purposes can be attained". (Anth 7: 270). Passions imitate rationality in the sense that they both calculate means to desired ends. One can observe this in Kant's analysis of greed. Kant explains this passion as the desire to have all that is good: "money is a password, and all doors, which are closed to the man of lesser means, fly open to those whom Plutus favours" (Anth 7: 274). While greed is a passion unrelated to the moral self-determination of an agent, it is related to a calculus of the means of obtaining everything materially worthy and opening all doors forbidden to the poor.

In the *Religion*, Kant maintains that inclinations are good, and that evil should be searched for in a rational principle. In the Anthropology, it is shown that both affects and passions may impede the will, either as tempestuous feelings that hinder the accomplishment of an action based on a moral maxim, or by factoring into the choice of the maxim itself. In both the *Religion* and in the *Anthropology*, Kant claims that the worst evil resides in a rational principle, not in a natural one. The evil principle should be searched for, then, not in man's nature, but in his rational perversion.

The extirpation of affects, however, is not Kant's purpose, and he even claims in that extirpation of inclinations would "not only be futile but harmful and blameworthy as well" (RGV 6: 58). However, we must undoubtedly extirpate passions, because they are not natural feelings or inclinations. That the evil of passions is worse than the evil of affects is attested to by many passages in the *Religion*. Kant even cites the Bible—"we have to wrestle not against flesh and blood (natural inclinations) but against principalities and powers, against evil spirits" (RGV 6: 60)—in order to asseverate that evil does not reside in sensible incentives. Affects can be the cause of weakness, but passions are the cause of true evil.

In his analysis of emotions and evil in Kant, Michael Rohlf correctly argues that, for Kant, "all passions are evil, and that all passions are social in content", but Kant "does not claim, and in fact he explicitly denies, that affects are evil, at least in the sense that passions are evil." (Rohlf 2013, p. 755). He considers that "affects, in contrast with passions, are not evil in the way passions are because they lack what makes passions evil, namely, a maxim opposed to the moral law" (Rohlf 2013, p. 759).

4 The Social Basis of Pure Evil

In order to emerge victorious in the battle against this evil, one must find its cause. If men investigate the circumstances that lead them to evil principles, they will discover that they are not related to their raw nature, but to the corruption of the will that one man produces over others. If a man consider himself poor, he does so "only to the extent that he is anxious that the other human beings will consider him poor and will despise him for it" (RGV 6: 94).

In their works on evil, both Allen Wood (2010) and Sharon Anderson-Gold (2001) call attention to the fact that evil in Kant has its source in our social condition. Since evil originates from social relations, combatting the evil of the passions implies an effort to build a new society able to counteract these passions.

In the chapter "Radical Evil" of the book *Political Emotions*, Martha Nussbaum also stresses the social feature of human evil in Kant. She says, "the fact that we are animals is not the primary source of our moral difficulty" and Kant's "key contention is plausible: the tempter, the invisible enemy inside, is something peculiarly human, a propensity to competitive self-love, which manifests itself whenever human beings are in a group" (Nussbaum 2013, p. 166).

While the nature of man can produce strong inclinations that are difficult to control, these inclinations do not lead to the corruption of the human heart. Kant is unequivocal in asserting that only the association of men is able to produce pure evil:

> Envy, addiction to power, avarice, and the malignant inclinations associated with these, assail his nature, which on its own is undemanding, as soon as he is among human beings. Nor it is necessary to assume that these are sunk into evil and are examples that lead him astray: it suffices that they are there, that they surround him, and that they will mutually corrupt each other's moral disposition and make one another evil. (RGV 6: 94)

This claim is unambiguous: the inclinations are not, by themselves. the source of evil, nor are our affects. The passions of envy, addiction to power and avarice are the result of interacting with other human beings, even if these others are not necessarily behaving immorally. Human beings are not evil because they are corrupted by already wicked people, but rather, ordinary social interaction makes human beings evil, because this interaction awakens the comparison between individuals. Kant claims that comparison, then, is the source of social evil: men feel that they are poor because they compare themselves to others, and their fear of being despised or dominated produces the evil passions of ambition and greed.

Nussbaum agrees with this very pessimistic Kantian viewpoint: "[E]ven when people are well fed and housed, and even when they are reasonably secure with respect to other prerequisites of well-being, they still behave badly to one another and violate one's other rights" (Nussbaum 2013, p. 167). In this way, evil is not a matter of social teaching: "Kant is surely right when he suggests that people require no special social teaching in order to behave badly, and indeed regularly do so despite the best social teaching" (Nussbaum 2013, p. 167).

5 Is Virtue Enough to Eradicate Evil?

Could virtue be a cure for evil? If evil arises from the weakness of the will, virtue can help strengthen the weak will. Weakness is the first degree of the propensity towards evil: it refers to the case in which one has a weak will and is susceptible to fall under the influence of a strong affect, thus losing rational control over one's decisions. However, such a lack of control is not, properly speaking, a vice, but rather a lack of virtue. In the *Religion*, this loss of control is termed frailty (*fragilitas*) of human nature, and consists in taking the moral law as the objective ground of action, even though it lacks sufficient subjective force when compared to inclinations (RGV 6: 30).

Virtue, as strength, could work as a cure for the undue influence of the affects, because affects are impermanent outbursts of feelings. As Kristi Sweet highlights: "There are numerous ways in which Kant defines virtue, and virtue itself is manifold in its constitution, perhaps first in Kant's understanding of it is that it is strength" (Sweet 2013, p. 85). As strength, virtue can work against inclinations and affects that make it difficult to maintain our resolve. Virtue implies not only abiding by the principle of moral law, but also fortitude in maintaining our decision to follow the moral law.

Could virtue also serve as a cure for the third degree of evil, malignity? Recently, some authors have pointed out that virtue can be the cure for all evil. Michael Rohlf states that "in general, virtue is the strength to comply with moral maxims in the face of our propensity to evil, understood as our tendency to prefer the satisfaction of inclinations", and an education focused on developing virtue "will promote not only a good heart and the adoption of fundamental moral maxims, which together constitute the intelligible character of virtue, but also the strength of will to comply with those maxims in the face of our propensity to evil" (Rohlf 2013, p. 762).

Because the evil of the passions is closely connected with society, however, this education designed to promote virtue can only fully occur in a society that is likewise based on the idea of virtue. In this way, only a social remedy can overcome these cancers threatening pure practical reason. If evil is social, the only way to overcome the evil of the passions is through a community based on the ideal of the moral good. Virtue, in the sense of individual strength, is insufficient to accomplish this task without also constructing a society designed to foster the rule reason over the passions.

6 The Overcoming of Evil Through the Creation of an Ethical Community

The social solution to evil is clearly stated in the following quote:

> Inasmuch as we can see, therefore, the dominion of the good principle is not otherwise attainable, so far as human beings can work toward it, than through the setting up and the diffusion of a society which reason makes it a task and a duty of the entire human race to establish in full scope. For only in this way we can hope for a victory of the good principle over the evil one. (RGV 6: 94)

This society is not a juridical-civil society, but an ethical society. While a juridical-civil, or political society, is the relation of human beings to one another under public juridical laws, an ethical-civil society is one in which they are united under the laws of virtue alone, without being coerced to follow these laws by force. Importantly, these two societies can coexist and be composed of the same members.

An association of human beings only under the laws of virtue, and ruled by this idea, can be called an ethical and, so far as these laws are public, an ethico-civil (in contrast to a juridico-civil) society, or an ethical community. It can exist in the midst of a political community and even be made up of the members of the latter—of course, without the foundation of a political community, it could never be brought into existence by human beings (RGV, 6: 94).

Kant points to an ethical community as the embodiment of virtue and of moral principles. This is not a political society, since even a perfect civil society will be unable to overcome passions and therefore defeat true evil by itself. Furthermore, this ethical community is a community of virtue, though not of individual virtue, but rather of shared virtue. It is—as Kant stresses in the aforementioned quotation—"an association under the laws of virtue". This association under the laws of virtue may help combat malignant social passions, while individual virtue can only control the pernicious influence of affects.

Kantian draws an analogy between this ethical community and a juridico-civil society—just as we can oppose the idea of the state of nature to civil society, we can also oppose the idea of an ethical state of nature to an ethical community.

In a political community, the political citizens are still in an ethical state of nature. The citizens cannot be coerced to enter an ethical state, but they can do so. These decisions rest on the individual's will, since the citizen of the political community remains free:

> The citizen of the political community therefore remains, so far as the latter's lawgiving authority is concerned, totally free: he may wish to enter with his fellow citizens into an ethical union over and above the political one, or rather remain in a natural state of this sort. (RGV 6: 96)

7 The Ineffectiveness of Political Institutions

Kant claims in the *Religion* that human beings cannot ground the eradication of evil only in the development of political institutions—in order to attain their moral destiny, humans will need to build an ethical community. Kant seems to have changed his mind regarding a possible progress of history based on the improvement of political institutions. In the *Idea for a Universal History*, he claims that: "[T]he greatest problem for the human species, to which nature compels him, is the achievement of a civil society universally administering right" (IaG 8: 22). In the *Idea*, just civil institutions are considered enough to develop the aim of human nature and to accomplish our moral end.

Paul Guyer remarks that there is already a shift between the text *Idea for a Universal History* (1784) and the appendix of *Perpetual Peace* (1795). He argues that, in the first, Kant claims that moral change will happen through a natural process, while in the second, Kant claims that only the free exercise of human will can lead to accomplishing the moral destiny of man (Guyer 2000, p. 408).

Muchnik claims that in order to understand Kant's conceptual shift, one must turn to the *Religion* (1793), "where the problem of radical evil receives its fullest expression" (Muchnik 2009, p. xxvii). He criticises, among others, Allen Wood, who has based his interpretation of evil in Kant only on the *Idea:* "Interpreters like Allen Wood have found in *Idea for a Universal History* the key to understanding the social dynamics of the propensity of evil, tracing the roots of Kant's view to his thesis about unsocial sociability" (Muchnik 2009, p. 2).

The idea of unsociable sociability plays an important role in the *Idea*, as an explanation of how immoral inclinations or passions can engender a moral outcome. This unsociable propensity, Kant affirms, "is this resistance that awakens all the powers of human being, brings him to overcome his propensity to indolence, and, driven by ambition, tyranny, and greed, to obtain for himself a rank among his fellows, whom he cannot stand, but also cannot leave alone" (IaG 8: 20).

Some commentators have found the main social evil in the idea of unsocial sociability. Kristi Sweet remarks that, "those who suggest that there is something in our unsociable nature that promotes evil are right" (Sweet 2013, p. 87). She goes further and associates social evil with the unsociable sociability of human beings: "[E]vil and the principle of self-love in which it is embodied is profoundly anti-social. This is highlighted in the way that unsociable sociability is expressed in one's desire to 'direct everything as to get his own way'" (Sweet 2013, p. 87).

In *The Idea for a Universal History with a Cosmopolitan Aim* (1784), unsociable sociability is an antagonism that will ultimately overcome our initial unsociable nature: a positive outcome will emerge from our morally bad origins:

> Thus happen the first true steps from crudity toward culture, which really consists in the social worth of the human being; thus all talents come bit by bit to be developed, taste is formed, and even, through progress in enlightenment, a beginning is made toward the foundation of a mode of thought which can with time transform the rude natural predisposition to make moral distinction into determinate practical principles and hence transform a pathologically compelled agreement to form a society finally into a moral whole. (IaG 8: 20)

In the *Religion*, on the other hand, Kant renounces the possibility of a moral outcome with an origin in immoral passions. There is no possibility that passions, left to their own devices, will naturally trend towards morality. In the *Religion*, Kant stresses another kind of evil, of a very different sort than unsociable sociability. It is not the tendency to flee from society, and thus loneliness, that leads to evil, but rather the passions that are aroused through comparison with others.

Thus, the *Anthropology* (1797) presents another way to overcome our evil inclinations: the formation of a cultivated society.

The summary of what pragmatic anthropology has to say regarding the true vocation (*Bestimmung*) of the human being is that he is destined (*bestimmt*), through his reason, to live in a society of human beings, and in this society, through the arts and sciences, to cultivate himself, civilise himself, and moralize himself (Anth, 7: 324).

Unlike the radical optimist of the *Idea*, in the *Anthropology*, Kant acknowledges that there is evil in men, which "is an inclination to desire actively what is unlawful, although he knows very well that it is unlawful" (Anth, 7: 324). He also recognises that passions are grave threats to reason and do not contribute to its development. Some hopefulness, however, still remains, because passions, although they are dangers to pure practical reason, can be overcome through the cultivation of the arts and sciences. This socio-cultural development, not of the individual, but of the species as a whole, will be able to counterbalance evil and accomplish the natural destiny of species: the attainment of complete rationality.

Neither the radical historical optimism of the *Idea*, nor the cultural confidence of the *Anthropology*, however, seemed to be enough to overcome evil. In the *Religion*, we see a new condition of this development—the establishment of an ethical community—which is not guaranteed by the cultivation of human being of the *Anthropology*, nor by the progress of history and of political institutions of the *Idea*.

A social solution, the ethical community, must provide a historical and cultural solution to evil, which a civil political society, no matter how perfect, will never fully attain. Wood explains how a moral community differs from every political community:

> Its laws cannot be statuses, derived from an arbitrary human authority, but must instead be purely moral laws, which recommend themselves to each man through his own reason. In addition to this, the very principle of a moral community of men will differ from that of a political one. The legislation of every political or juridical state 'proceeds from the principle of limiting the freedom of each to those conditions under which it can be consistent with the freedom for everyone'. (Wood 1978, p 189)

The laws of the political community are always coercive laws and a moral community should promote moral relationships between its members. Good laws can compel men to an outward legality, but not to a true internal improvement of their moral character. Without a moral community, we may have external conformity to the law but will never attain the full development of morality.

Allen Wood did not realize that a moral community is only necessary because evil in society is not unsociable sociability but rather pure evil, which will never be eliminated by the development of political and cultural history. However, he is correct in demonstrating the necessity of a moral community to eradicate evil, due to the fact that outward legality is insufficient to attain the full development of morality.

Because the roots of evil are social, and are the result of passions that are stimulated through social interaction, only an ethical community is truly able to overcome evil. Political institutions are necessary, but not sufficient conditions—they can compel man to external legality, but not to an improvement of their heart.

Bibliography

Anderson Gold, Sharon (2001): *Unnecessary Evil*. Albany: State University of New York Press.

Anderson-Gold, Sharon and Muchnik, Pablo (2010): *Kant's Anatomy of Evil*. New York: Cambridge University Press.

Elster, Jon (2000): *Strong Feelings: Emotion, Addiction, and Human Behavior (Jean Nicod Lectures)*. Cambridge: MIT Press.

Guyer, Paul (2000): *Kant on Freedom, Law and Happiness*. Cambridge: Cambridge University Press.

Kant, Immanuel (1900): *Kants Gesammelte Schriften*. Königlich Preussischen Akademie der Wissenschaften (Ed.). Berlin: De Gruyter.

Louden, Robert (2010): *Kant's Impure Ethics*. Oxford: Oxford University Press.

Nussbaum, Martha (2010): *Political Emotions*. Cambridge: Harvard University Press.

Muchnik, Pablo (2009): *Kant's Theory of Evil: An Essay on the Dangers of Self-Love and the Aprioricity of History*. Lanham: Rowman & Littlefield Publishers.

Rohlf, Michael (2013): "Emotion and Evil in Kant". In: *The Review of Metaphysics* 66. No. 4, 749–773.

Shakespeare, William (2005): *The Oxford Shakespeare: The Complete Works*. Stanley Wells, Gary Taylor and John Jowett (Eds.). Oxford: Oxford University Press.

Sweet, Kristi (2013): *Kant on Practical Life*. Cambridge, New York: Cambridge University Press.

Wood, Allen (2010): "The Intelligibility of Evil". In: Sharon Anderson Gold and Paul Muchnik (Eds.): *Kant's Anatomy of Evil*. New York: Cambridge University Press.

Wood, Allen (1978): *Kant's Moral Religion*. Ithaca, London: Cornell University Press.

Section 2: **Critical Emotions: On Kant's Aftermath**

Igor Cvejić
Intentionality *Sui Generis* of Pleasure in Mere Reflection

Abstract: In the following chapter, I will attempt to argue that feelings, and, above all, pleasure in mere reflection, ought to be understood as intentional states, and moreover, as feeling-intentionality *sui generis*. In the first portion of the text, I present the fundamentals of the Kantian understanding of feelings, and attempt to demonstrate why we should reject some of the conclusions of interpretations offered by Paul Guyer and Rachel Zuckert. In part two, I outline some of the particulars of pleasure in mere reflection. In part three, I detail problems relating to the question of the object of pleasure in the context of mere reflection. Finally, in part four, I propose an approach in which intentionality of pleasure in mere reflection can be understood as feeling-intentionality *sui generis*, explain why this understanding should be ascribed to Kant, and discuss how this might resolve some of the problems surveyed in part three.

Keywords: Kant, intentionality, judgment of taste, aboutness, consciousness

The question of intentionality in Kant's philosophy is a difficult one, mostly because the term has assumed significance within philosophy only after his death. Furthermore, although the concept was the subject of seminal works by Franz Brentano and Edmund Husserl, there is still no agreement regarding the precise meaning of the term. Many authors believe Kant treats feelings as intentional states, while drawing on quite simplistic notions of intentionality. Thus, in a discussion with Paul Guyer, Henry Allison writes: "Although I cannot here enter into a debate about the nature of intentionality, I believe it plausible to understand intentionality as the directedness or aboutness characteristic of consciousness" (Allison and Guyer 2006, p. 130). I intend to show that such an understanding of intentionality is not only too general, but also misguided. If we attempt to apply the concept of intentionality to Kant's philosophy, we would have to make a distinction between consciousness being about something and being directed at something. The label 'aboutness' is easily recognized in the elements of our cognitive states (representations, beliefs or cognitive judgments) that express something about some object. Kant insists that of feelings (*Gefühl*)

Igor Cvejić, Univ. of Belgrade, Serbia

https://doi.org/10.1515/9783110720730-008

say nothing about an object (not even the state of the subject), thus obviously stripping feelings of their character of 'aboutness'.

Notwithstanding previous difficulties in understanding feelings as intentional states, I will attempt to argue that feelings, and above all, pleasure in mere reflection, ought to be understood as intentional states, and moreover, as feeling-intentionality *sui generis*. In this way, we resist reducing feeling-intentionality to cognitive elements (i. e., beliefs or representations). We can find some indication of understanding affective intentionality as *sui generis* in the late Husserl (2000, p. 8–9.), Edith Stein (1917, p. 10, 109–116), Heidegger (1992, p. 89 ff) and Sartre (1994). Today, it is explicitly discussed by authors such as Peter Goldie (2000), Jan Slaby, Achim Stephen (Slaby 2008; Slaby and Stephan 2008), etc. I intend to show that we can find clear indication of this designation even earlier, in the work of Kant.

In the first part of the chapter, I provide an overview of Kant's understanding of feelings, and attempt to show why we should reject some of the conclusions of interpretations offered by Paul Guyer and Rachel Zuckert. In part two, I outline some of the particulars of pleasure in mere reflection. In part three, I detail problems regarding the question of the object of pleasure in the context of mere reflection. Finally, in part four, I propose an approach in which intentionality of pleasure in mere reflection can be understood as feeling-intentionality *sui generis*, explain why this understanding should be ascribed to Kant, and discuss how this may resolve some of the problems surveyed in part three.

1 Kant's Thoughts on Feelings of Pleasure and Displeasure

In his critical works, Kant offers three definitions for feelings of pleasure and displeasure. The first, found in the Preface of the *Critique of Practical Reason*, runs as follows:

> Pleasure is *the presentation of the agreement of the object or of the action with the subjective conditions of life*, i. e., with the power [consisting] of *the causality of a presentation in regard to the actuality of its object* (or [in regard to] the determination of the subject's forces to action in order to produce the object). (KpV 5: 9–10)

A second definition is taken from the unpublished First Introduction to the Critique of the Power of Judgment:

> *Pleasure* is a *state* of mind in which a representation is in agreement with itself, as a ground, either merely for preserving this state itself (for the state of the powers of the mind reciprocally promoting each other in a representation preserves itself), or for producing its object. (EEKU 20: 231)

The third definition is the most reliable, given that it is found in a central part of the *Critique of Judgment:*

> The consciousness of (*Das Bewußtsein des*) the causality of a representation with respect to the state of the subject, *for maintaining* it in that state, can here designate in general what is called pleasure; in contrast to which displeasure is that representation that contains the ground for determining the state of the representations to their own opposite (hindering or getting rid of them). (KU 5: 220)

Taken together, in all three definitions, Kant combines the mysterious phrase "causality of representation," to which we will return shortly, with words of psychological and political connotation (agreement, *Übereinstimmung*), as well as with vocabulary specific to physics (promotion/hindering of life/powers, *Beförderung/Hindernisse*). Although we cannot pursue this question further here, we should note that Kant uses these various different registers to define what is essentially the same phenomenon: "Pleasure and displeasure is a feeling of agreement or disagreement, and what is the same, of promotion or obstruction of life" (V-Met/Mron 29: 894).

While this would seem to point to a univocal definition, interpretations of Kant's definitions have conspicuously differed from one another. We will present two main interpretations, by Paul Guyer and Rachel Zuckert, and examine their weaknesses; then we will present what we consider to be an appropriate interpretation.

Guyer's Causal Model

In his marvelous interpretation of third *Critique*, Paul Guyer presents several radical readings of Kant's characterization of feeling. First, he proposes that feelings are opaque sensations, which cannot be explained other than through the effects that produce them. The various representations (sensations, intuitions (*Anschauung*) or concepts) tied to feelings, are connected only by their causes. Accordingly, we can designate various causes or effects of feelings, but not discern qualitative differences in the feelings of pleasure and displeasure themselves. In this way, Guyer deprives feelings of their intentional character.

There are any number of moments in Kant's writing that seem to support Guyer's interpretation. (Guyer 1997, p. 94) There are also, however, numerous criticisms of this position. (Aquila 1979, Zuckert 2007, etc.) To avoid repeating these criticisms, I will focus here on one I have rarely found in other authors, and which I consider to be crucial.

Despite Kant's explicit claim regarding the difference between sensations (*Empfindung*) and feelings (*Gefühl*) (KU 5: 206), Guyer insists on treating them as equivalents, given that Kant did not successfully justify the distinction. There are, however, at least two convincing reasons why feelings cannot be equated to sensations in Kant's psychology. Sensations appear as impressions to our outer senses, and, as such, belong to the (lower) faculty of cognition. There is no discussion of "inner sensations" in Kant's texts from the critical period. Thus, to say that feelings are sensations is to confuse two different faculties, namely, feelings of pleasure and displeasure with the (lower) faculty of cognition. This is clarified further in the second reason why feelings are not the same as sensations. In the *Critique of Pure Reason*, Kant explains that the only material for inner sense are outer sensations; (KrV 3: 23.70; Allison 1983, 277) feelings, on the contrary, do not provide new material to inner sense. (V-Met/ Dohna 28: 673) It is therefore impossible to hold that feelings are somehow new sensations that appear in our inner sense; feelings, above all, are the way in which the already given sensations appear or are arranged.

Zuckert's HOC (Higher Order Consciousness) Model

Rachel Zuckert is a critic of Guyer's model, and advocates the thesis that Kant takes feelings to be intentional mental states. I have chosen to focus on her work because she gives a more detailed account (in comparison with other authors) of how feelings can be understood as intentional states. According to Zuckert, and, in particular, her reading of § 10 of the *Critique of the Power of Judgment*, feelings can be understood as second-order consciousness, that have, as their contents, any other kind of representation (sensation, intuition or concept). Feelings represent a formal relational characteristic of this content, with a tendency to persist:

> It can have different "contents" (whatever representation we're having), and represents (is "consciousness of") a formal, relational characteristic of that content, indeed one concerning relations in time, the universal form of intuitions. For pleasure is the consciousness of a representation's tendency to persist (into the future) or its future directedness. (So I read our "consciousness of [...] causality [...] so as to keep us in that state.") (Zuckert 2007, p. 234).

Since Zuckert's interpretation is more recent, I will present the basic objections to it in slightly more detail. The first set of objections regards her reading of *Erhalten* (maintain, keep up) as future directedness. Thomas Höwing raises the objection that Kant's definition tends to be transcendental—meaning that it contains only pure concepts, without determinations in time (Höwing 2013, p. 96). This criticism is probably too harsh, because even the concept of state (*Zustand*) marks determination in time, and yet is still only a concept and not a concrete determination. Nevertheless, it seems that there is no indication that 'maintaining' could indeed be understood as 'future directedness' (see Guyer 2009, p. 207). Additionally, in his early writings, Kant shows that the persistence of the state of force does not indicate its specific directedness, but rather a fundamental characteristic of it, as seen in Kant's definition of pleasure: "There would be no force, if there is no aspiration to maintain the state in itself" (GSK, 01: 141).

A second set of objections is more serious, and refers to Zuckert's thesis that feelings are second-order states. Höwing points out that Zuckert neglects the definition from the *First Introduction* which states that pleasure is "a state of the mind in which a representation [...]." However, pleasure being a second-order state about a representation, along with its tendency to maintain itself, is entirely different from pleasure being, as the definition indicates, a state in which a representation has a tendency to maintain itself (Höwing 2013, p. 96). Guyer also holds that this interpretation leads to infinite regress, if we accept that pleasure is a state we want to prolong—since it is not clear, in Zuckert's account, which state we actually wish to prolong (Guyer 2009, p. 208).

Furthermore, in my opinion, Zuckert also fails to address the second part of the definition from § 10, that is, the definition of displeasure: "displeasure is that representation that contains the ground for determining the state of the representations to their own opposite." Her reading is based on the thesis that the beginning of the definition of pleasure—"Consciousness of [Das Bewußtsein des Kausalität] causality of representation"—be read as objective genitive: second-order consciousness about causality of representation. However, it is impossible to read the definition of displeasure (meant as a parallel of pleasure) in this way, because it is obvious that displeasure is defined as what Zuckert calls a first-order state, with its formal characteristic being "that representation that contains the ground for determining the state of the representations to their own opposite". Thus, it is plausible to read the phrase "Das Bewußtsein des Kausalität" as subjective or *Eigenschaft* genitive. Accordingly, the definition of § 10 should be read as follows: The causality of a representation with respect to the state of the subject, for maintaining it in that state, is the very kind of consciousness that can here designate what is generally called pleasure. This suggests that Kant did not believe that causality of representation demanded higher-order-consciousness for our awareness of it, but rather that it is one of the ways in which we come to be aware, and itself manifests as awareness.

Zuckert's interpretation also fails, as does Guyer's, due to a confusion of faculties. Unlike Guyer, Zuckert differentiates feelings from sensations, and yet like Guyer, she correctly emphasizes that feelings are not discursive representations (Zuckert 2007, p. 236). However, in her reading, feelings are representations, and their main function is cognitive, representational (Zuckert 2007, p. 233)—exactly what the faculty of feeling does *not* do. The crucial challenge set by Kant is to characterize feeling as a *sui generis* mental state, meaning a mental state that is not a representation. Both Zuckert and Guyer miss this point. In what follows, I will attempt to show that some of the advantages of Zuckert's interpretation can be preserved, if we keep to the formal structure that consists of representation and its relational property (to maintain its state), while avoiding the contradictions that emerge with the introduction of second-order consciousness.

Three Basic Faculties of the Soul

It is well-known that Kant thought that there were three basic (irreducible) faculties of the soul: the faculty of cognition, the faculty of desire, and feelings of pleasure and displeasure. This thesis was directed against that of Christian Wolff, who held that the soul has only one basic force, that is, to represent the world (*vis representativa universi*), and that all other powers of the soul were derived from it (*vis derivativa*). Kant denied Wolff's metaphysical conclusions even in his earlier work, in which he was working with a different understanding of substance and force. In the *Critique of the Power of Judgment*, Kant attempted to ground the basic faculties in the principles of higher faculties of cognition (understanding, power of judgment and reason). Unfortunately, Kant presents a precise psychological determination of his understanding of various mental states only in his lectures. I will focus only on one of his later lectures, known as *Metaphysik Dohna*, held at the same time as he was working on the *Critique of the Power of Judgment*. I have chosen this moment in particular because it is here that Kant makes his most careful distinction between different mental states, and offers his most precise explanation of "causality of representation", which is used to define feeling and desire.

In *Metaphysik Dohna*, Kant first distinguishes between kinds of determinations within our soul: "they are either representations themselves (e.g. understanding), or they have reference to representations (e.g. will)" (V-Met/Dohna 28: 672). After reminding the reader, once again, of Wolff's erroneous thesis, Kant shows various ways in which certain mental states are not representations of themselves: "Our representations can themselves become efficient causes (and to that extent are not cognition)" (V-Met/Dohna 28: 675).

Further, he delineates kinds of causality of representation while also indicating the difference between feelings and desires:

The causality of representation is:

First, subjective – they are causes for producing themselves, maintaining themselves.
Second, objective – they become a cause of the production of objects.
[...] Thus a representation which produces the effort (*conatum*) for maintaining its state of representation (*statum repraesentativum*) is called *pleasure* [...]. (V-Met/Dohna 28: 675)

Thus, we see that Kant fairly easily differentiates among three kinds of mental states: representations themselves (cognition), subjective causality of representations (feelings of pleasure or displeasure) and objective causality of representations (desires) (Table1). It is important to note that in Kant's definition of pleasure, he is not speaking of either new sensations nor of second-order consciousness (as they themselves would both be representations). The key point is that this is not a new kind of representation, but a tendency of one representation to maintain its state of representation.[1]

Table 1: Basic faculties of the soul and corresponding determinations within the soul

Kinds of determinations of the soul	Representations themselves	Determinations which have reference to representations	
		Subjective causality of representations	Objective causality of representations
Basic faculties of the soul	Faculty of cognition	Feeling of pleasure and displeasure	Faculty of desire

Feeling as Subjective Causality of Representation

The thesis I am advancing, which I will now attempt to elaborate, can be understood as a significant modification of Zuckert's interpretation. According to this thesis, subjective causality of representation is not a mental state of which we are aware by way of higher-order consciousness (designated by Zuckert as feel-

---

1 As far as I can tell, my interpretation is closest to that of Hannah Ginsborg, although she offers less detail in explaining her understanding of the phenomenological structure of feeling (Ginsborg 1991, pp. 300–303).

ing). Rather, it is itself the means by which we are aware of a mental state, that is, subjective causality of representation, which manifests itself phenomenologically as consciousness, even without a second-order representation, that is, as feeling of pleasure or displeasure.[2] In this sense, the supposition of higher-order mental states or representations is completely unnecessary. On the other hand, this does not mean that feelings are a kind of sensation that can in no way be further explained (other than through their own causes); rather, feelings have a complex phenomenological structure that consists of two components: (1) a cognitive component consisting of representations themselves (sensation, intuition or concept) and (2) a causal component, consisting of its tendency toward maintaining its state of representation (subjective causality). These two components in one feeling are of course, inseparable. Subjective causality of representation is not a new, additional layer on top of the representation itself, but rather a subjective characteristic (*Beschaffenheit*) of a cognitive state, one, albeit, which cannot be reduced to the cognitive state itself.

It is important to note that causality here does not mean the relation between two things, one of which (the cause) precedes the other (the effect) in time—as the Humean paradigm suggests. At least in this case, we can apply Eric Watkins' interpretation, according to which causality ought to be understood as the exercise of causal power of one substance (Watkins 2005), which we call the cause, or the determination of a power of some substance to determine effects. (V-Met/Mron 29: 845) Thus, in the case of subjective causality of representations, causality is not a relation between a representation and its potential effects, but rather the exercise (or determination) of the causal power of representation to maintain its state. We can see that this is indeed the case from Kant's explanation of the phrase "objective causality of representation" in his definition of the power of desire. (KU 5: 177–178, EEKU 20: 230–231)

This interpretation regarding explanations of intentionality has one major advantage—it accounts for a much more intimate relationship between feeling and relevant cognitive states (representations), which is not the case with the causal model explanation. While feelings, in a strict sense, do not have a character of aboutness, (which Kant reserves for cognition), they are intimately related to the representations in which they are grounded, because they are the exercise of the causal power of that representation. Additionally, in my opinion,

---

2 Kant's main characterization of conscious states is that in it we are able to differentiate objects. It is important to note that Kant calls feeling of pleasure and displeasure "entirely special faculty of discriminating" (KU 5: 203).

the causality of representations also contributes to intentionality in a specific way (outside of cognition).

Kinds of Feelings

Kant gives at least three ways to distinguish feelings of pleasure. The first is according to the representations that ground them. According to the division of representations into sensations, intuitions and concepts, there are also three kinds of feelings: (1) gratification/pain (pleasure/displeasure in sensation); (2) pleasure/displeasure in a mere reflection (in intuition); and (3) intellectual pleasure (through concepts) (the most specific and genuine kind of intellectual pleasure is moral pleasure based on the idea of a moral law, or more precisely moral feeling and/or feeling of respect) (KU 5: 209). Parallel with this division, Kant adds that feelings differ according to the life force they affect: (1) gratification (*animal*), (2) feeling in taste (*human*) and (3) moral pleasure (*spiritual*)³ (V-Met/Pölitz 28: 248, KU 5: 210). Kant also speaks of a general division, according to which pleasure in the agreeable and pleasure in the good are bound to the faculty of desire, and thus to the interest in the existence of its object, while pleasure in reflection is disinterested pleasure.

In my opinion, another two clear distinctions can be made. The first is in the kind of subjective causality of representation. Sensations can exercise physical causality to maintain their states, however, concepts exercise a different type of causality—as purposiveness: "the causality of a *concept* with regard to its *object* is purposiveness (*forma finalis*)" (KU 5: 220). Pleasure in a reflection is related to purposiveness without purpose. Thus, it can be said that pleasure in the agreeable, pleasure in the good and pleasure in reflection (taste) have different causal components—a different subjective causality.

---

3 Several authors claim that there is no qualitative difference in feelings of pleasure (and displeasure) in Kant, except whether they are pleasure or displeasure (Beck 1960, p. 93; Guyer 1997, p. 103). They mostly refer to a sentence from the *Critique of Practical Reason:* "the agreeableness, the gratification (*Vergnügen*) [...] is nonetheless of the same kind. It is so not only insofar as it can always be cognized merely empirically, but also insofar as it affects one and the same vital force manifesting itself in our power of desire." (KpV 5: 23) The reader should note that for feeling, Kant in this place uses *Vergnügen*, which refers to only one kind of pleasure (*Wohlgeffalen*, *complacentia* is a wider concept), meaning that these authors assume what they have yet to demonstrate: that every type of pleasure is the same as gratification (*Vergnügen, voluptas*). Also, it is obvious that only gratification affects one and the same vital force, while other kinds of feelings affect other vital forces.

Finally, feelings can be differentiated according to the intentional object and the way the object is constituted. The object of pleasure in a sensation is something which is pleasant, the object of pleasure in mere reflection is beautiful, and the object of intellectual pleasure is something useful (or in the case of moral pleasure, good) (see KU 5: 266). While an argument can be made for each kind of feeling, this is beyond the scope of our topic, and for this reason, in what follows, we will focus only on the case of pleasure in mere reflection.

2 Pleasure in Mere Reflection

To begin, we will give a few basic characteristics of pleasure in mere reflection. The first is that the cognitive component is neither sensation nor concept, but the pure form of intuition—something yet to be explained. Pleasure in mere reflection, in contradistinction to pleasure in the agreeable and pleasure in the good, is disinterested. The subjective causality (causal component), in this case, is not pure mechanical causality, but that of purposiveness without purpose. This pleasure is not grounded in the senses nor in the determination of the will, but in reflection. Finally, and most difficult to explain, it is bound to the play of the imagination and the understanding.

Reflection

Here we can only briefly sketch some of the basic characteristics of reflection and the reflecting power of judgment. In Kant, reflection appears, above all, in the *Logic*, in the context of the construction of empirical concepts. Kant defines the function of an act of reflection as follows: "as to how various representations can be conceived in one consciousness," further adding the explanation: "I reflect on that which they [various representations] have in common among themselves." (Log 9: 95) Kant designates the reflecting power of judgment in a similar way: "If [...] the particular is given, for which the universal [*Allgemeine*] is to be found, then the power of judgment is merely *reflecting*" (KU 5: 179). A deeper explanation is far more complicated. From what we can tell, there must be a presentation (*Darstellung*) through the imagination upon which an act of reflection is directed. A target of reflection is not an external object nor a content of that presentation, but only the way it is apprehended in the imagination—which begs the question whether this singular *in concreto* presentation has a universal (*Allgemeine*) form whose source could be attributed to the understanding (KrV 3: 215; see Refl 16: 558). In the *Critique of the Power of Judgment*, Kant presents the principle for the reflecting power of judgment: the principle of formal purposiveness of nature (without a purpose). Without further consideration of this problem, what is relevant for us here that reflection is not a "black box" (Zuckert 2007, p. 283). Indeed, reflection is deduced according to a given principle (of formal purposiveness), has a *target* towards which it is directed (a form of apprehension of a presentation through the imagination), and has a formal object. This constitutes the way in which it is directed at its target, and explains the universality (*Allgemeinheit*) of this singular presentation of the imagination.

Difficulties in the Interpretation of § 9

In § 9 of the *Critique of the Power of Judgment*, Kant introduces the thesis that in judgments of taste, judgment (*Beurtheilung*) must precede a feeling of pleasure, and that universal communicability of this state is related to the harmony of a free play of the imagination and the understanding.

Guyer draws our attention to a problem that can be gleaned intuitively from § 9. The basic thesis of the paragraph is that judgment precedes a feeling of pleasure. However, a judgment of taste, like any other aesthetic judgment, ought to be a judgment grounded in feeling. Guyer therefore concludes that pleasure simultaneously follows judgment, while also logically preceding it, which, if regarded a single act of judgment, would be obviously absurd (Guyer 1997, p. 99 and p. 134).

Guyer finds a solution in the introduction of a two-act theory, according to which we are speaking of two different acts of reflection: one which produces the pleasure of the aesthetic response, and another which determines that the feeling of pleasure occasioned by the given object is such a pleasure, and thus validly attributed to anyone perceiving that object (Guyer 1997, p. 97). Thus, according to Guyer, the second act is really about the feeling of pleasure, by determining the cause based on which we attribute universal communicability to that feeling (this argument is, of course, compatible with the causal model advocated by Guyer).

There are various objections to this thesis, but perhaps the strongest is that the judgment of taste as the result of the second act would not be an aesthetic judgment at all, but rather an empirical theoretical judgment about our mental history (Aquila 1979, Ginsborg 1991). For the purposes of this chapter, we will concentrate on Hannah Ginsborg's criticism and attempted solution. In place of Guyer's two-act theory, Ginsborg introduces the theory of a self-referential act of reflection. She focuses on one sentence: "Thus it is the universal capacity for the communication (*allgemeine Mitteilungsfähigkeit*) of the state of mind in the given representation which, as the subjective condition of the judgment of taste, must serve as its ground and have the pleasure in the object as a consequence" (KU 5: 217). Guyer finds that a literal reading of this sentence leads to the absurd notion that universal communicability of a mental state of pleasure is the cause of that pleasure (Guyer 1997, p. 137). Instead of arriving at this conclusion, Ginsborg offers her own reading in which it is a self-referential act of reflection during which, in the very act of judgment, I am taking judgment of the object to be universally communicable—an act which manifests phenomenologically in a feeling of pleasure in that object (Ginsborg 1991, p. 299).

Still, there are a few problems that need mentioning, and which make me think that neither Guyer nor Ginsborg are entirely correct. First, in § 9, Kant is not speaking of a relation of cause and effect, but of ground and consequence. Ground (*Grund*) is a wider concept, which, in addition to cause, (*ratio fiendi*) also encompasses ground of cognition (*ratio cognoscendi*) and ground of possibility (*ratio essendi*) (V-Met/Dohna 28: 648). If we read this paragraph as having to do with the ground of possibility, then it is much easier to avoid the problems indicated by Guyer, since there is nothing contradictory in the fact that there is judgment in the ground of possibility of pleasure with pleasure being judgmental (in the same way that wood being grounds for the possibility of a wooden house does not mean that a wooden house is not made of wood) (see Zuckert 2007, p. 314).

Another problem is that Guyer and Ginsborg read the expression "*allgemeine Mitteilungsfähigkeit*" as having to do with a property of a mental state (which the similar expression "*allgemeine Mitteilbarkeit*" in the same paragraph does indeed designate). In German, the term "*Mitteilungsfähigkeit*" commonly designates one's rhetorical capacity to make oneself understandable to a wider audience. If we read Kant's text in this way, it indicates something quite coherent: if pleasure (a mental state) in taste must be universally communicable, then it must be its grounding in one's capacity that makes it possible. The capacity to find a universal for a particular constitutes the power of judgment. Thus, Kant is saying that reflective power of judgment (or aesthetic judgment) grounds the possibility of pleasure in taste. He repeats this conclusion a few lines later: "Now this merely subjective (aesthetic) judging of the object [...] is the ground of this pleasure in the harmony of the faculties of cognition" (KU 5: 218).

A third problem is the way in which both Guyer and Ginsborg introduce the characteristic (*Merkmal*) of universality (*Allgemeinheit*) of the mental state. Both Guyer's second act theory and Ginsborg's idea that reflection reflects on its own universality are additions that have no basis in Kant's texts. Moreover, it seems that they could be better ascribed to a theorist attempting to justify her claim on taste, rather than to one aesthetically judging an object with pleasure. They both overlook that universality of a particular representation is a formal object of nor-mal reflection, that is, the way we are engaged with an object when judging it. However, this does not mean that every presentation we judge has the character of universality. One possible interpretation—which I find rather plausible and which corresponds with Kant's claims that forms of universality are given by the understanding (Log 9: 91) and that the universality of the judgment of taste has its source in the understanding (Anth 7: 241)—is that the understand-ing, in the free play of the imagination, applies its functions without determined concepts (one of these being the form of universality). Kant is quite clear on this question in several places (KU 5: 219, 222).[4]

Definition of Pleasure in § 12

In § 12, Kant defines pleasure in mere reflection as follows:

> The consciousness of [*Das Bewußsein des*] the merely formal purposiveness in the play of the cognitive powers of the subject in the case of a representation through which an object is given is the pleasure itself, because it contains a determining ground of the activity of the subject with regard to the animation of its cognitive powers, thus an internal (*innere*) cau-sality (which is purposive) with regard to cognition in general[...] [This pleasure] has a cau-sality in itself (*in sich*), namely that of *maintaining* the state of the representation of the mind and the occupation of the cognitive powers without a further aim. (KU 5: 222)

In accordance with his causal model, Guyer thinks that here we ought to speak not of one, but two different causalities. He claims that "internal" (*innere*) cau-

---

4 One objection that is difficult to avoid is that reading Kant may lead to the conclusion that all objects are beautiful. Kant claims that the beauty of an object can be justified by simply demand-ing only correspondence of the cognitive faculties necessary for cognition in general. (KU 5: 392). The implication of this position is that any form that fulfills the necessary condition for cogni-tion – practically every form in our experience – fulfills this requirement. I think that it is im-portant not to explain the harmony of the faculties in cognitive terms (nor pre-cognitive, nor meta-cognitive). Correspondence between imagination and understanding is a necessary condi-tion for cognition, but that one particular form in itself *in concreto* exemplifies formal purposive-ness (as its source is in some concept) is neither necessary nor useful for cognition. For example, it is not necessary for cognition that this particular tree exemplify the concept of tree, with all its characteristics – I will compare it with other representations and subsume imagination under the hegemony of understanding. If it is still the case, then it is adherent beauty. And if one un-determined presentation, a pattern on a sea-shell, for example, exemplifies in itself *in concreto* form as its source is in some concept, that is not useful for cognition – because I cannot make an objective concept without comparison with other various representations.

sality is the power of representation to produce pleasure, while "intrinsic" cau-sality (*in sich*) is the ability of the feeling of pleasure itself to produce a tendency toward its own continuation (Guyer 1997, p. 194). However, in order to read this definition in such a way, Guyer had to modify the translation. While Kant's text must be read such that "consciousness [es] contains a determining ground [...] thus an internal causality," Guyer substitutes the pronoun *es* with the phrase "an aesthetic judgment:" "[A]n aesthetic judgment involves a determining ground [...] thus and internal causality" (Guyer 1997, p. 193)—there is no basis for this in the original German text.

Furthermore, Guyer overlooks the main point of § 12, which concerns a mo-ment of relation in an aesthetic judgment. For Kant, an inner (*innere*) relation is one where the determining ground of predication is found in a (logical) subject (Longuenesse 2003, p. 155). An example of outer causality would be all the phys-ical causal relations in nature (KrV 3: 224; OP 21: 419), while a good example of inner causality would be Leibniz's monads or the causality of free will men-tioned in the same passage. Thus, Kant says that merely formal purposiveness in the play of cognitive powers contains in itself a determining ground for its cau-sality to maintain its state.

Zuckert finds Kant's definition "a slip," since "Kant thus suggests that aes-thetic pleasure has "causality" or that we linger in judging the beautiful because it is pleasurable," which would imply that pleasure precedes judging, a notion altogether incoherent with the rest of Kant's claims (Zuckert 2007, p. 311n). Yet this problem emerges only if Zuckert insists on her interpretation that feelings are a second-order consciousness *about* an inner causality of judging. Converse-ly, if we read this paragraph such that reflection is structured as a tendency to-ward maintaining its state (formal purposiveness in play) and that this very state is by definition a feeling of pleasure (which has causality), then the problem dis-appears. This pleasure is grounded in judgment, but pleasure is nothing other than this judgment structured as a tendency toward maintaining its state.

Reflection Structured as a Feeling of Pleasure

According to my reading, pleasure in mere reflection is a state of judgment, structured as formal purposiveness in faculties' play. As such, this state exercises a subjective causal power (which is purposive) and which is grounded in the free play of imagination and understanding incited in a reflection. Simply put, reflec-tion is phenomenologically structured as the feeling of the pleasure-tendency to maintain its state.

The first thing necessary for any judgment of taste is a representation given empirically for the apprehension in imagination. In addition to being empirically given, however, it is necessary for the imagination to apprehend a form of the representation as ordered according to law, lawful without law. The target of reflection is a form of representation in imagination. Still, reflection is not arbitrary, but unfolds according to the transcendental principle of formal purposiveness, such that it is the universality of a particular formal object of judgment. In order for the form of representation to truly be structured as purposive, neither presentation in imagination nor reflection are sufficient—it is also necessary for the imagination to somehow agree with the understanding and its function of universality. In other words, it is also necessary for the understanding to have an impact on the acts of the imagination as if the form of apprehension has its source in some concept. The agreement of imagination and understanding with the power of judgment simultaneously promotes the process of judgment, that is, the formal purposiveness in judgment. Namely, the agreement in the act of judging a representation, in which the imagination and understanding are in mutual play, with the acts of reflecting power of judgment, simultaneously designates the promotion of purposive causality in judging, and what is seen as an active state of the subject, and a tendency to maintain this state, that is, the feeling of pleasure. In this sense, the characterization of merely formal purposiveness in the play of cognitive powers corresponds to practically all Kant's definitions of pleasure: (a) first, it designates agreement with the subject's conditions of life (of the subject who judges), (b) then, it designates promotion of life (in judging, [KU 5: 244]), and finally (c) it designates a subjective causality (purposiveness) to maintain its state of representation.

3 Problems in Understanding How a Form of an Object is Beautiful

There are a number of places where Kant underscores that, in taste, we have pleasure in a form of an object (not in a state of subject, [KU 5: 279, V-Met-K3E/Arnoldt 29: 1009]). At the same time, Kant hints at pleasure being a way that we become aesthetically aware of the harmonious play of the faculties (KU 5: 218), which could imply that this harmony is its internal object.

The question of form of an object immediately opens two problems inherent in Kant's description of judgment of taste: (1) why is the form presented in the imagination a form of an object; (2) why is it at all one unified (identical) form, when it is not determined by the concept of an object, nor by the objective rules of synthesis (categories)? According to Kant's epistemology, in order for the manifold of representations to refer to an object, it must be unified in a concept of object as a rule for the synthesis of the manifold. This means that the concept is ascribed as a predicate to some intuition, constituting the cognition of an object (KrV 3: 112). However, in a judgment of taste, *ex hypothesi*, the predicate is only the subjective feeling of pleasure, not a concept. The question, thus, arises, why the form is presented by imagination as the form of an object at all, rather than merely a subjective apprehension of imagination. This brings us to a second question. Since Kant says that the manifold of representation can be presented as unified only if it is unified in the consciousness as a concept, how can there be a unity of this manifold that constitutes the form of an object?

Guyer sought the solution to this problem in a metacognitive interpretation of the harmony of the faculties. In this reading, the form of an object is grounded in some concept (and the cognition of the object), while, for taste, what goes beyond this cognition is relevant (Guyer 2006). And while we agree with Guyer that, in some cases the harmony of the faculties can be understood as metacognitive (e.g. when a rose is beautiful), it is clear that Kant offers examples in which there is no presupposition of (conceptual) cognition of an object: for example, in the interplay of sounds one feels as musical composition (KU 5: 225).

Ginsborg, as mentioned, introduces the thesis that an act of reflection is self-referential. This allows her to seamlessly explain why the feeling of pleasure is intentional both regarding the state of the subject as well as the object. However, Ginsborg spends significant effort trying to explain how the form presented by the imagination is the form of the object. She proposes that it is a presentation by the imagination which is lawful, and as such, presents an example of the rule for judging that object. More specifically, given her self-referential understanding of the act of reflection, a person judging an object simultaneously also takes their judgment to be the standard way this particular presentation should be judged (lawfully, free of sensations, etc.). That is to say, the judgment sets the standard of how the individual presentation ought to be judged as an object. In this way, the normativity of reflection also carries with it the identity of form of an object. Yet, Ginsborg's interpretation is problematic because of the shift away from the normativity of subjective universality (of judging) towards judging this particular presentation as an object (Ginsborg 1997, p. 2006).

Zuckert also attempts to answer the question of why the manifold of representations is at all unified in one form. Zuckert emphasizes that aesthetic judgment unfolds according to the (subjective) principle of purposiveness without purpose. This activity aims at or strives for unification of the manifold, through which we are able to grasp the beautiful object as unified (Zuckert 2007, p. 300). In order to explain this activity, she draws on the thesis about the anticipated whole: by representing these properties as presented at different moments, and also as part of an anticipated future whole (Zuckert 2007, p. 302). Furthermore, as we mentioned, Zuckert understands the feeling of pleasure as consciousness of the tendency toward maintaining the state of representation. In this way, the feeling of a singular representation, according to Zuckert, has the role of marking the unity of consciousness (Zuckert 2007, p. 317–318; see KrV 3: 109). Continuing this line of thinking, feeling, for Zuckert, is also self-awareness about the future directedness of the subject's state.

The first problem with Zuckert's reading, however, is that although it can explain aesthetic judgment as an activity in which a future whole is anticipated, it fails to explain the exact moment of judgment when the manifold of sensations indeed presents as a unified form (identity of form of an object), that is, the moment of pleasure in reflection (see Zinkin 2012). Put somewhat differently, it would seem that Kant is proposing that there is indeed one unified and identical form of an object (KU 5: 288), and not (merely) an anticipated whole. Further complicating matters is that this allows for the skeptical argument that it is not possible to shift from a subjective principle of judgment to the representation of an object as unified.

4 Intentionality *Sui Generis* of Pleasure in Mere Reflection

In my opinion, some of these problems can be resolved by a different understanding of how a feeling of intentionality *sui generis* is constituted by the judgment of taste. In pleasure in mere reflection, the identity of an intentional object is not constituted primarily in the cognitive component. Rather, it is precisely the causal component, the tendency to maintain that state in a purposive activity, which is responsible for the constitution of an identity of an object.

This reading allows us to immediately explain why the form presented by the imagination is one unified and identical form. This is because judgment is structured as a tendency toward maintaining this state of representation. That is, during the exercise of (purposive) subjective causality in aesthetic judgment, the activity of the imagination and the understanding (that is, their harmonious play) is maintained, thus holding a given form of the apprehension, and making the form one and identical. In other words, this form, as a target of reflection, could be considered identical only when judgment is structured as feeling of pleasure (cf. Zinkin 2012).

Nevertheless, this still does not explain why this form is designated as the form of an object. For Kant, an object is "that in the concept of which the manifold of a given intuition is *united*" (KrV 3: 111). However, while we are not dealing with a concept, there is still a causality that is grounded in some (undetermined) concept. This subjective causality comprises the structure of the state of aesthetic judgment, and is ascribed to a reflected form as its predicate. Lest we forget, purposiveness is "causality of a *concept* with regard to its *object*" (KU 5: 220). Put differently, the unity of the manifold of perception is reflected in aesthetic judgment in such a way as if it is unified in a concept of an (undetermined) object. This does not mean that this state can be said to be about an object (aboutness). With regard to cognition, it is not confused or incomplete knowledge of the object, but rather simply does not fulfill the minimal requirement to refer to the object (it lacks a concept). Because this relation is merely aesthetic, we can only say that we are directed toward a form seen in a reflection as the form of an object. Thus, an object of pleasure is not an object of cognitive, but rather of particular aesthetic intentionality, that is, of feeling intentionality *sui generis*.

The thesis presented by Zuckert, then, that the feeling of a singular representation stands in the place of the concept as a sign of the unity of consciousness, requires modification. This is to say, what makes the identity of a manifold of representations in the consciousness is not a representation (since this would always have to be some concept), but rather an identical subjective purposiveness (subjective causality) that is applied to a form of the manifold of representations. Thus, it is the subject that is directed toward the manifold of representations as subsumed under one causality, that of purposiveness without a purpose. Judgment of taste can, therefore, be explained analogously with the form of logical judgment, as a way of bringing given representations under formal purposiveness, or as a synthesis of intuition with its subjective causality that can be executed *a priori* (see KU 5: 286–287, 290; KrV 3: 114).

Self-awareness has not entirely dropped out of the picture, but it should not be understood as an introspective consciousness about our mental states, nor as consciousness about the harmony of the faculties (since that would be cognition).[5] I hold that this is an entirely different kind of intentionality. First, it is important to mention the thesis, common in contemporary literature, that emotional self-awareness cannot be taken as a distinct component from emotional engagement toward the object: "While afraid, you experience something as dangerous and at the same time 'you' feel vulnerable in the relevant respect. But

---

[5] This mistake, in my opinion, is also made by Allison (2011, p. 54, p. 69 and p. 130). (See Zuckert 2007, p. 313n).

your experience of danger is not separate from, but rather consists in your feeling thus vulnerable" (Slaby 2008, p. 439). The situation is the same with pleasure in mere reflection, when I feel myself as someone who, in reflection (*a priori*) takes account of everyone else's way of representing, evaluating above mere private interests (KU 5: 293). These are not two experiences: in the case of pleasure in mere reflection, judging an object with pleasure consists in feeling oneself as someone who (*a priori*) takes account of everyone else's way of representing and vice versa. However, this does not mean that we feel pleasure because our state is universal, as that would then be empirical interest in beauty (which can be objected to Ginsborg, see Allison 2001, p. 114): we feel pleasure because of the promotion of formal purposiveness in judging a form of representation, and in this pleasure, we feel ourselves as someone who takes everyone else's way of representing into account.

5 Conclusions

In this text, I have elaborated the interpretation of feelings as *sui generis* mental states, which I think better suits Kant's viewpoint. Based on this interpretation, I claim that pleasure in mere reflection is actually an act of reflection structured as pleasure. Additionally, I point out some potential advantages of this reading of *Critique of the Power of Judgment*, above all the definition from § 12. Thus, I explained the intentionality of this pleasure as *sui generis* feeling-intentionality, through which a beautiful object is constituted (I think that most interpreters have failed to distinguish this correctly from the type of intentionality usually found in cognition). It can be concluded that, in that regard, I agree with Guyer, that pleasure in taste has no cognitive intentionality. This, however, does not mean that there is no intentionality in pleasure at all, but rather that this intentionality is of a special kind.

Bibliography

Allison, Henry E. (1983): *Kant's Transcendental Idealism*. New Haven, London: Yale University Press.
Allison, Henry E. (2001): *Kant's Theory of Taste. A Reading of the Critique of Aesthetic Judgment*. New York: Cambridge University Press.
Allison, Henry E. and Guyer, Paul (2006): "Dialogue: Paul Guyer and Henry Allison on Allison's *Kant's Theory of Taste*". In: Rebecca Kukla (Ed.): *Aesthetic and Cognition in Kant's Critical Philosophy*. New York: Cambridge University Press, pp. 111–137.

Aquila, Richard E. (1979): "A New Look at Kant's Aesthetic Judgment". In: *Kant Studien* 70. No. 1, 17–34.

Beck, Lewis White (1960): *A Commentary to Kant's Critique of Practical Reason.* Chicago: University of Chicago Press.

Ginsborg, Hannah (1991): "On the Key to Kant's Critique of Taste". In: *Pacific Philosophical Quarterly* 72, pp. 290–313.

Ginsborg, Hannah (1997): "Lawfulness without a Law: Kant on the Free Play of Imagination and Understanding". In: *Philosophical Topics* 25. No. 1, pp. 37–82.

Ginsborg, Hannah (2006): "Thinking the Particular as Contained under the Universal". In: Rebecca Kukla (Ed.): *Aesthetic and Cognition in Kant's Critical Philosophy.* New York: Cambridge University Press, pp. 35–60.

Goldie, Peter (2000): *Emotions: A Philosophical Exploration.* New York: Oxford.

Guyer, Paul (1997): *Kant and the Claims of Taste.* Cambridge: Cambridge University Press.

Guyer, Paul (2006): "Harmony of the Faculties Revisited". In: Rebecca Kukla (Ed.): *Aesthetic and Cognition in Kant's Critical Philosophy.* New York: Cambridge University Press, pp. 162–193.

Guyer, Paul (2009): "The Harmony of the Faculties in Recent Books on the *Critique of the Power of Judgment*". In: *The Journal of Aesthetics and Art Criticism* 67. No. 2, 201–221.

Heidegger, Martin (1992): *Der Grundbegriffe der Metaphysik: Welt, Endlichkeit, Einsamkeit (GA 29/30).* Frankfurt am Main: Vittorio Klostermann.

Höwing, Thomas (2013): *Praktische Lust. Kant über das Verhältnis von Fühlen, Begehren und praktischer Vernunft.* Berlin, Boston: De Gruyter.

Husserl, Edmund (2000): *Aktive Synthesen :Aus der Vorlesung "Transzendentale Logik" 1920/1921 (Hua XXXI).* Berlin: Springer.

Longuenesse, Beatrice (2003): "Kant's Theory of Judgment, and Judgments of Taste: On Henry Allison's *Kant's Theory of Taste*". In: *Inquiry* 46. No. 2, pp. 143–163.

Sartre, Jean-Paul (1994): *Sketch for a Theory of the Emotions.* London, New York: Routledge.

Slaby, Jan (2008): "Affective Intentionality and the Feeling Body". In: *Phenomenology and the Cognitive Sciences* 7. No. 4, pp. 429–444.

Slaby, Jan and Stephan, Achim (2008): "Affective Intentionality and Self-Consciousness". In: *Consciousness and Cognition* 17, 506–513.

Stein, Edith (1917): *Zum Problem der Einfühlung.* Halle: Buchdruckerei des Waisenhauses.

Watkins, Eric (2005): *Kant and Metaphysics of Causality.* New York: Cambridge University Press.

Zinkin, Melissa (2012): "Kant and the Pleasure of 'Mere Reflection'". In: *Inquiry* 55. No. 5, pp. 433–453.

Zuckert, Rachel (2007): *Kant on Beauty and Biology.* New York: Cambridge University Press.

Serena Feloj

Exemplary Emotions: A Discussion of Normativity in Kant's Aesthetic Judgment

Abstract: In this chapter I will argue that the sentimentalist elements of Kant's account call for a revision of its normative interpretations, a better framing of its subjective universalism, and finally for a reconsideration of aesthetic normativity in favour of regulativity. We will notably see that when reference is made to a wide notion of normativity a few non-negligeable problems arise: 1. Based on Kant's aesthetic judgment, no value is attributed to an object, as it is rather a feeling that is expressed; the main question is: can a feeling be normative? 2. How is it possible to combine the regulative character, essential to Kant's judgment of taste, with aesthetic normativity? Is it possible to speak about normativity without rules, norms and standards (normal ideas)? 3. Is it still possible to discuss normativity while entirely renouncing prescriptions? My chapter aims to discuss the normative character of aesthetic emotions in Kant's third Critique by calling upon the notions of regulativity and exemplarity.

Keywords: aesthetic judgment, feeling, aesthetic normativity, exemplarity, subjective universalism

In light of the current debate surrounding aesthetic normativity, the key role played by emotions, and in particular, the feeling of pleasure within Kant's account has potentially major implications. The notion of normativity has been key to an improved understanding of subjective universality that, for Kant, characterizes aesthetic judgment. In scholarly literature, however, there is little discussion (somewhat unsurprisingly), of what exactly we should understand by normativity within the context of Kant's aesthetic. In general terms, the question ensuing from the discussion on normativity in aesthetics can be simplified as follows: how can an emotion, that is to say, a subjective state of mind, be expressed in a communicable and universally valid judgment? In this regard, it is true that to a certain extent, the notion of aesthetic normativity finds suitable ground in Kant's theory of taste, lending Kant's aesthetic judgment a high-ranking position within the contemporary debate. Recent trends show the tendency to take normativity very broadly, even to the point of nuancing most of its core meaning.

Serena Feloj, Univ. of Pavia, Italy

https://doi.org/10.1515/9783110720730-009

Because of how we speak about normativity in aesthetics, we seem to have indeed accepted that every kind of evaluative process is normative.

In this chapter I will argue that the sentimentalist elements of Kant's account call for a revision of its normative interpretations, a better framing of its subjective universalism, and a reconsideration of aesthetic normativity in favour of regulativity. We will see that when reference is made to a broad notion of normativity, a few non-negligeable problems arise: 1. Based on Kant's aesthetic judgment, no value is attributed to an object, as it is rather a feeling that is expressed. This begs the question: can a feeling be normative? 2. How is it possible to combine the regulative character, essential to Kant's judgment of taste, with aesthetic normativity? Is it possible to speak about normativity without rules, norms and standards (normal ideas)? 3. Is it still possible to discuss normativity while entirely renouncing prescriptions? My contribution discusses the normative character of aesthetic emotions in Kant's third Critique by calling upon the notions of regulativity and exemplarity. This argument not only provides an alternative reading of certain elements of Kant's aesthetics of acute relevance in the contemporary debate, but also aims to underline the peculiarity of the aesthetic experience as an experience characterized by spontaneity and communicable to others through a judgment with an essential character of indeterminacy.

Among Kantian scholars, two principal opposing views have been upheld on this topic: the first, promoted mainly by Paul Guyer (1979), views Kant's theory of aesthetic pleasure as opaque and non-intentional, while the second, "intentionalist" position, championed mainly by Henry A. Allison (1998), understands the function of aesthetic pleasure as making us conscious of the activities of our faculties.[1] It should be noted that both Guyer and Allison are considered eminent voices in Kantian studies, and should also be added that in the past decade, due to the influence of analytic philosophy, much of the issues connected to Kant's notion of aesthetic pleasure have been referred to the notion of aesthetic normativity. Such a reference to normativity seems to grant the possibility of grounding the normative validity of aesthetic judgments in Kant's transcendental philosophy, provided the normative nature of Kant's notion of emotion is taken for granted. An example of this perspective can be seen in the article "Aesthetic Judgment", by Nick Zangwill for the *Stanford Encyclopedia of Philosophy*, especially in its revisited edition of 2014 (Zangwill 2014), in which he applies the most recent findings of the contemporary Kantian debate to the definition of aes-

---

1 These authors argued their respective cases in Allison and Guyer 2006; see Tomasi 2008, pp. 17–18.

thetic judgment. What stands out here is how the normative character of Kant's aesthetic judgment is taken for granted—the assumption that Kant's aesthetic is normative ensues nonetheless from the idea that pleasure in beauty has an intentional content. However, as mentioned previously, this is not an entirely uncontroversial interpretation.

1 Aesthetic Normativity: Between Norm and Ideal

The normative essence of Kant's aesthetic judgment is usually evidenced by the universal validity of aesthetic claims and by the shareable and communicable nature of these kinds of judgments. A peculiar aspect of Kant's aesthetic theory is the aspiration to a universal validity of taste, which would seem to suggest that in matters of taste and beauty others "should" share our judgment (see Feloj 2018). As a result, Kant's account seems to ground basic normativity in the principle of the adequacy of aesthetic judgment, ensuring that when I say "X is beautiful", my judgment is correct, or at least appropriate. This is also what leads many scholars to think that Kant's aesthetic could be interpreted as exemplifying the normativity of the aesthetic judgment. Any claim regarding correctness in an aesthetic judgment is, however, problematic and in no way self-evident as, in Kant's understanding, beauty is not an attribute of the object, but rather a feeling of the subject. For this reason, the subjective nature of aesthetic universality, as well as the meaning of the aesthetic "should", have generated, and continue to generate, many interpretive problems. After careful assessment of the elements at stake, we will see that when Kant mentions an element of universality in this context, what he is really referring to is something ideal, different from "normal" universality, and that in the *Critique of the Power of Judgment*, Kant provides a distinctive definition of the aesthetic "should" (*Sollen*) (§ 19) which departs in some important respects from regular accounts of normativity.

From the outset, by establishing the first maxim of taste as "thinking for oneself" (*Selbstdenken*), Kant makes it clear that in the aesthetic experience, the adequacy of our emotional response is not related to the judgment of the majority. While trying to reconcile this kind of statement with the normativity suggested by Kant's reference to what also others "should" judge, Zangwill states that "a judgment of taste makes a claim to correctness", which implies a "shift from the problematic 'should' that is involved in a judgment of taste to a problematic 'correctness' or 'betterness'. This may be inevitable. We are dealing with a normative notion, and while some normative notions may be explainable in terms of others, we cannot express normative notions in non-normative terms" (Zangwill, 2014). This interpretation is the least problematic, for various reasons.

First, speaking about correctness in the absence of a verification criterion sounds implausible. An aesthetic judgment is, in fact, not an epistemic statement about an object, but an expression of subjective feelings—it would be more plausible to speak about appropriateness to a community of judging people. Secondly, even when shifting from the problematic aesthetic "should" to the perhaps even moreso "correctness", we can ascribe a normative nature to aesthetic judgments only if this is understood in a very wide (and vague) manner, without any references to prescriptions.

Before addressing the peculiar "should" (*Sollen*) involved in aesthetic judgments, it is useful to review the distinction between aesthetic ideals and norms. This is one of the most important points of disagreement between Kant and Hume's *Standard of Taste*. According to Hume's empiricism, when surveying the historical evolution of art, we notice that some works of art are universally appreciated. This is not due to some attribute of the objects, but to a regularity of our aesthetic feeling, or to the so-called "standardization of taste". This is the core of Hume's sentimentalism.[2] From Hume's point of view, our attitude toward works of art is not a matter of satisfaction, but "we affirm our preference as valid" (Scruton 1979, p. 105). This is why we demand the same feelings from others and take any judgment that differs with ours as the expression of a defective sensibility (Hume 1757, p. 230)—we think that our response is more appropriate than its opposite. In the wake of Hume's sentimentalism, some contemporary authors state that, in aesthetics, "the normativity of judgment derives from the normativity of feeling" (Zangwill 2014).[3]

It is unclear, however, how the normativity of judgments of taste can be inherent in feelings, and how feelings can be more or less veridical. Hume's solution rests on common sense and on a "subjective normativity", based on which, if "I get the idea or sentiment and you don't, in contemplating the same object, either you or I may be 'abnormal,' but there is no sense in which either of us can be 'wrong' or 'right,' which is to say, 'mistaken' or 'correct'" (Kivy 2016). Kant famously rejects Hume's "normality criterion" and he replaces it with the notion of aesthetic ideal. In the *Critique of the Power of Judgment* (§ 7) Kant anticipates the core topic of the *Deduction* as he claims that if one "pronounces that something is beautiful, then he expects the very same satisfaction of others: he judges not merely for himself, but for everyone, and speaks of beauty as if it were a property of things" (KU 212: 98). What should be emphasized here is that when I demand

---

2 See Hume's *Treatise* and *The Standard of Taste*.
3 In recent years, many interesting studies have been published about the normativity of taste in Hume and Kant, see Carrol 1984; Kulenkampff 1990; Falkenstein 1998; Railton 1999; Costelloe 2004; Phillips 2005; Allison 2008; Dorsey 2008; Guyer 2012; Shelley 2013; Graham 2014.

the agreement of others as to what I call beautiful, my request is neither a pre-scription nor a matter of facts.[4] It is an ideal agreement (see Borutti 2017) based on which all judging people are meant to speak with a universal voice. What is clear is that, when it comes to judgments of taste, there is no concept that can grant universal validity, in contrast with the case of epistemic or moral judg-ments. In Kant's own words, beauty is represented as an object of universal sa-tisfaction without concepts.

The ideal nature of the universality of taste is even more strongly outlined further on in § 17. The distance from Hume, the standard of taste, and an empiri-cal search for regularity becomes more pronounced as we read on and the legiti-macy of normativity-based readings of Kant's aesthetic appears increasingly slim. Kant offers a discouraging warning to anyone seeking the source of aesthet-ic normativity in his theory of taste: "There can be no objective rule of taste that would determine what is beautiful through concepts. For every judgment from this source is aesthetic, i.e., its determining ground is the feeling of the subject and not a concept of an object. To seek a principle of taste that would provide the universal criterion of the beautiful through determinate concepts is a fruitless undertaking, because what is sought is impossible and intrinsically self-contra-dictory" (KU 5: 231; Kant 2000, p. 116).

Since the "determining ground"[5] of judgment is the feeling of the subject, an aesthetic judgment has to do with the communicability of the emotion. This is rather peculiar insofar as it is neither granted by a concept—as happens with normative moral judgment and the good—nor just derived from some kind of em-pirical regularity—as happens with the agreeable and the descriptive affirmation of one's own preferences. What defines the judgment of taste is neither fully nor-mative nor clearly descriptive. It is rather defined by its exemplarity.

The aesthetic subjective universality is taken as ideal, as it is determined by the spontaneity of an emotion that cannot be prescribed to anyone, but that can be requested from others. There is no sign or guarantee of an effective agree-ment, but there is a possibility. The ideality of the aesthetic emotion therefore provides an opportunity for the universality of the judgment of taste. Upon closer inspection, the ideal of beauty is defined in the following terms: as the exhibi-tion of a rational idea, it is an example of judgment through taste and is "some-thing that we strive to produce in ourselves even if we are not in possession of it"

---

4 See what Kant writes in § 7: "does not count on the agreement of others with his judgment of satisfaction because he has frequently found them to be agreeable with his own, but rather de-mands it from them" (KU 5: 212–213; Kant 2000, p. 98).
5 Not to be mistaken for the "transcendental ground", this latter being identified with the free play between imagination and understanding.

(KU 5: 232; Kant 2000, p. 117). In this way, the ideal of beauty is created by the faculty of imagination. As Terry Pinkard writes: "we do not, as it were, walk into a museum armed with a definite and precise concept of the beautiful and then examine each painting to see if it is subsumed under that concept" (Pinkard 2002, p. 69).

The ideal of beauty is furthermore carefully differentiated from the "normal idea". By *Normalidee* Kant means the measure (*Maße*), derived from the average resulting from the associations of imagination (see Chiodo 2015). The normal idea provides the rules for the evaluation of beauty, which are ultimately determined and derived from the realm of experience, – which is not the archetype of beauty. The normal idea only gives us the correctness of the representation: "It is, as was said of Polycletus's famous Doryphorus, the *rule* (*Regel*)" (KU 5: 235; Kant 2000, p. 119). The key word here, *Regel*, calls upon regularity and its measurement by an average size, which is indeed determined by empirical rules. Far from being a *Gesetz*, the "rule" is not comparable to the a priori moral norm.

It is also clear that Kant excludes both the concept and the rule from aesthetic judgment. The notion of "ideal" does indeed display some affinities with the exemplarity of genius (§ 46), which is defined as an ability to create without any concept and without any rule, by merely contemplating the aesthetic idea. This also explains why in both §17 and §46, imitation is banned from the aesthetic experience: everyone must judge with their own taste.

It is, finally, safe to say that the ideal of beauty, as investigated by Kant, implies several challenges when it comes to the discussion of its normativity. While excluding any correctness criterion, it leads to the claim that there are no empirical rules, no rational concepts, and no norms granting the aesthetic judgment's universality, and furthermore that no normal idea will be enough to explain the communicability of feelings. One may well wonder whether it still makes sense to discuss normativity when all these elements are excluded from aesthetic judgment. One element persists, however—the element of necessity. The ideal of beauty is archetypical and exemplary "in accordance with which he must judge everything that is an object of taste, or that is an example of judging through taste, even the taste of everyone" (KU 5: 232; Kant 2000, p. 116 – 117). The normativity of the judgment of taste can still be validated, then, to a certain extent, by means of the aesthetic "should".

2 A Non-prescriptive Necessity: The Aesthetic "should"

As we have seen, from a Kantian point of view, addressing aesthetic normativity is more problematic than one would imagine. Kant's aesthetic theory is congruent with Hume's standard of taste in that the judgment of taste is determined by a feeling; it is however well known that Kant abandons Hume's empirical perspective in favor of a transcendental theory in which the communicability of the judgment is granted by the free play of the cognitive faculties.[6] Based on Kant's aesthetic theory, the spontaneity of emotions is preserved—they have no rules, no concepts, no correctness and no normal criterion. Nevertheless, emotions are universally valid, can be communicated, and determine our judgment.

In the contemporary debate on Kant's aesthetic, within the realm of the polarized discussions between intentionalists and non-intentionalists, Andrew Chignell has supported the normative nature of Kant's aesthetic judgment starting from its subjectivity and with reference to aesthetic ideas.[7] Chignell is convinced, in contrast to Guyer, that in his "subject-based theory, Kant clearly did not intend to give up the idea that judgements of taste are normative" (Chignell 2008, p. 416). Chignell's proposal tries to solve the problem of aesthetic normativity by showing that the subjective basis of the normativity of the aesthetic judgment is not at variance with the theory of aesthetic ideas (Chignell 2007, p. 419). Chignell's interpretation duly recognizes the ideality of subjective universality and he convincingly argues for bringing Kant's formalism back to the forefront of the discussion. We should not forget that Kant illuminates the way we experience an object regardless of the content of the object of our experience. Less convincingly, Chignell's line of argument takes for granted the normativity of aesthetic emotions and does not question how Kant's aesthetic normativity should be understood.

Chignell reads the ideality of the intersubjective validity of taste mainly based on the last paragraphs of the *Critique of the Aesthetic Power of Judgment* (§§ 49 – 59), and his argumentation aims to demonstrate how these texts are not at odds with the main topic of the entire *Deduction*, that is, the subjective universality of taste (Chignell 2007, p. 423). I agree with him as he underlines the con-

---

6 In Kant's perspective, the transcendental guarantee of the universality of our judgment is given by the presence of the same faculties with the same functions in every subject.
7 For another interesting perspective on Kant and normativity see Ginsborg 2015. I will not discuss here Ginsborg's complex interpretation though.

tinuity between these paragraphs, however I am also convinced that a different path better explains the key features of aesthetic normativity in Kant. I suggest establishing a comparison between the fourth moment of the *Analytic of beauty* and the conclusion of the *Critique of the Aesthetic Power of Judgment*. This comparison indeed allows stressing the importance of the regulative use of emotions in aesthetic judgment. Before venturing into a discussion of regulativity, however, it is useful to understand how the normative claim can be crucially combined with the element of ideality. If the normativity of taste can rest only on the "should" that characterizes aesthetic intersubjective validity, and has no rules nor concepts as guarantee, it will be very useful to understand what kind of necessity is here at stake. It is my belief, as previously anticipated, that in this respect the ideality of the aesthetic demand should not be disregarded.

On the topic of the intersubjective validity, Kant clarifies that aesthetic necessity is set in the field of possibility (§ 18). In contrast with objective theoretic necessity and practical necessity, aesthetic necessity is peculiar in that it can only be called exemplary. In this sense, any rule of taste can be potentially inferred, and the necessity of the aesthetic feeling is far from being apodictic: "[A] necessity of the assent of all to a judgment that is regarded as an example of a universal rule that one cannot produce. Since an aesthetic judgment is not an objective and cognitive judgment, this necessity cannot be derived from determinate concepts, and is therefore not apodictic" (KU 5: 237; Kant 2000, p. 121). This also entails that, in aesthetics, the feeling of pleasure and the expression of a judgment are not two separate moments, but rather two elements of the same experience.

Furthermore, the exemplarity of taste defines not only its necessity but also the distinctive "should" implied in aesthetic judgments. The aesthetic "should" is conditional, as it is granted only by the faculties we have in common. This entails that a subjective "should" does not describe an actual agreement nor prescribe the approval of others, but rather places universality in ideality and possibility. This ideality of the aesthetic "should" is linked to the determining function of emotions. When we experience and judge aesthetically, we can only appeal to others to share our emotions. At the same time, the subjective universality of emotions, granted by common sense, assumes the form of a peculiar "should" that is more an expectation than a prescription. The unique "should" Kant is describing here may sound almost oxymoronic, as it is a non-prescribing "should". In this sense, the judgment of taste "determines what pleases or displeases only through feeling and not through concepts, but yet with universal validity" (KU 5: 238; Kant 2000, p. 122).

The determining function of emotions means that aesthetic feelings are non-private—in spite of their unavoidable subjective nature, they are shareable and universally communicable. The determining function of emotions does not mean, however, that feelings follow rules or prescriptions, or can be correct or incorrect. Moreover, Kant makes it clear that we do not choose to feel or not to feel—feelings do not depend on our will. The spontaneity of emotion is fully preserved.

Finally, the difficulties of a "should" grounded in emotions are openly admitted by Kant in the controversial §22. The solution to these difficulties, however, is not given here. In §2, Kant explicitly states that aesthetic judgments entail a "should" (*Sollen*): "[I]t does not say that everyone will concur with our judgment but that everyone should agree with it" (KU 5: 239; Kant 2000, p. 123). Remarks of this kind justify the enthusiasm of many interpreters regarding the attempt to anchor aesthetic normativity in Kant's theory of taste. However, as previously outlined, the aesthetic "should", as defined by Kant, is no ordinary "should"—it is determined by emotions, it is ideal, and it is exemplary.

As Kant attempts to better elucidate his aesthetic "should", he adds another element (§22). The aesthetic "should", taken as, "I ascribe exemplary validity" to my judgment of taste, relies on a form of common sense that is "a merely ideal norm" (KU 5: 239; Kant 2000, p. 123)—we have already shown what Kant understands by "ideality of taste". What is added here, however, is the qualifying remark presenting the judgment of taste as an "indeterminate norm" (*unbestimmte Norm*). From a Kantian point of view, indeterminacy is a recurring feature in aesthetics: no determined concept lays the ground for a judgment, which is ultimately determined only by emotions. This kind of sentimentalist theory could, in my opinion, provide an interesting approach for contemporary aesthetics, although it clearly requires a revision of the normative assessment of the aesthetic judgment. Kant himself seems to admit the difficulty of this revision by asking whether common is to be understood as "as a constitutive principle of the possibility of experience" or "whether a yet higher principle of reason only makes it into a regulative principle for us first to produce a common sense in ourselves for higher ends" (KU 5: 240; Kant 2000, p. 124). In light of other sections of the third Critique (§48–59), Kant seems to prefer the latter solution. This leads to other complex questions: the judgment of taste, "with its expectation of a universal assent", becomes "in fact only a demand of reason to produce such a unanimity in the manner of sensing" (KU 5: 240; Kant 2000, p. 124), as he famously claims.

This has important consequences on the definition of the aesthetic "should", as it must be understood only as a possibility: "the 'should', i.e., the objective necessity of the confluence of the feeling of everyone with that of each, signifies only the possibility of coming to agreement about this, and the judgment of taste only provides an example of the application of this principle". Kant cautiously postpones the solution to these problems, as he writes: "this we would not and cannot yet investigate here" (KU 5: 240; Kant 2000, p. 124). I am nevertheless confident that some answer is provided at the end of the *Critique of the Aesthetic Power of Judgment*, when Kant analyses the notion of regulativity.

3 A Subjective Requirement: From Normativity to Regulativity

In the fourth part of the *Analytic of Beauty*, while defining aesthetic necessity, Kant resorts to the notion of "indeterminate norm", in order to stress the determining function of emotions in aesthetic judgment. This may sound controversial, as emotions determine the judgment of taste and thus give it an indeterminate norm. I believe, however, that we can better understand this controversial point if we abandon a strict notion of aesthetic normativity, a notion that is not Kantian but contemporary, in favour of the possibly more complex notion of regulativity. This notion allows us to conserve the ideality and indeterminacy that are distinctive features of aesthetic judgment.

The complexity of Kant's aesthetic theory leads some contemporary scholars to claim that Kant does not provide many clues regarding the nature of the normativity implied in aesthetic feelings (Zangwill 2014). For instance, Kant may point to the problem of aesthetic normativity, but leave us without a full characterization of the notion of normativity he is attempting to explain. Here I hope to demonstrate that while Kant offers us many elements that help us understand the complex notion of subjective universality, these elements do not necessarily fit with the stricter and more rigid contemporary notion of normativity. Interesting results can also ensue from implementing, in contemporary terms, the more indeterminate notion of regulativity, possibly as a peculiar kind of normativity, that preserves the ideality, exemplarity, indeterminacy and, ultimately, the emotional nature of aesthetics.

As is well known, the regulative use of reason is defined in the first Critique (KrV A 670/B 698: 605. See Feloj 2015) and developed further in the *Introduction* to the third Critique – here it determines the nature of the principle of the reflective power of judgment, the principle of purposiveness. This latter is presented as a subjective principle that reflects on nature and which is prompted by a requirement of reason (*Bedürfnis*) (KU 5: 184; Kant 2000, p. 70–71). It is possible to argue then, that Kant places his notion of aesthetic universality in the footsteps of the same theory of the regulative use of reason, where the expectation of universal approval is meant as a demand of reason, and the aesthetic "should" signifies only the possibility of coming to an agreement. In the *Introduction,* Kant provides some evidence to support this idea. He writes, in fact, that the combination of the feeling of pleasure with purposiveness is the result of the need of our understanding to find order in nature (§ VI). The feeling of pleasure is, therefore, a presupposition of the reflective power of judgment: "This presupposition of the power of judgment is, however, so indeterminate" (KU 5: 188; Kant 2000, p. 74), and must remain so if we hope to differentiate between judgment between epistemic judgment, due to the fact that, "because we can certainly determine boundaries with regard to the rational use of our cognitive faculties, but in the empirical field no determination of boundaries is possible" (KU 5: 188; Kant 2000, p. 75).

Aesthetic feeling is then combined with the representation of the form of an object with a particular kind of necessity, as it derives from the agreement between the cognitive faculties that we have in common with others: "the faculty for judging through such a pleasure (consequently also with universal validity) is called taste" (KU 190: 76). This pleasure remains however ideal and contingent. It is a pleasure which "can never be understood through concepts to be necessarily combined with the representation of an object, but must always be cognized to be connected with this only through reflected perception, and consequently, like all empirical judgments, cannot promise any objective necessity and make a claim to a priori validity" (KU 5: 190 – 191; Kant 2000, p. 76 – 77). The judgment of taste only makes a "claim to be valid for everyone" (KU 5: 191; Kant 2000, p. 77).

In the *Introduction* to the third Critique, Kant clarifies his point of view by means of an analogy; the subjective universality of the judgment of taste may sound "strange and anomalous", but we must keep in mind that it is "a feeling of pleasure (consequently not a concept at all) which, through the judgment of taste, is nevertheless to be expected of everyone and connected with its representation, just as if it were a predicate associated with the cognition of the object" (KU 5: 191; Kant 2000, p. 77). This expectation "in spite of its intrinsic contingency, is always possible" (KU 5: 191; Kant 2000, p. 77) in virtue of the humanity intrinsic in every subject.

Furthermore, in the *Methodology of Taste* Kant sums up the relation between the ideality and the universal validity of taste also clarifying the role of norms: creation and enjoyment of art cannot follow norms nor prescription but must cultivate the humanity we share with others. This is the meaning of the regulativity of taste described in the *Introduction* and this is what grants the communicability of our aesthetic feeling. In the aesthetic experience, there are no "universal rules" and no prescriptions; on the contrary "there must be regard for a certain ideal that art must have before its eyes, even though in practice it is never fully attained" (KU 5: 355; Kant 2000, p. 229). Therefore, aesthetic examples cannot be taken as "prototypes and models for imitation", otherwise "thus smothering the genius and together with it also the freedom of the imagination even in its lawfulness, without which no beautiful art nor even a correct personal taste for judging of it is possible" (KU 5: 355; Kant 2000, p. 229).

Any concept or norm prescribed to the subject would thereby nullify the freedom of the imagination, which is the essence of the aesthetic experience. The notion of subjective universality as mere possibility should instead preserve the indeterminacy that defines aesthetics. In this regard Kant writes:

> [T]he propaedeutic for all beautiful art, so far as it is aimed at the highest degree of its perfection, seems to lie not in precepts, but in the culture of the mental powers through those prior forms of knowledge that are called *humaniora*, presumably because *humanity* means on the one hand the universal *feeling of participation* and on the other hand the capacity for being able to *communicate* one's inmost self universally, which properties taken together constitute the sociability. (KU 5: 355; Kant 2000, p. 229)

In conclusion, Kant seems to understand the "indeterminate norm" that ideally guides our aesthetic feeling as the promotion of humanity that, in transcendental terms, is the vivification of the cognitive faculties we share with others. This complex meaning of norms in the context of the aesthetic experience allows us to reassess the meaning of normativity in Kant's aesthetic theory. More precisely, the ideality of taste, despite being mentioned by Chignell in order to demonstrate the normative nature of Kant's aesthetic judgment, is what single-handedly calls for a revision of the normativity claim; the ideality of taste shows, in fact, how aesthetic normativity is a mere subjective need of our reason. In comparison with moral judgment, where I can have the prescription of the moral law but can also decide to behave in a morally wrong way, in aesthetics I feel pleasure and simultaneously express a judgment of taste without any prescription and without the mediation of any concept. If we take thus into consideration the ideality, the exemplarity and the indeterminacy of the aesthetic judgment, it is not as easy to claim that Kant would have defined subjective universality through the normativity of emotions. On the contrary, it is much more likely that he would have emphasised their regulativity.

Bibliography

Allison, Henry E. (1998): "Pleasure and Harmony in Kant's Theory of Taste: A Critique of the Causal Reading". In: Herman Parret (Ed.): *Kants Ästhetik-Kant's Aesthetics-L'Esthétique de Kant*. Berlin, New York: De Gruyter, pp. 466–483.

Allison, Henry E. (2008): "'Whatever Begins to Exist Must Have a Cause of Existence': Hume's Analysis and Kant's Response". In: *Philosophy and Phenomenological Research* 76. No. 3, pp. 525–546.

Borutti, Silvana (2017): "We-Perspective on Aesthetic Grounds: Gemeinsinn and Übereinstimmung in Kant and Wittgenstein". In: Michela Summa, Thomas Fuchs and Luca Vanzago (Eds.): *Imagination and Social Perspectives. Approaches from Phenomenology and Psychopathology.* New York: Routledge.

Carrol, Noël (1984): "Hume's Standard of Taste". In: *The Journal of Aesthetics and Art Criticism* 43. No. 2, pp. 181–194.

Chignell, Andrew (2007): "Kant on the Normativity of Taste: The Role of Aesthetic Ideas". In: *Australasian Journal of Philosophy* 85. No. 3, pp. 415–433.

Chiodo, Simona (2015): "The Ideal as an Inclusive Tool. From Kant's Aesthetics to Contemporary Ethical Puzzles". In: *Studi di estetica*, pp. 139–170.

Costelloe, Timothy M. (2004): "Hume's Aesthetics: The Literature and Directions for Research". In: *Hume Studies* 30. No.1, pp. 87–126.

Dorsey, Dale (2008): "Hume's Internalism Reconsidered. In: *Journal of Ethics & Social Philosophy* 2. No. 3, pp. 2–23.

Falkenstein, Lorne (1998): "Hume's Answer to Kant". In: *Noûs* 32. No. 3, pp. 331–360.

Feloj, Serena (2015): "From 'World' to 'Organism'. The Schematism of the Regulative Use of Reason". In: *Studi di estetica* 48, pp. 87–108.

Feloj, Serena (2018): Il dovere estetico. Normatività e giudizi di gusto, Milano: Mimesis.

Ginsborg, Hannah (2015): *The Normativity of Nature. Essays on Kant's* Critique of Judgement. Oxford: Oxford University Press.

Graham, Gordon (2014): "Aesthetics as a Normative Science". In: *Royal Institute of Philosophy Supplement* 75, pp. 249–264.

Guyer, Paul and Allison, Henry (2006): "Dialogue: Paul Guyer and Henry Allison on Allison's *Kant's Theory of Taste*". In: Rebecca Kukla (Ed.): *Aesthetic and Cognition in Kant's Critical Philosophy*. New York: Cambridge University Press, pp. 111–137.

Guyer, Paul (1979): *Kant and the Claims of Taste*. Cambridge: Harvard University Press.

Guyer, Paul (2012): "Passion for Reason: Hume, Kant, and the Motivation for Morality". In: *Proceedings and Addresses of the American Philosophical Association* 86. No. 2, pp. 4–21.

Hume, David (1985): "On the Standard of Taste (1757)". In: E.F. Miller (Rev. ed.): *Essays: Moral, Political, and Literary*. Indianapolis: Liberty Classics.

Hume, David (2007): *A Treatise of Human Nature*. D.F. Norton and M.J. Norton (Eds.). Oxford: Clarendon.

Kant, Immanuel (1911/1998): *Kritik der reinen Vernunft*. In: Königlich Preussischen Akademie der Wissenschaften (Ed.): *Kants Gesammelte Schriften*, Vol. 3, Berlin: Reimer. Paul Guyer and Allen Wood (Trans.), *Critique of Pure Reason*. Cambridge: Cambridge University Press.

Kant, Immanuel (1913/2000): *Kritik der Urteilskraft*. In: Königlich Preussischen Akademie der Wissenschaften (Ed.): *Kants Gesammelte Schriften*, Vol. 5, Berlin: Reimer. Paul Guyer (Trans.), *Critique of the Power of Judgment*. Cambridge: Cambridge University Press.

Kivy, Peter (2016): "Hume's Taste and the Rationalist Critique". In: Paul Russell (Ed.): *The Oxford Handbook of Hume*. Oxford, New York: Oxford University Press, pp. 531–545.

Kulenkampff, Jens (1990): "The Objectivity of Taste: Hume and Kant". In: *Noûs* 24. No. 1, pp. 93–110.

Phillips, David (2005): "Hume on Practical Reason: Normativity and Psychology in *Treatise* 2.3.3". In: *Hume Studies* 31. No. 2, pp. 299–316.

Railton, Peter (1999): "Normative Force and Normative Freedom: Hume and Kant, But Not Hume *versus* Kant". In: *Ratio* 12. No. 4, pp. 320–353.

Scruton, Roger (1979): *The Aesthetics of Architecture*. London: Methuen.

Shelley, James (2013): "Hume and the Joint Verdict of True Judges". In: *The Journal of Aesthetics and Art Criticism* 71. No. 2, pp. 145–153.

Tomasi, Gabriele (2008): "Sul valore rappresentativo del piacere per il bello in Kant". In: *Studi Kantiani* 21, pp. 17–32.

Zangwill, Nick (2014): "Aesthetic Judgment." In: E.N. Zalta (Ed.): *Stanford Encyclopedia of Philosophy*. https://plato.stanford.edu/entries/aesthetic-judgment/, accessed on 29 December, 2017.

Daniela Angelucci
"An Emotion That Seems to Be No Play": Deleuze on Kantian Sublime

> [...] [T]he feeling of the sublime is a pleasure that only arises indirectly, being brought about by the feeling of a momentary check to the vital forces followed at once by a discharge all the more powerful, and so it is an *emotion* that seems to be no play, but a serious matter in the exercise of the imagination.
>
> Immanuel Kant, *Critique of Judgment*, § 23, my italics

Abstract: The intent of the present chapter is not to provide an exhaustive account of Gilles Deleuze's reading of Kantian aesthetics, but rather to show how Kantian thought, and in particular, the concept of sublime, reappear in Deleuze's books on cinema. The sublime appears both in the first volume, "The Movement-Image", where it is explicitly mentioned, as well as in the second, "The Time-Image", where it is a sort of precursor to the focus of this volume: the idea of time in itself. My main claim is that Kant can be considered an antecedent to the crystal-image, that is, the genetic moment of the time-image—one of the most powerful concepts created by Deleuze.

Keywords: sublime, feeling, aesthetics, cinema, crystal-image, time-image

In the book *What is Philosophy* (1991), written with Félix Guattari, and the last monograph Deleuze published before his death, Kant's *Critique of Judgment* is defined as an "unrestrained" and free work. The direct question posed by the title of the volume regarding the nature of philosophy can be addressed, according to the two authors, only in old age, when one has given up on style and artifice, and has acquired the liberty necessary to ask direct, sober and concrete questions. With Kant, as with other authors, thinkers, and artists, the work composed in old age is characterised by a particular autonomy of thought: in the case of his third *Critique*, Kant has finally acquired the strength and unscrupulousness necessary to overcome the limits of the mind's faculties, the accurate identification of which had been the aim of the texts written in his prime. The admiration of Deleuze and Guattari for Kant is evident in their acknowledgement of Kant as one of the most important and free "creators of concepts", cited several times in this regard in the 1991 book, where, for instance, when speaking of the need for philosophy to open up heretofore unexplored realms of thought, they claim that Kant "is less a prisoner of the categories of subject and object

Daniela Angelucci, Univ. of Roma Tre, Italy

https://doi.org/10.1515/9783110720730-010

than he is believed to be, since his idea of Copernican revolution puts thought into a direct relationship with the earth" (Deleuze and Guattari 1994, p.85).[1] Yet Deleuze himself, almost thirty years earlier, in 1963, dedicated a text to the German philosopher, *Kant's Critical Philosophy*, intended to illustrate the modalities and mechanism of the philosopher's thought, which he later—in a letter to Michel Cressole—defined as "a book on an enemy". A complex and continuous confrontation unfolds between the opposite poles of admiration and explicit recognition of a theoretical opponent, that, in addition to the book cited, is articulated in the lectures on Kant delivered by Deleuze in Vincennes in 1978, as well as in his 1984 article *On Four Poetic Formulas Which Might Summarise the Kantian Philosophy.*[2]

The intent of the present chapter is not to provide an exhaustive account of Gilles Deleuze's reading of Kantian aesthetics, but rather to show how Kantian thought, and in particular, the concept of sublime, reappear in Deleuze's books on cinema. The sublime appears both in the first volume, "The Movement-Image", where it is explicitly mentioned, as well as in the second, "The Time-Image", where it is a sort of precursor to the focus of this volume: the idea of time in itself.

It is in the 1985 book, *The Time-Image*, in fact, that we can recognise the characteristics of the sublime at that initial moment of thought—a moment of suspension, of seriousness, almost violent—which determines the appearance of a pure and not chronological temporality. In illustrating such a perspective, it is interesting that Deleuze chooses the Kantian term "emotion" (*Rührung*), which appears sporadically in place of the term "feeling" (*Gefühl*) in the *Analytic of the Sublime* to emphasise, "a momentary check to the vital forces followed at once by a discharge" (Kant 2007, p. 76). The use of this term, which refers to an unreflexive and precipitous reaction to something unexpected, denotes the subject's increased passivity during this experience, confirming our reading of Deleuze and the argument proposed in these pages. Moreover, in the *Analytic of the Beautiful*, Kant states that

---

1 Deleuze proposes "a machinic portrait of Kant" (Deleuze 1994, p. 45), along the lines of the machines by the artist Tinguely. In general, in many quotations, Deleuze questions the transcendental of Kant in the explanation of his plane of immanence; to this regard see Luisetti (2011); according to the author the approach of Deleuze is still quite Kantian.
2 The article dating to 1963 must be also cited, *L'idée de genèse dans l'esthétique de Kant*, (which appeared in "Revue d'esthétique"), and the passages on Kant in *Difference and Repetition* and in *The Logic of Sense*. On the relationship between the two philosophers see: Willatt and Lee (Eds.) (2009); Lord (2012); Crevoisier. (2016); Palazzo (2013).

Emotion – a sensation where an agreeable feeling is produced merely by means of a momentary check followed by a more powerful outpouring of the vital force – is quite foreign to beauty. Sublimity (with which the feeling of emotion is connected) requires, however, a different standard of judging from that which underlies taste. (KU 5: 76; Kant 2007, p. 57)

But let us proceed in order, and first follow the vicissitudes of the sublime found in Deleuze's contributions on Kant.

1 Enemies

The 1963 text, *Kant's Critical Philosophy*, focuses on the relationship between the faculties in the three *Critiques*. Deleuze identifies a first sense in which the term "faculty" is used in works by Kant, that is, as a type of relationship between subject and object. From this perspective it is possible to identify the faculty of knowledge, related to the object from the standpoint of conformity; the faculty of desire, related to the object in a causal relationship; and the feeling of pleasure and pain, in which the representation affects the subject, intensifying or weakening its vital force. Kant's aim is to define the higher form of these faculties, meaning the situation in which the faculty is autonomous and legislative, and in which it finds its own law in itself. There is, however, a second sense of the word "faculty", which denotes not the different relationships of a representation, but the source of these representations—the three faculties of imagination, understanding and reason. The relationship between these two different meanings of the word, "faculties", in its systematic variations, produces what Deleuze defines as a "real network" of the transcendental method. For instance, the faculty of knowledge, in its higher form, entails a legislative understanding which however does not prevent the imagination and reason from retaining a role, defined by Deleuze as "entirely original".

It is in this framework that Deleuze dedicates particular attention to the faculty of feeling of the third *Critique*, given that its higher form presents two "paradoxical characteristics". Firstly, unlike knowledge and desire, the feelings of pleasure and pain do not define any interest of reason, speculative or practical; on the contrary, these feelings are completely disinterested. Secondly, these feelings do not legislate over objects, being indifferent to their existence, but only over themselves, which means that the faculty of feeling is not autonomous but "heautonomous". Concerning the faculties as understood in their second, higher sense, which refers to the source of representations, Deleuze states that the third *Critique* presents yet another peculiarity: the imagination, in its free accord with understanding as indeterminate, does not schematise as such, but rather reflects the form of the object, and thus becomes productive and sponta-neous. Aesthetic common sense is, for this reason, "a pure subjective harmony where imagination and understanding are exercised spontaneously, each on its own account. Consequently, aesthetic common sense does not complete the two others; it provides them with a basis or makes them possible" (Deleuze 1984, pp. 49 – 59). In this way, aesthetic common sense shows that the faculties are indeed capable of this harmony. This claim, however, leads to another prob-lem, that is, the question as to whether the free accord of the faculties that founds common sense must be presupposed or rather produced or generated – a problem that will be at the centre of *The Idea of Genesis in Kant's Aesthetics*, an article composed by Deleuze the same year.

In order to solve this problem, Deleuze turns to another type of aesthetic judgment, that of the sublime. Deleuze is certainly not the only twentieth century author to have considered the sublime as a proving ground for the judgment of the beautiful and of the entire *Critique*. One need only recall Lyotard (1993; 1994), who sees in the *Analytic of the Sublime* and in its brevity—defined as a "meteor dropped into the work"—proof of Kant's awareness of the capacity of the sublime (which is interested, serious, it involves reason) to cloud the argument of the *An-alytic of the Beautiful*, effectively ending the hopes of the philosophical unifica-tion of the *Critique*. For Deleuze, the relevance and problematic nature of the concept of sublime for Kant is also evident, as seen in this text dating to the six-ties. Deleuze holds that the particular relationship between the imagination and reason produced by the sublime, in its immensity and power, shows how the ac-cord between faculties is a point of arrival, generated in the discord and contra-diction between the demands of reason and those of the imagination typical of the experience of the sublime. If, in the sublime, reason forces the imagination to confront its own limits, the imagination, awakening reason, overcomes its subordination to a determining faculty (the intellect, whether it regulates it or harmonises with it) and thus increases its power. The pleasure of the sublime, made possible by pain, allows an accord between faculties to emerge "at the bot-tom of the dissension", and in this way generates it, produces it: "It can then be seen that the imagination-reason accord is not simply assumed: it is genuinely engendered, engendered in the dissension" (Deleuze 1984, p. 51).

The search for an accord that may re-establish the unity of the faculties is where Deleuze differs from Kant and, as the former wrote in 1968 in *Difference and Repetition*, is what makes the latter a "philosopher of common sense". How-ever, according to Deleuze—these are indeed some of the conclusions of his book *Kant's Critical Philosophy*—the reflective judgment of the third *Critique*, and in particular the relationship between the faculties generated by the *dissension* ex-perienced between the power of imagination and the demands of reason typical to the feeling of the sublime, manifests something that had remained hidden in the determining judgment: "the principle of its originality", according to which, "despite the fact that *our faculties differ in nature*, they nevertheless have a free and spontaneous accord" (p. 61). It is necessary to highlight how already in this text Deleuze addresses the issue concerning the possibility of an encounter between terms that are by nature heterogeneous; this is an issue that will reappear in many key concepts of later works, which we will discuss later on.

2 "Aware of the catastrophe"

In 1978, Deleuze delivered four talks on Kant in Vincennes, which revolved around a new conception of time developed by the German philosopher. This was not only a decisive conception of time for modern consciousness, but an extraordinary invention generated within an "amazing architecture", in which "a thinking machine", creator of concepts, can be seen at work, according to Deleuze. Deleuze's first two lectures are mostly dedicated to describing how, in Kantian philosophy, time is liberated from all forms of cosmological or psychological subordination, and released from nature or the soul, to become a pure, a priori form. To indicate time's liberation from matter, from changes in space, and from movement, Deleuze uses the Shakespearian formula "time is out of joint": time is disjointed, unhinged, free—it does not depend on action that unfolds within it, but rather everything is subordinated to time, which is a pure form and interior limit of thought.

> With Kant there is an indescribable novelty. It's the first time that time is liberated, stretches itself, ceases to be a cosmological or psychological time, whether it's the world or the soul makes no difference, to become a formal time, a pure deployed form, and this will be a phenomenon of extreme importance for modern thought. This is the first great Kantian reversal in the theory of time. So I take Hamlet's formula literally to apply it to Kant: 'the time is out of joint'. (Deleuze 1978, p. 14)

From this characteristic of time, Deleuze shifts towards a radical interpretation of the subject in Kant: if the obstacle of thought—that which is impossible to think—is now interior to thought itself, the Kantian subject, simultaneously empirical and transcendental, is a fractured subject, traversed and broken by the concept of time, according to Deleuze. This condition of alienation can be best described with Rimbaud's poetic formula, "I is another". Beyond the difference in tone and atmosphere that such a reading implies with regard to Kantian philosophy, [3] of interest here is the reason for this turn, or rather, once again, Deleuze's interest in the limits of thought, and the possibility of imagining an encounter between two dimensions that are different by nature. In this case, these two dimensions are the subject as phenomenon, who inhabits time, and the subject as unifying activity of thought, which operates through the pure a priori forms of space and time, as well as through the categories. As Deleuze states in the Vincennes lectures:

> We find a sort of tension between two forms: the active form of spontaneity, or if you prefer, the 'I think' as form of active determination, or form of the concept, since 'I think' is the formal unity of all concepts, so on the one hand the active form of determination, on the other the intuitive or receptive form of the determinable, time. The two are absolutely heterogeneous to each other, and yet there is a fundamental correlation: the one works in the other. (Deleuze 1978) [4]

Deleuze returns to and radicalises the idea of the fractured subject, torn between a dual nature, both conceptual and empirical, in *On Four Poetic Formulas Which Might Summarise the Kantian Philosophy*, in which Deleuze argues that Kant surpasses Rimbaud in affirming a split subject. He writes,

> I am separated from myself by the form of time, and nevertheless I am one because the I [*Je*] necessarily affects this form by carrying out its synthesis, [...], and because the Ego [*Moi*] is necessarily affected as content in this form. The form of the determinable means that the determined ego represents determination as an Other. (Deleuze 1984, p. IX)

The identification of a time that is liberated from things and their movements is thus followed by the discovery of a split subject, in which the I and the Ego are traversed by the line of time, which both separates and connects them, under the condition, however, of a fundamental difference.

During the third talk on Kant, held March 28, 1978, Deleuze returns to and crystallises the issue concerning the relationship between time and thought:

> Time has become the limit of thought and thought never ceases to have to deal with its own limit. Thought is limited from the inside. There is no longer an extended substance which limits thinking substance from the outside, and which resists thinking substance, but the form of thought is traversed through and through, as if cracked like a plate, it is cracked by the line of time. It makes time the interior limit of thought itself, which is to say the unthink-

---

3 This radicalisation has not gone unnoticed by interpreters: against this reading are Cassinari (1993), but also the curator of the Italian edition of Deleuze's lessons on Kant, see Palazzo (2004).
4 Schema and synthesis are defined this way, the two fundamental acts of understanding.

able in thought. From Kant onward, philosophy will give itself the task of thinking what is not thinkable, instead of giving itself the task of thinking what is exterior to thought. The true limit traverses and works thought from within. (Deleuze 1978)

It is at this point that Deleuze returns to and underlines the issue of the fractured subject, divided between "I think", the form of active determination (form of the concept), and "I am", the receptive form of the determinable (in time). It is here that the notion of the sublime appears, an experience that renders any synthesis between these two levels impossible.

With his *Critique of Judgment*, written in old age, Kant becomes "aware of the catastrophe", in which aesthetic comprehension and synthesis of perception are compromised, which constitutes the experience of the sublime. "Instead of a rhythm, I find myself in chaos" (Deleuze 1978), because I cannot apprehend the parts of an object, I cannot reproduce them nor can I recognise them, and the imagination is confronted by its own limit. This limit of the imagination, however, allows us to discover something more powerful: the faculty of the Idea, the super-sensible. The point of arrival of Deleuze's interpretation of Kant, and the conclusion of the fourth lecture, is that at any moment, phenomena may occur in time and space that undermine aesthetic comprehension, that is, the basis of the synthesis of the imagination, destroying its rhythm, the accord between things to be measured and unit of measure. The "adventure of the sublime"—a serious, indeed catastrophic emotion—exposes the fragility of the ground on which the activity of the imagination rests—it faces an obstacle, and begins to falter in front of the immense ocean, the infinite skies, the avalanches, the tempests.[5] This failure of schematism, however, as we have seen, also implies a great reward.

This same adventure of the sublime as clash between the faculties is described by Deleuze in an essay composed in 1984, with another poetic formula, again borrowed from Rimbaud: "a disorder of all the senses" (Deleuze 1984, p. XI). [6] The portrait Deleuze traces is that of a Romantic Kant, or better still, of Kant as founder of Romanticism, who, in the third *Critique*, is intent on pursuing the extraordinary task of identifying the possibility of extremely free relation-

---

5 Gianni Carchia, in his essay on the imagination in Kant, claims that "the possibility of reflectively grasping the sublime stems not from disarticulation, but from the ruins of the faculties of representation". See Carchia (2006, p. 68).

6 This is the fourth poetic formula, which follows the third, borrowed from Kafka, which is "the agony of being governed by laws that are unknown to us" which refers to the *Critique of Practical Reason*. In this text these two formulas are added to the first two, which we have mentioned (see Deleuze 1984).

ships between the faculties. Once again, it is in the sublime that the discord between the imagination and reason allows the faculties themselves to go beyond, because in this clash one pushes the other towards its limit. In this short text, a link emerges between the image of Kant as the "enemy" of Deleuze's 1963 book, a work that revolved around the variation of the relationships between the faculties, as well as the description of Kantian thought as an endless production of concepts, which becomes evident the moment the accord between faculties loses its regularity and becomes either a free play or fierce clash. The encounter between the two philosophers, however, is possible insofar as Deleuze highlights the most problematic and dissonant traits of Kantian thought: if the failure produced by the apparition of the formless in the sensible domain is a moment of arrest for Kant, who seeks to heal this wound by forging a new accord, this same arrest represents the only possible starting point for Deleuze, who conceives of thought as the outcome of a violent impact with the Outside.[7] In Deleuze's reading of Kant, the sublime is a decisive turning point, in which dissonance becomes emancipated from accord.

3 Recognition Fails, Action is Suspended

In the first half of the 1980s, Deleuze published two volumes dedicated to cinema, *The Movement-Image* (1983) and *The Time-Image* (1985). The thesis inspiring the two works, reaffirmed with even greater force by their conclusions, is that philosophy and cinema are closely linked: both are, in fact, conceptual practices, creative activities. Philosophy and cinema respond to the same needs, though each in its own domain, and by different means: the former by creating concepts, the latter by producing images. If, however, a creative intent is common to all arts, cinema is the most philosophical among the arts, in that it has an inclination—unexpected as much as it is evident—to manifest the life of thought. In particular, cinema exposes temporality, which the first volume, dedicated to classical cinema (from its origins to the end of World War II), articulates as change, a movement of things through action, while the second, dedicated to modern cinema, as exhibition of temporality per se. The way Deleuze's thought has been summarised here is purposefully partial, and it puts the issue

---

7 This description of the activity of thought is present throughout Deleuze's work, from the text on Proust of 1962 to *What is Philosophy?* of 1991. The polemical objective is classical rationalist philosophy, and its belief that truth can be reached through methodical decision and practice. To this idea Deleuze opposes that of the involuntary nature of a necessary thought, the fate of which depends precisely on the relationship with the outside.

of temporality in the foreground, in a way that already alludes to what the following pages will address.[8] In fact, after having examined some of the theses advanced in Deleuze's two books on cinema, (including their commentary on the philosophy of Bergson) I will attempt to show how Kant's legacy resurfaces, in particular in the presentation of the time-image, protagonist of cinematographic modernity.

In the first lines of the preface to *The Movement-Image*, Deleuze states that the intent of the work is not to compose a history of cinema, but to propose a taxonomy, a classification of cinematographic images. In fact, the passage from one period to another in the history of cinema is stylistic and theoretical, rather than merely historical and chronological. Firstly, cinema is the most Bergsonian art of all, it is, in other words, the art that exhibits a world made up of images in continuous movement, that is, a world that is incessantly transformed. This, it must be noted, despite Bergson's dislike of cinema, which, in the final chapter of his *Creative Evolution* (1907), is defined as the prototypical example of false movement in that it is made up of photograms subsequently put together by a projector. In fact, Deleuze claims that Bergson did not grasp the potential of this *dispositif* for understanding that same duration, the indivisible and always new becoming that his philosophy sought. Every film sequence is, in fact, described as a dynamic system in itself, and every change in the frame implies a transformation of the entire image.

The editing of the sequences typical in classical cinema allows time to emerge as a narrative through movement, a succession of scenes connected by a causal link. Using the analyses and lexicon of Bergson's first chapter of *Matter and Memory* (1896), Deleuze identifies a system that he defines as "sensory-motor", made up of actions and feelings linked together in a linear narrative, in which the passage of time is shown through the unfolding of the plot. According to Deleuze, this "organic" system began to weaken as a result of political, social and economic changes in the mid-forties after World War II, when the first signs of transformation and crisis—images no longer indispensable and motivated by the progress of the plot—began to appear in the linear and well-connected narrative of the films of the period (comedies, westerns, noir films). With the crisis of the classical genre, visible in Italian neo-realism, and which reaches its peak with the Nouvelle Vague, new kinds of characters emerged in films, "who saw rather than acted": invalids, children, elderly, simple witnesses who

---

8 For a summary, which is not impartial but is more exhaustive, I would like to refer to my work (Angelucci 2013). For a useful and articulated study of the sublime in the text by Deleuze on cinema, see Cantone (2008).

are unsuited for action and who render the plot of the film increasingly empty and disconnected, a plot that can no longer be described in terms of an opposition between perception and action, cause and effect.

From this impotence originates the possibility of a new type of image, which allows a direct vision of time and thought.

> A pure optical and sound situation does not extend into action, any more than it is induced by an action. It makes us grasp, it is supposed to make us grasp, something intolerable and unbearable. [...] It is a matter of something too powerful, or too unjust, but sometimes also too beautiful, and which henceforth outstrips our sensory-motor capacities. (Deleuze 1989, p. 18)

The pure optical and sound image referred to by Deleuze above is the protagonist of the second volume dedicated to cinematographic modernity. In this volume, Deleuze also deploys the characters of the new aesthetic regime, by commenting on *Matter and Memory*.

In the second chapter of this book, entitled *Of the Recognition of Images. Memory and Brain*, Bergson identifies two types of recognition, defined as concrete acts with which we grasp the past in our present. The first, which has to do with perception and the plane of actuality, is that "of which the body is capable by itself": it is an automatic memory characterised by repetition and habit. Bergson explains that this type of recognition, in its immediacy, is an action and not a representation, since recognizing an object we perceive as usual or familiar generally consists in using it, or at least in a tendency to display a sensory-motor reaction. In addition to this habitual memory, with its organised motor accompaniment—which can be compared to the way an herbivorous animal recognises grass immediately and reacts mechanically to this identification—there is, however, another modality, which is not repetitive or automatic, but attentive and reflective. Every time an inhibition intervenes, the mechanism regulating the spontaneous motor response is blocked, whereby the subject is forced to make an effort to search for the appropriate reaction to the present situation in the past, distancing itself from its actuality to become immersed in memory, in pure thought. This "pure past" is visible in dreams, for example, or in certain pathological states—it appears only when action is blocked, when attention for life is lost, when the search for a particular image fails. [9]

---

9 In chapter IX of his book, Lapoujade (2017) underlines how the two volumes on cinema are articulated and revolve around the crisis of action, connecting the issue of a subject separated from its power of acting to the political dimension.

In turning to these analyses by Bergson, Deleuze, who is interested in borderline states, highlights the moments these states seem to bring about a vaguely disturbing atmosphere, marked by the frequency of expressions such as fractures, blockages, inhibitions, illness, disturbances, and failures in recognition. If, in the case of the automatic relationship between perception and action typical of habitual recognition, we have identified a similarity with the cause and effect chain of classical narratives, the suspended atmosphere of inhibited action predominates in modern cinema, which abandons linear narration and the automatic succession of scenes to show "a-centred" movements, still images, disconnected planes, emptied situations and spaces, and characters whose actions are obstructed. All this is produced following a cognitive blockage, that is, the suspension of recognition that Bergson would have defined as habitual, mechanical, spontaneous, caused by the fact that the immediate response to the perceptive stimulus is interrupted. However, this same impediment is precisely what, as in the case of the experience of the sublime, allows a direct contact with the virtual—with temporality, memory, thought. Time exhibited indirectly through action seems to be more akin to the "time in things" of classical philosophy, that which appeared through the change of phenomena, while time in itself, detached from movement, and which appears in the images of the modern cinematographic regime, is defined as being out of joint, freed from its hinges, liberated from action—just as Deleuze had defined Kantian time.

> Over several centuries, from the Greeks to Kant, a revolution took place in philosophy. The subordination of time to movement was reversed. [...] Time is out of joint. [...] It could be said that, in its own sphere, cinema has repeated the same experience, the same reversal, in more fast-moving circumstances. The movement-image of the so-called classical cinema gave way, in the post-war period, to a direct time-image. (Deleuze 1989, p. XI)

4 The Sublime and the Crystal

The "modern" cinematic experience, in which the narrative, the identity of characters and of place, and even temporal linearity itself are derailed, is described by Deleuze as a failure of the cognitive system, which allows a consideration of the time-image among the contemporary descendants of the Kantian sublime. Already in the first volume of his work on cinema, *The Movement-Image*, Deleuze cited Kant and the two typologies of the sublime, mathematical and dynamical, in reference to classical cinema. The film production of the French school of the twenties and thirties is, in this sense, a mathematically sublime cinema, with its need to give an overall vision of nature and its movements rising above the empirical condition, as can be seen for example in the films of Abel Gance. The unit of measurement is here so great, so extended, that the imagination is unable to grasp it, and thus, according to Deleuze, it must give way to a speculative faculty. The dynamical sublime, on the other hand, is visible in German cinematographic expressionism, in its use of light and contrast to show powerful movements of intensity. This intensity made powerful, with its immeasurable lines, its dark areas, and its oblique perspectives, annihilates viewers by terrifying them and making them participate in the inorganic, impersonal life of things.[10] This direct reference to the sublime, however, seems too literal, and not powerful enough, in comparison with the experience of the clash of the faculties as a result of the time-image of cinematographic modernity and its ability to free time from narrative and from action.

Images unbound from the narrative sequence, typical of a certain genre of modern cinema, with its characteristically powerful and purely aesthetic images, are defined by Deleuze as "pure optical and sound images". These images possess an unrestrained force, an abnormal dynamic, which is both the effect and the cause of questioning the structures of our normal sensible, empirical and organic condition. This arrest, however, does not mark the end of thought—on the contrary, according to Deleuze, it constructs its beginning, and represents the only possibility of entering into direct contact with pure temporality, made visible in images. Deleuzian cinematographic examples of time-images are multiple, but also quite different one from another, in contrast with the more easily identifiable genres corresponding to typologies of image-movement, thus confirming the impossibility of giving an objective form to the sublime vision of a time appearing "in itself".

What prevents an adequate reaction to an extreme situation—too painful or intense, for example—is precisely what allows the subject to go beyond the habitual relationship with the world (a movement which displays the same duplicity as the Kantian sublime, being the reverse of failure), thus also allowing a vision of time freed from its actuality, a time that Deleuze also calls, in line with Bergson, pure virtuality or thought.

This chapter, at the outset, highlighted that one of the recurrent traits of Deleuze's thought is the search for assemblages (*agencement*), that is, of encounters between dimensions that are heterogeneous or different by nature. As we have seen, the 1963 text by Deleuze on Kantian philosophy focused on the relationship between different faculties which address different worlds, and on the feeling of the sublime, in which the accord Kant sought becomes an explicit clash, a

---

10 See Deleuze (1986, chapter III).

dissension between the imagination and reason. This point also emerges strongly in the concept of time-image:

> The essential point, in any event, is that the two related terms differ in nature, and yet 'run after each other', refer to each other, reflect each other, without it being possible to say which is first, and tend *ultimately* to become confused by slipping into the same point of indiscernibility. (Deleuze 1989, p. 46)

This duality (one might say a reflective aspect) of an image that is both actual and virtual is highlighted by another conceptual invention, that of the "crystal-image": the point of indiscernibility between actual and virtual, and the genesis of a direct presentation of time. Another perspective to describe the establishment of the time-image emphasises the particular relationships between actuality and virtuality, or between present action and the search within the subject's memory. To use Bergsonian terms, in the failure of automatic recognition, the subject abandons the dimension of its actuality, and goes in search of the memory it needs in the past dimension, in virtuality: by becoming immersed in memory it is possible to come into contact with thought, which becomes purer the more the search for a particular memory results in failure. This, however, is how a series of "memory-circuits" are established that go from the actual to the virtual and then back to the starting point, in a relationship of mutual tension between the two areas. The crystal-image is the most contracted circuit, an immediate, virtual, and always reversible reflection of the actual—a point of indiscernibility between two ontologically different dimensions. "The crystal-image, or crystalline description, has two definite sides which are not to be confused. [...] indiscernibility constitutes an objective illusion; it does not suppress the distinction between the two sides, but makes it unattributable" (Deleuze 1989, p. 69).

The challenge here is to grasp the nature of the momentum that allows the transition to virtuality in its irreducible ontological difference from actuality: it is certainly not an intellectual process, nor is it a psychological one, but rather is concerned with a dismantling, a suspension of what is habitual, which renders time "out of joint". On the other hand, this detachment from actuality is never total, insofar as between the two dimensions—which cannot be discerned simultaneously—there is a continuous circuiting. The image of a crystal effectively emphasises the supra-personality, the a-subjectivity of time in Deleuze. With its inorganic nature, and its refractions, the conceptual character of the crystal allows Deleuze to describe a non-harmonic encounter between matter and memory, and between thought in itself and the phenomenal, suprasensible, and natural world. This encounter is still marked by discord and by violent traits, yet its consequence is the impossibility of distinguishing between the two dimensions.

We may ask: who, in the modern cinematographic regime described by Deleuze, is blocked from reacting, and thus enters into contact with the dimension of the sublime that is "out of joint" and unthinkable? Who is experiencing that feeling of impediment of the vital forces, that "emotion that is no play"? The answer to these questions displays the starkest differences between the thought of Kant and Deleuze, and contrasts two different theories regarding the status of the subject. The possibility of grasping time in itself, pure thought, belongs to characters and spectators together, and images are part of matter, constitutive both of the film and of the whole world. While the Kantian sublime is an experience of the subject even more subjective than the pleasure derived in judging something beautiful, in that it lacks an objectual correlative endowed with form, cinematographic aesthetics as described by Deleuze have no subject, it is not an aesthetics of the spectator or of the creator. There is no Kantian subject in Deleuze's ontology, one that entails the reciprocal immanence of being and entity. Furthermore, the notion of "gaze" typical of cinematographic aesthetics, which would reintroduce a representative distance against which the philosopher battles, is abandoned and replaced by the notion of a gaze that is "already in things".[11]

In spite of this undeniable distance, the old enemy, with his thought-machine, seems to resurface in the pages Deleuze dedicates to modern cinema, which re-propose an experience (paradoxically lacking a subject) of the clash between dimensions that are different by nature—an experience that is, at the same time, the only possible genesis of thought. In the 1960s Kant was, for Deleuze, an adversary to be understood and also combatted, because of his imprisonment within a philosophy of common sense. Later, the French philosopher resumed a confrontation with Kant which highlighted his closeness to his own thought. Both philosophers discussed the lack of a spontaneous agreement between faculties; the proposal of a divided subject; and above all, the appearance of the sublime as a negative emotion, which disturbs the ordinary organization of faculties and the possibility of recognition. In Deleuzian philosophy, such failure of the faculties, caused by the impact with a particular type of (cinematographic) image, becomes the genesis of the direct presentation of time, and therefore of the contact with thought itself. In conclusion, it can certainly be said that the serious emotion of the Kantian sublime is, if not the only one, one of the most

11 An in-depth analysis of this difference between Kant and Deleuze regarding the status of the subject can be found in the already cited Cantone (2008, pp. 133–136).

significant philosophical antecedents of the time-image in general. In particular, it can be considered a precursor of the crystal-image, that is, the genetic moment of the time-image—one of the most powerful concepts created by Deleuze to describe the accidental beginning of a necessary thought.

Bibliography

Angelucci, Daniela (2013): *Deleuze and the Concepts of Cinema*. Edinburgh: Edinburgh University Press.

Cantone, Damiano (2008): *Cinema, tempo, soggetto. Il sublime kantiano secondo Deleuze*. Milano: Mimesis.

Carchia, Gianni (2006): *Kant e la verità dell'apparenza*. Torino: Ananke.

Cassinari, Flavio (1993): "Dottrina delle facoltà, monismo ontologico e questione fondativa: Deleuze lettore di Kant". In: *Fenomenologia e società* 2, pp. 97–111.

Crevoisier, Michaël (2016): "Réflexion et expérimentation. Deleuze lecteur de Kant. Philosophique. Numéro monographique". In: *"La réflexion"* 19, pp. 1–31. https://journals.openedition.org/philosophique/931, accessed on 16 March, 2021.

Deleuze, Gilles (1963) : "L'idée de genèse dans l'esthétique de Kant". In: *Revue d'esthétique* 16. No. 2, 71–85.

Deleuze, Gilles (1978): *Lectures on Kant*. http://deleuzelectures.blogspot.com/2007/02/on-kant.html, accessed on 15 May, 2019.

Deleuze, Gilles (1984): *Kant's Critical Philosophy*. London: Athlone Press.

Deleuze, Gilles (1986): *Cinema 1. Movement-image*. London: The Athlone Press.

Deleuze, Gilles (1989): *Cinema 2. The Time-Image*. London: The Athlone Press.

Deleuze, Gilles and Guattari, Félix (1994): *What is Philosophy?* New York: Columbia University Press.

Kant, Immanuel (2007): *Critique of Judgment*. Nicholas Walker and James Creed Meredith (Ed.) (Trans.). Oxford: Oxford University Press.

Lapoujade, David (2017): *Aberrant Movements. The Philosophy of Gilles Deleuze*. Cambridge, London: The MIT Press.

Lord, Beth (2012): "Deleuze and Kant". In: Daniel W. Smith and Henry Somers-Hall (Eds.): *The Cambridge Companion to Deleuze*. Cambridge: Cambridge University Press, pp. 82–102.

Luisetti, Federico (2011): *Una vita, Pensiero selvaggio e filosofia del'intensità*. Milano: Mimesis.

Lyotard, Jean-François (1993): "The Interest of the Sublime". In: *Of the Sublime: Presence in Question*. Albany: State University of New York Press.

Lyotard, Jean-François (1994): "Comparison of the Sublime and Taste". In: *Lessons on the Analytic of the Sublime: Kant's Critique of Judgment*. Stanford: Stanford University Press.

Palazzo, Sandro (2004): "La catastrofe di Kronos". In: Gilles Deleuze: *Fuori dai cardini del tempo. Lezioni su Kant*. Milan: Mimesis, pp. 26–27.

Palazzo, Sandro (2013): *Trascendentale e temporalità. Gilles Deleuze e l'eredità kantiana*. Pisa: ETS.

Willatt, Edward and Lee, Matt (Eds.) (2009): *Thinking Between Deleuze and Kant*. London: Continuum.

Section 3: **Kant's Emotions and Contemporary Philosophy of Mind**

Pedro Jesús Teruel

The Ambiguity of Kantian Emotions: Philosophical, Biological and Neuroscientific Implications

Abstract: Neither the term 'emotion', nor its current meaning, can be found in Kant's writings. In this chapter I identify one strategy for exploring the realm of emotions by delineating the German notion of *Erregung*, its German-Latin counterpart *Motion*, and its semantic field. I argue that there is a link between the embodied aspect of emotions and the classic question of *pathos*, and that the Kantian approach to emotions is related to the stoic idea of *ataraxia*. Following the subsequent discussion of *akrasia*, I turn to its neuroscientific implications, in order to show that weakness of will in general, and especially its role within Kantian philosophy, can be understood from a naturalised model of causation.

Keywords: emotion, mood, passion, weakness of will, naturalism

In Kant's understanding, anthropology is to moral philosophy as applied geometry is to pure geometry: anthropology provides a cartography necessary for a true understanding of human action (V-Anth/Mron 25/2: 1212).[1] Following that theory *nolens volens*, the role of emotions has attracted increasing attention during the last few decades. Indeed, while often overlooked, emotions are an increasingly relevant topic in numerous branches of philosophy, with deep epistemological, psychological, ethical and anthropological implications. In recent years, Kantian studies have also incorporated many approaches to the subject,

---

Acknowledgement: This contribution is part of the Scientific Research and Technological Development Project FFI2016-76753-C2-1-P, financed by the Ministry of Economy and Competitiveness of the Government of Spain, of the Project PID2019-109078RB-C22, financed by the Ministry of Science, Innovation and Universities, and of the activities of the excellence research group PROMETEO/2018/121 of the Valencian Government

1 Robert B. Louden has rightly observed that Mrongovius reversed here the intended analogy: Kant's position is that anthropology is to moral philosophy as geodesy (applied geometry) is to pure geometry. See Louden (2000, p. 202, n32).

Pedro Jesús Teruel, Univ. of Valencia, Spain

https://doi.org/10.1515/9783110720730-011

with significant contributions from various linguistic areas of study.[2] The natural-scientific aspect of the question, however, has rarely been considered—this is the aspect I hope to contribute to in the present chapter.

Various significant definitions of what Kant understood by emotions have been proposed. Here, I follow the useful classification offered by Alix Cohen. Some scholars (John Sabini, Maury Silver) identify emotions with brute forces such as pain, over which we have no control; in contrast, others (such as Marcia Baron) focus on individuals' responsibility for their own emotions. Beyond these control-based models, other authors (Janelle DeWitt or Rachel Zuckert, for example) consider emotions in terms of conative judgments. Still others (for instance, Maria Borges or Patrick Frierson) underline the phenomenological diversity of emotions, which are unified by affective, cognitive and desiderative aspects.[3] Cohen herself considers the meaning of 'emotion' to be more complex than in the former models and more specific than in the latter. I agree with Cohen that emotions are affects of a certain type, because they imply both basic sensations (pain, pleasure) but also cognitive processes involved in evaluative and often desiderative judgments. In this chapter, I examine how emotions may have cognitive content, paying special attention to their link to practical propensities. This approach takes me beyond the writings of Kant to consider the naturalised hermeneutics of transcendental philosophy.

My aim in this chapter is to identify the treatment of emotion in Kant's works by following a conceptual path along which to address the aspects of affects rooted in moods, thereby demonstrating the way emotion is connected to both the classic concept of "passions", as well as to the modern sphere of evolutionary biology. I will argue that Kant's approach can be understood from a naturalised perspective, consistent with his understanding of emotions, in which notions such as the connection with the brain's functional areas and neuronal facilitation play a crucial role.

This is a new contribution in a series of studies in which I show the possibilities and boundaries of understanding transcendental philosophy within the

---

2 The works of N. Sherman (1989) and R. B. Lauden (2000) have opened hermeneutic paths that have proved relevant in new approaches to the relationship between emotion and reason. Other ground-breaking studies include those of Maria de Lourdes Borges (2004, 2012, 2019). Special mention should be made of the papers published in *Kant on emotion and value* (2014), edited by Alix Cohen. Nuria Sánchez Madrid has approached the affective, sentimental and emotional sides of Kantian philosophy in a series of works (see, for instance, 2016). Scholars such as Ana Marta González (2015) have identified the links and differences between emotions and passions in an interpretative path that I attempt to explore in the second section of this contribution.
3 These references can be found in Cohen (2017, p. 665–666).

natural sciences. I have previously attempted to understand psychological subjects, such as dreams and their meaning (Teruel 2018a), as well as moral matters
such as radical evil (2015) and its projection in the anthropological sphere of the
fragilitas (2018b). The present chapter is conceived as a continuation of this latter
question.

1 Etymology of "emotion": Addressing the Problem

We must first identify the roots of the word 'emotion', in order to delimit the semantic field under consideration. I will argue that ambiguity in its usage, exemplified by the Kantian approach, lies in its very origin.

1.1 Etymology and Semantics

The modern English word 'emotion' comes from the Middle French 'esmotion'
(modern 'émotion') and is linked to 'esmovoir' (modern 'émouvoir'). These
stem from the Latin roots *motio* and *motus*, 'movement', and 'emovere' ('exmo-
vere' in Vulgar Latin). Hence *esmovoir*, 'to set in motion', 'to stir up', is not only
understood in the physical sense, but also in the psychological-figurative sense
(Trésor 1994). This meaning was first recorded in modern European languages at
the end of the sixteenth century. Initially used in English between 1570 and 1580
(Harper 2000), in Spanish it dates back to 1640 (Coromines 2001), although it did
not enter into general use until the nineteenth century; its first entry in the Spanish Dictionary of the Royal Academy was in 1843 (RAE 2014).

The Latin prefix e-/ex-, added to the modern French version from the Vulgar
Latin, highlights the effects of 'motion': far from being an intimate, merely subjective change, it is perceptible to the observer. An emotion is therefore a change
of mood, the results of which are manifested in the agent's behaviour.

The emotion is thus linked to psychological states and represents changes or
transformations of said psychological states. Here, another important word related to emotions appears, this time taken from the Greek: one characteristic and
highly significant human mood is called τό πάθος or τό πάθημα, from
πάσχειν: 'to experience, to go through'. Like many other Greek words, this,
too, is highly polysemic. The more one's mood escapes individual self-control,
the more it falls into a logic of *pathos*, a pathology, and deliberation no longer
has power over it. This classic problem is known as ἀκρασία (or ἀκράτεια). Aris-

totle addresses this from multiple angles: both within the context of the individual way of life in the *Nicomachean Ethics*; as well as with respect to the external influence on mood, through his theory of tragedy in the *Poetics*. The Greek *pathos* eventually gave way to the Latin *passio* and the modern versions of the word (English *passion*, Spanish *pasión*, Catalan *passió*, Portuguese *paixão* or Italian *passione*). From the sixteenth century onwards, the word 'emotion' slowly began to cover the semantic field of 'passion', 'sentiment' and 'affect', coming into generalised use in the 1830s (Dixon 2003).

Although there is no trace of the word *emotion* in the writings of Kant, we find significant terms related to its semantic field. Most of them, like *Begierde*, *Neigung* or *Leidenschaft*, are simply misleading, since each one has a specific meaning and translation. Other concepts such as *Affekt*, *Gefühl* or *Rührung* call for accurate delimitation. I will focus on the German *Erregung* and the Latin-German *Motion*, still used today to designate the semantic field of emotion (Schischkof 1991).

The term *Regung* refers to movement, with the implications of the Latin *motus:* not only a physical change but also a deep change in mood that is apprehended by the observer. The Grimm brothers provide many examples of this use of the concept in the literature of Kant's time. The word *Erregung* is also linked to this semantic field, and lends the nuance of excitement, arousal, incitation, and inner commotion; it also appears in Luther's German translation of the Bible (Grimm 1854 – 1961).

1.2 Kantian Reception of the Duality Motion/Erregung

In Kant's writings we find both expressions in relation to the human mood. He speaks of mood motion, *Motion des Gemüths* (Kant, Refl 1504 15: 809), motion with the mood, *Motion mit dem Gemüth* (Refl 612 15: 262), motion of the spectator's mood, *Motion (des Gemüthes) des Zuschauers* (Anth 7: 232), or inner motion, *innere/innigliche Motion* (KU 5: 332; Refl 1526, 15: 952; Anth 7: 261). On occasion it also appears in connection with the mood's movement or shift, *Gemüthsbewegung* (KU 5: 274).

The word *Erregung* denotes a change that can be the result of physical causes. In Kant's pre-critical writings, we find a particularly physical use of the term, associated with earthquakes, *Erregung der Erdbeben* (FBZE 1: 467), or bodies of water, *Erregung der inländischen Seen* (VUE 1: 426). In his translations of two Latin works of 1755 regarding physical processes, J.H. von Kirchmann rendered both the deponent verb *urgentur* and the substantive *sollicitatio* as *Erregung* (Kirchmann 1901; Kant, Di 1 380; PND 1: 407).

This physical nuance is also exhibited in the critical period dating to the beginning of the 1780s, as well as in Kant's correspondence, for example in relation to warmth (PG 9: 248). In a letter to Johann G. Kiesewetter (February 9, 1790), Kant associates *Erregung* with an excitation of the nerves, *Erregung des Nervenreizes* (Schöndorffer 1792, p. 938). In his posthumously published writings, particularly the 12th Convolut (July 1797-August 1799), *Erregung* is related to physical dynamics: *Erregung eines Stoßes* (OP 22: 568), to materials: *Erregung eines Stoffs* (OP 22: 562, 403; OP 21: 79, 226, 229), and to matter itself: *Erregung der Materie* (OP 21: 327, 383, 463; OP 22: 169, 194). Kant characterises *Erregung* as "movement in general that exercises by itself its act in any direction whatsoever" and translates it into Latin as *agitatio* (OP 21: 199–200). A few months later he renders it as *incitation* (OP 22: 194, 469).

Together with this 'mechanical' meaning, there is also a 'practical' sense of the word (VNAEF 8: 413). The representational sense clears the way for the transition from the mechanical to the practical connotations of *"Erregung"*. Kant addresses this representational sense of the word by writing about the living force, *Erregung der Lebenskraft* (Anth 7: 175), the sense organs, *Erregung der Sinnesorgane* (OP 21: 573; 22, pp. 551, 110), or the empirical representation itself: *Erregung der empirischen Vorstellung* (OP 22: 400). He also applies it to the realm of feeling in general, *Erregung des/eines Gefühls* (Anth 07: 261; EEKU 20: 249), or to the excitement of mood states like disgust, *Erregung des Ekels* (Anth 7: 149), or dissension: *Erregung der Mishelligkeit* (ZeF 8: 375; VAZeF 8: 191). He refers to the incitation of moral ideas within the context of aesthetic experience: *Erregung moralischer Ideen auf das Gemüth* (KU 5: 482, note), and also of passion, *Erregung der Leidenschaften* (Refl 1516. 15: 861).

1.3 Intrinsic Duality

The analysis of the two terms *Motion* and *Erregung* shows the structural duality characteristic of discussions of mood. With 'mood'—also translated into English as 'psyche', 'spirit' or 'mind' in the context of Kantian studies—the author refers to the biological-psychological structure which replaces the transcendent notion of 'soul' of rational psychology. Mood is the unitary, psychological, biologically-rooted structure that all human faculties are related to. The transition from the heavily metaphysical notion of soul (*Seele*) to the functional, transcendental idea of mood (*Gemüth*) is one of the main achievements in the development of transcendental philosophy (Teruel, 2013).

Concepts linked to mood are typically characterised by a two-faceted anthropological structure. This is also the case with *Gemüthsbewegung* or *Erregung*. The intrinsic duality of mood, linked to the sphere of mental affects as well as to a network of physical causes, is also found in the passions. While passions refer to temporary changes in mood, they can also occasion a tendency towards a more prolonged state of passion (Anth 7: 275).

It thus seems important to distinguish between changes in mood and states of passion. At first glance, changes in mood are somewhat transitory and do not necessarily correspond to the structure of affective and moral dispositions of the individual; in turn, states of passion are permanent and affect this structure in a pathological way. The strong influence of the Stoic doctrine of the passions in shaping Kant's practical views is well documented. For this reason, an overview of Stoic ideas regarding the passions can be a useful way to help clarify the Kantian position.

2 (Un)healthy Emotions, Passion and Reason

Kant's knowledge of the Greek Stoa, and of its reception in Latin antiquity, can be traced back to his formative years. The conceptual architecture of many Kantian insights bears the mark of Stoicism. Here I will focus on the key concept of ἀταραξία. Because of its connection with the Epicurean doctrine, we shall examine them both together.

2.1 Greek Semantic Field

The Epicurean doctrine has its roots in the crucial role of pleasure for the achievement of a good, flourishing life (εὐδαιμονία). Pleasure, the first and highest good, must be sought in concordance with the type of object that arises in each specific circumstance. For example, natural, necessary, pleasure must therefore be preferred to the natural but unnecessary, or the artificial and vain, and the absence of pain must take preference over the result of a search driven by desire (Epicurus 1925, p. 127). Absence of physical pain (ἀπονία) and mental disturbance (ἀταραξία) constitute the highest good: the sage "will direct every preference and aversion toward securing health of body and tranquillity of mind, seeing that this is the sum and end of a blessed life" (Epicurus 1925, p. 128).

Despite the proximity of the Epicurean notion of ἀταραξία to Stoic ethics, two remarks are pertinent. The first is related to the ethical aspect: for the Stoics, the highest good is not pleasure—understood as the absence of physical and mental disturbance—but living according to the goals of human nature. The second remark concerns the anthropological-psychological aspect: ἀταραξία is indeed a condition for achieving εὐδαιμονία, but it is derived by avoiding unhealthy emotions and thus from ἀπάθεια. The Stoic ideal of ἀπάθεια implies emotional detachment from all external conditions of life, so that the individual can liberate him or herself from the powers that lie beyond his or her control, and shape the only space for human freedom allowed by universal determination. It is the "inner citadel" (Hadot [1992] 2001), the mental state of the sage who can say, like Stilbo—or Bias of Priene—"I have all my goods in me!" (Seneca 1917, letter 9, p. 18).

Because of Kant's coherence and understanding of the mental conditions necessary for a virtuous life (MS 6: 484), and despite the general incompatibility of eudemonistic ethics and Kant's practical philosophy, there is a remarkable link between Kantian ethics and the Stoa. The Stoic ideal of ἀπάθεια as a condition for ἀταραξία indeed indicates the way human independence is forged by avoiding internal and external demands. This independence, in turn, is necessary to create the conditions for freedom: for the Stoics, in coherence with the goals of human nature; for Kant, in self-responsibility and rational autonomy (KU 5: 272). This helps explain why Kant considers απατηεια to be a necessary condition for virtue (MS 6: 408; Anth 7: 253).

A crucial transition at the dawn of ethical thought was the shift from the metaphysical, determinant notion of δαίμων, to the external, normative concept of ἔθος, and finally to the immanent, individual notion of ἦθος. Heraclitus' statement (ca. 535–475 BCE): "ἦθος ἀνθώπῳ δαίμων", represents this increasing consciousness of independence (Diels and Kranz 1951, p. 22 B 119). The need to ensure autonomy from internal demands of the passions is what underlies the thorny problem of weakness of will (ἀκρασία).

The Stoic perspective was significant for Kant in that it pointed to the struggle against unhealthy emotions and the formation of the "inner citadel" of the human being. In *The Conflict of the Faculties*, Kant considers the Stoic dietetic discipline of abstinence as the philosophical way of life that can best promote self-control (SF 7: 100–101). Kant expands the notion of 'dietetics' to make it the epitome of moral intervention in the dispositions human beings share with all creatures, including the moderation of pleasure: it is a "dietetics of thought" (Refl 15: 491).[4]

---

4 For the Kantian definition of pleasure as coincidence between object and "subjective conditions of life", see KpV 5: 9, footnote.

2.2 Kantian Cartography

Consistent with the aforementioned conceptual frame, Kant distinguishes the realm of passions from that of emotions. Together with 'inclination', *Neigung* (MS 6: 408), 'passion', *Leidenschaft* (KU 5: 272, note) belongs to the semantic field of 'desire': *Begehrung, Begierde* (MS 6: 408; Anth 7: 251; KU 5: 272, note). 'Emotion', in turn, belongs not to the field of sensation, *Wahrnehmung* (Anth 7: 134, note), which is an empirical representation, nor to feeling (*Gefühl*), which is not a representation but its subjective result and may at times be disinterested (MS 6: 211, note), but rather to affection, *Affekt* (Anth 7: 251), arising through bodily and affective motion, which is linked to the sensation of pleasure and displeasure, *Lust/Unlust* (KpV 5: 9, note). Despite their proximity, sentiment and emotion should not be combined in the theoretical frame nor used synonymously. Sentiment should be regarded as a by-product of reason; in the aesthetic experience of beauty or sublimity, it is related to disinterest (KU 5: 257–258, 267).

While Kant does not spell this out explicitly, I would suggest that, when they motivate action, emotions belong to impulsive causes (*causae impulsivae*) and specifically to sensitive causes (*stimuli, Bewegursachen, Antriebe*) that move the will through their connection to pleasure and displeasure, insofar as this depends on the way the object affects the mood through empirical representation. The *Stimuli* exercise either a determining force (*vis necessitantem*) in the case of non-rational animals, or a moving force (*vis impellentem*) in the case of human beings (V-Met-L2/Pölitz 28: 254–255).

2.3 Reformulation of the Problem

In contemporary language, but consistent with Kantian insights, I suggest that an emotion is an embodied, stereotyped, psychical and conscious reaction to internal or external solicitudes. My definition is only an attempt to express the sense of a notion that is difficult to grasp. I agree with Schacter et al. that any definition of emotion must include two aspects: "First, the fact that emotional experiences are always good or bad, and second, the fact that these experiences are associated with characteristic levels of bodily arousal" (Schacter et al. 2011, p. 375). Affective evaluation and physical reaction are therefore substantive elements of the emotion. Any attempt to define emotion which excludes the embodied reactive element thus fails to grasp its specific identity and risks confounding it with feeling (see, for example, the definition of emotion in *The Oxford Diction-*

ary as "a strong feeling deriving from one's circumstances, mood, or relationships with others").

As long as the motions of the mood do not threaten the position of moral dispositions as the highest good grounded in the concordance of virtue and happiness, nor even contribute to them, as in the case of aesthetic experience, they are potentially consistent with practical reason. The problem arises if they permanently modify those dispositions by linking them to desiderative objects that lead to a divergence from the conditions necessary to achieve the highest good. It should be noted here that we are not dealing with an intellectual difficulty in conceiving the good, but rather an inner conflict between practical judgment and dispositions of the will. The issue of the role of passion in the practical sphere raises, once more, the classic problem of ἀκρασία.

When an emotion is beyond an individual's control and becomes an established threat to his or her character, it is a passion. In Kant's words, it is "the inclination that can be barely defeated, or not defeated at all, by the subject's reason" (Anth 7: 251). When it negatively affects practical judgment, because this judgment depends on internal or external elements that are heteronomous in regard to the moral consciousness, then the passion implies a deliberate choice of evil (*Bösartigkeit, vitiositas*). When this happens in spite of the fact that practical judgment has embraced the opposite moral maxim, it is a case of weakness of will or fragility (*fragilitas*).[5]

The transition from affects to passions lies in the Kantian notion of propensity. This is the object of analysis in the *Religionsschrift* of 1793; significant contributions are also made in the *Anthropology* (1798). Propensity is "the subjective fundament of the possibility of a tendency" (RGV 6: 29). Propensity to evil can coexist with the individual determination to follow the moral principle. This is the subjective state that Kant calls *fragilitas* (see Teruel 2018).

3 Propensity, Fragility and Neuroscience

I have addressed Kant's keen interest in research on the human brain and the nervous system elsewhere. This interest gave him a deeper insight into what I

---

5 See RGV 6: 29. This is the case of passion and not of affection in general or emotion in particular, not only for Kant but also for the Stoics; see, for example, Seneca, 1917, letter 9, 3.13.15.17. Hence I disagree with N. Sánchez (2016, p. 47–48, p. 68) in her undervaluing of the Stoic doctrine of affective inclinations; I would suggest that this statement is the result of not making a sharp distinction between the notions of sentiment, inclination and emotion, on one side, and passion, on the other.

term—inspired by Colin McGinn—the epistemological closure of his theoretical point of view on subjectivity. On this subject, his epilogue to the work of Thomas Sömmerring *Über das Organ der Seele* (1796) is clear enough (see Teruel 2008). On the other hand, Kant's knowledge of the relationship between the nervous system and organic motions—based on the work of August Unzer—led him to an understanding of mental disorders that could be considered functionalist *avant la lettre* (see Teruel 2013). Kant identified powerful strategies with which to control the passions and edify the "inner citadel" (see Teruel 2014). I now turn to the theoretical framework of his approach from a naturalised perspective.

3.1 The Issue of Propensity

Understanding how a propensity to evil fits within the framework of practical reason is a thorny question. It was already so in Antiquity—as the problem of ἀκρασία eloquently testifies—and so it is for Kant. The individual tends towards the goals his or her dispositions are oriented towards; the doctrine of dispositions (*Anlagen*) plays an important and often under-recognised role in Kantian writings (see Teruel 2016). Kant distinguishes between dispositions towards the animal condition, for example, preservation of the self and the species; dispositions towards humanity, i.e., the achievement of rational goods in the frame of social existence; and dispositions of the personality, related to the exercise of spontaneity and to pure reason insofar as it is also practical (RGV 6: 26).

The mystery of moral weakness (*Gebrechlickheit, fragilitas*) lies in the fact that the individual prefers the object of generic dispositions towards the animal condition over specifically human dispositions towards the personality, and does so despite having adopted a moral maxim (RGV 6: 36–37). This is the first meaning of moral evil in the important first section of the *Religionsschrift* (RGV 6: 29).

I believe propensity should be considered as the counterpart to the natural predispositions of mood (*natürliche Gemüthsanlagen*) referred to in the *Metaphysik der Sitten*. These are "subjective conditions of the receptivity towards the concept of duty" (MS 6: 399). Propensity is, as we know, the "subjective fundament of the possibility of a tendency". Both terms—predisposition and propensity—identify possible realisations of an agent that is potentially moral. Human discretion (*menschliche Willkür*) can be influenced by both the side of pure will (*reiner Wille*) or by the pathologically affected will; in this case, an ethical evaluation should consider the possible influence of weakness of will as a mitigating element (MS 6: 413, 228).

3.2 Biological-evolutionary Link Between Emotion and Propensity

The question is: how can emotion lead to propensity to evil? Here, the issue lies in the 'raw nature' of the human being (Anth 7: 325). I suggest that the biological-evolutionary perspective can shed some light on this issue from three complementary strategies: the phylogenetic, the ontogenetic and the neuroscientific, at the structural as well as the dynamic level.

Trophic dependence on resources, the search for sexual partners, and defence against predators or environmental threats give rise to evaluation processes and stereotyped psycho-physical reactions—emotions—that are ontologically embodied but also phylogenetically favoured, because of their relevance not only to the individual's survival but also—and essentially—to the preservation of the species. The structural, organic correlate of this ontogenetic and phylogenetic process is the shaping of the human brain. Over the last two million years, throughout the transition from *homo erectus* to its modern day descendants, synaptic reinforcement has led to patterns related to functions that are vegetative-trophic, psychical-social and subjective-reflexive: this triad corresponds to evolutionary levels as well as to the actual structure of the main brain sections (MacLean 1989). There are two aspects—structural and dynamic, respectively—the relevance of which I wish to highlight.

The functional areas of the brain, as they have been shaped ontogenetically and phylogenetically under selective pressure in the interaction with the environment, are reciprocally related. The more recently developed neocortex areas, that survey the reflexive processes, are linked to the older phylogenetic limbic areas connected to emotional experience (Swanson 1987). Neuronal projections such as the Papez and Yakovlev circuits exemplify the connection between the two processes. The ground-breaking studies of Klüver and Bucy (1939) showed the important role of the amygdala in shaping emotional responses; this is demonstrated by the multiple afferent and efferent fibres connecting it with the cortical and subcortical areas, and supported by clinical research on apes and human patients with severe brain damage. Recent research has highlighted the role of the *nucleus accumbens* in reinforcing emotions, addictions and behavioural diseases (Sturm et al. 2003; Puigdemont et al. 2012). I have previously dealt with this issue from the neurophilosophical perspective (Teruel 2013b). Emotions are deeply neurophysiologically involved in human deliberation and decision making. This structural, phylogenetically shaped network of connections is based on ontogenetic patterns. Here, it is important to emphasise the rule of the processes of synaptic long-term facilitation. Repetition of biologically favoured (re)actions leads to increased conductivity in the neuronal network and shapes embodied patterns at both the electric-chemical and the behavioural levels (Bliss et al. 1993).

In other words, it is the behavioural patterns, oriented towards self-preservation, that are rewarded through long-term synaptic facilitation in the phylogenetic shaping of species that possess a nervous system. This leads to stereotypical reaction patterns, strongly oriented towards the welfare of the individual—biologically marked through pleasant experiences, and related to crucial ontogenetic and phylogenetic processes—and thus towards selfish behaviour. This does not exclude the adoption of communal or group survival patterns, as Darwin noted in his ground-breaking work of 1871, but strongly orients them towards the achievement of selfish goals.

3.3 Back to Kant

The ontogenetic and phylogenetic origins of patterns related to pleasure and survival goals explain the strong psycho-physiological reactions underlying propensities. This is the side of the emotions rooted in mood, with neuroscientific implications that can be identified in brain structures and neuronal network processes and that go beyond the Kantian understanding of the question. In fact, Kant refutes the cognitive character of emotions on the basis of the organic dependence of mood changes:

Now every affection is blind, either in the choice of its purpose, or, if this be supplied by Reason, in its accomplishment; for it is a mental movement which makes it impossible to exercise a free deliberation about fundamental propositions so as to determine ourselves thereby. It can therefore in no way deserve the approval of the Reason. (KU 5: 272, p. 112 of J.H. Bernard's translation.)

The side of emotional experience we have dealt with is rooted in a change in mood that occurs prior to any deliberation. However, that does not mean that it is blind—that is, arbitrary or non-teleological—in the choice of its purpose. Kant recognises that nature, in its wisdom, provides us with emotions before we can rationally judge (Anth 7: 253). By discovering harmony among empirical phenomena and the transcendental conditions of knowledge, pleasure has always been present in human beings' relationship with the world, to the point that, without it, experience would be impossible (KU 5: 187).

Continuing this line of thought, Sánchez Madrid (2016, p. 49, 67) beautifully alludes to pleasure as the 'hinge' upon which the distinction between the knowable and the unknowable swings. I also agree with Angelica Nuzzo (2014, p. 102) —if by 'emotion' she means the organic affection rooted in one's mood, and not an imprecise notion mixed with 'sentiment'—when she states that emotion shapes our cognitive exploration within nature. The kind of pleasure emerging from harmony felt between the faculties—cognition, feeling and desire—leads to advancement of life, *Beförderung des Lebens* (KU 5: 244). This statement can be taken further when linked to the mediatory role played by feelings through their connection to reason, and by emotions through their embodied, mood-rooted character.

Evolutionary epistemology demonstrates that emotional experience is a largely a priori set of stereotyped reactions where the phylogenetic history of successful, cognitively loaded interaction with the environment is encrypted.[6] This explains not only the intentional side of mood-rooted reactions, but also its non-intentional side as it arises in the notion of temperament (Anth 7: 235). From this point of view, naturalistic hermeneutics supports a consistent reading of the Kantian doctrine of emotions. I would say that this revised theory is located in the place that Ana M. González (2015, p. 94 f.) describes as 'intermediate' between "feeling" theories of emotion (such as Whitting's) and cognitive theories of emotion (such as those of Robert, Kenny or Solomon). Approaching Kant from the perspective of evolutionary epistemology is a significant contribution, but not without its difficulties, which I have dealt with elsewhere (Teruel 2015). In my approach, it is fully compatible with the non-reductionist aspects of transcendental philosophy.

One underlying aspect related to the history of concepts remains. The semantic field under consideration, closely connected to current understanding of emotion, is the result of the modern reductionism of the broader, pre-modern comprehension of mood changes (Solomon 1983). Contemporary attempts to include the cognitive dimension and link it to reason in the sphere of emotions is a reversal of that reductionist conceptual operation. In some way, our attempt to find unity in the apparently fragmentary web of references to emotions in Kant's writings is the search for the unified field that underlies the human experience of emotion.

4 Conclusion

Although Kant did not use the word *Emotion* or its derivations, we have identified some terms—to which we have added the German-Latin *Motion* and the German *Erregung*, both related to the human mood—that belong to the same semantic

---

6 See the ground-breaking work on this in Lorenz 1941. For an introduction to its epistemological implications, see Popper 1990.

field. In analysing these terms I have argued that there is a link between the Kantian approach to the psycho-physical, embodied side of mood-rooted, pleasure-receptive changes, whose reactions go beyond the deliberative instances of the individual, and the classic issue of πάθος, more closely connected to the views of the Stoics. From the difficult conceptual problem of ἀκρασία which then arises, I have moved on to its projections in the Kantian subject of *fragilitas* (*Gebrechlichkeit*).

I have shown that weakness of will in general, and its Kantian version in particular, can be understood from a biological-evolutionary perspective on three reciprocally related levels: the ontogenetic, the phylogenetic and the neuroscientific. In addressing the neuroscientific level, I have emphasised the centrality of the brain's connections between cortical and limbic areas in shaping deliberation and decision processes, as well as the ontogenetic and phylogenetic support of processes of neuronal facilitation. There are strong links between this model and the correlative explanation of the place of emotion in moral life, on one side, and the Kantian doctrine of emotion and its relationship with the notions of propensity and moral fragility, on the other. The result is a naturalised approach to the psycho-physiological, embodied aspect of morality.

Of course, this is only one aspect in the shaping of human experience. Emotions play a dual role in this process. They are messengers sent from our phylogenetic past and advisers of our biological, psychical and moral present. They can overwhelm us through their mood-rooted power; yet they can also be a powerful support in advancing human life in all its richness. Emotions are creatures of two worlds, precisely because of their ambiguity.

Bibliography

Bliss, Tim V.P. and Collingridge Graham L. (1993): "A Synaptic Model of Memory: Long-term Potentiation in the Hippocampus". In: *Nature* 361, pp. 31–39.

Cohen, Alix (Ed.) (2014): *Kant on Emotion and Value*. London: Palgrave McMillan.

Coromines, Joan (2001): *Diccionario crítico etimológico castellano e hispánico*. Madrid: Gredos.

Diels, Hermann A. and Kranz, Walther (1951–1952): *Die Fragmente der Vorsokratiker* 6th ed. Weidmann: Hildesheim.

Dixon, Thomas (2003): *From Passions to Emotions: The Creation of a Secular Psychological Category*. Cambridge: Cambridge University Press.

Epicurus (1925): "Letter to Menoeceus". In: *Lives of the Eminent Philosophers by Diogenes Laërtius*, Vol. 2. Bk. X. Robert D. Hicks (Trans.). Cambridge, London: Loeb Classical Library.

González, Ana Marta (2015): "Emoción, sentimiento y pasión en Kant". In: *Trans / Form / Ação* 38. No. 3, pp. 75–97.

Greene, Joshua (2008): "The Secret Joke of Kant's Soul". In: Walter S. Armstrong (Ed.): *Moral Psychology*. Cambridge: MIT Press, pp. 35–79.

Grimm, Jacob and Grimm, Wilhelm (1854–1961): *Deutsches Wörterbuch, digitalisierte Fassung im Wörterbuchnetz des Trier Center for Digital Humanities*, Version 01/21. https://www.woerterbuchnetz.de/DWB, accessed on 30 April, 2021.

Hadot, Pierre (2001): *The Inner Citadel: The "Meditations" of Marcus Aurelius* [*La citadelle intérieure. Introduction aux Pensées de Marc Aurèle*. 1992]. Michael Chase (Trans.). Paris: Artheme Fayard.

Harper, Douglas (2000): *Online Etymology Dictionary*. Lancaster, Pennsylvania.

Kant, Immanuel. *Gesammelte Schriften*, v. 1–22, Berlin: Preussische Akademie der Wissenschaften, Vol. 23, Berlin: Deutsche Akademie der Wissenschaften; vols. 24–, Göttingen: Akademie der Wissenschaften. [Akademie-Ausgabe, AA]

Kant, Immanuel ([1784–1785] 2012): "Anthropology Mrongovius". In: Allen W. Wood and Robert B. Louden (Eds.): *Lectures on Anthropology*. Robert R. Clewis and G. Felicitas Munzel (Trans.). Cambridge, New York: Cambridge University Press.

Kirchmann, Julius Hermann von (1901): *Immanuel Kants Sämtliche Werke*. Leipzig: Felix Meiner Verlag.

Klüver, Heinrich and Bucy, Paul (1939): "Preliminary Analysis of Functions of the Temporal Lobes in Monkeys". In: *Archives of Neurology and Psychology* 42, pp. 979–1000.

Lorenz, Konrad Zacharias ([1941] 1983): "Kants Lehre vom Apriorischen im Lichte gegenwärtiger Biologie". In: Konrad L. Lorenz and Franz M. Wuketits (Eds.): *Die Evolution des Denkens*. Munich: Piper & Co., pp. 95–124.

Louden, Robert B. (2000): *Kant's Impure Ethics: From Rational Beings to Human Beings*. Oxford: Oxford University Press.

MacLean, Paul D. (1989): *The Triune Brain in Evolution: Role in Paleocerebral Functions*. New York: Plenum Press.

Nuzzo, Angelica (2014): "The Place of Emotions in Kant's Transcendental Philosophy". In: Alix Cohen (Ed.): *Kant on Emotion and Value*. Hampshire: Palgrave McMillan, pp. 88–107.

Pérez Zafrilla, Pedro Jesús (in press): "The dual process model of moral judgement. A divided mind or a myopic methodology".

Popper, Karl R. (1990): *A World of Propensities*. Bristol: Thoemmes.

Puigdemont, Dolors, Pérez-Egea, Rosario, Portella, Maria J. and Molet, Joan (2012): "Deep Brain Stimulation of the Subcallosal Cingulate Gyrus: Further Evidence in Treatment-Resistant Major Depression". In: *The International Journal of Neuropsychopharmacology* 15. No. 1, pp. 121–133.

RAE (2014): *Diccionario de la Real Academia*. Madrid: RAE.

Sánchez Madrid, Nuria (2016): "Resonancias emocionales de la razón en Kant". In: *Princípios. Revista de filosofia* 23. No. 41, pp. 33–74.

Schacter, Daniel L., Gilbert, Daniel T., Wegner, Daniel M. and Hood, Bruce M. (2011): *Psychology. European Edition*. Basingstoke: Palgrave Macmillan.

Schöndorffer, Otto (1972): *Kants Briefwechsel. Auswahl und Anmerkungen von Otto Schöndorffer*. Hamburg: Felix Meiner Verlag.

Seneca, Lucio Anneo (1917): "Epistulae morales ad Lucilium". In: *Moral Letters to Lucilius*, Vol. 1. Richard Mott Gummere (Trans.). Cambridge, London: Loeb Classical Library.

Solomon, Robert C. (1983): *The Passions: The Myth and Nature of Human Emotions*. Notre Dame: University of Notre Dame Press.

Sturm, Volker, Lenartz, Doris and Koulousakis, Athanasios (2003): "The *Nucleus Accumbens: A Target for Deep Brain Stimulation in Obsessive-compulsive- and Anxiety-disorders*". In: *Journal of Chemical Neuroanatomy* 26. No. 4, pp. 293–299.

Swanson, Larry W. (1987): "Limbic System". In: Gerald Edelman (Ed.): *Encyclopaedia of Neuroscience*. Basel: Birkhäuser, pp. 589–591.

Teruel, Pedro Jesús (2008): *"Das Organ der Seele*. Immanuel Kant y Samuel Thomas Sömmerring sobre el problema mente-cerebro". In: *Studi kantiani* 21, pp. 59–76.

Teruel, Pedro Jesús (2013a): "Die äußere Schaale der Natur. Eine Fußnote zum *Versuch über die Krankheiten des Kopfes* (1764)". In: *Kant-Studien* 104. No. 1, pp. 23–43.

Teruel, Pedro Jesús (2013b): "La encrucijada neurocientífica entre naturalismo y humanismo. Análisis filosófico de algunos tratamientos psiquiátricos por estimulación eléctrica del sistema límbico". In: *Daimon. Revista Internacional de Filosofía* 59, pp. 103–113.

Teruel, Pedro Jesús (2014): "Das Hippocratische Geschäft. Significado, sentido y ubicación estructural de la medicina en la filosofía kantiana". In: *Estudos kantianos* 2. No. 2, pp. 217–240.

Teruel, Pedro Jesús (2015): "Crítica de la leicología pura. El enfoque lorenziano como punto d partida para una posible hermenéutica naturalista de la filosofía transcendental". In: Antonio Campillo and Delia Manzanero (Eds.): *Los retos de la Filosofía en el siglo XXI. Actas del I Congreso internacional de la REF*, Vol. 12. Madrid, València: Red Española de Filosofía, Universitat de València, pp. 23–29.

Teruel, Pedro Jesús (2016): "Significado, sentido y ubicación estructural del término *Anlage* en la filosofía kantiana". In: Juan Manuel Navarro, Rafael V Orden and Rogelio Rovira (Eds.): *Nuevas perspectivas sobre la filosofía de Kant*. Madrid: Escolar y Mayo, pp. 83–89.

Trésor (1994): *Le Trésor de la Langue Française informatisé*. Nancy, Paris: Université de Lorraine, CNRS.

Dina Mendonça

Calibration Hypothesis: Rethinking Kant's Place for Emotion and the Brain's Resting State

Abstract: The chapter begins by presenting how contemporary developments in neuroscience and cognitive science show several links to Kant's work, and more specifically how the predictive mind hypothesis can be seen as having its roots in the Kantian project. Following these initial considerations, the chapter next describes the renewed examination of the role of emotions in Kant's ethics, in order to propose that the Kantian system includes a mediate control over the emotional landscape.

Keywords: neuroscience, cognitive science, predictive mind hypothesis, emotions, brain

This chapter suggests that the renewed analysis of Kantian reflection on emotions enables a novel hypothesis concerning the regulation of emotions. Following contemporary Kantian scholars who have indicated Kant's contributions to our understanding of emotions (Borges 2004), and in line with the recent developments in cognitive science and neurophilosophy, we suggest a novel focus on the role of the brain's resting state in regulating and controlling one's general emotional structure. This, in turn, allows for new ways to mediate control of emotions and thus for the ongoing cultivation of excellence of character.

This chapter begins by presenting how developments in neuroscience and cognitive science have several links to Kant's work (Fazepour and Thompson 2015), and more specifically how the predictive mind hypothesis can be seen has having its roots in the Kantian project. This enables us to highlight the importance of understanding what exactly happens in the human brain's resting state, and the implications that the brain's continued activity during its resting

Acknowledgement: This work is supported by national funds through FCT – Fundação para a Ciência e a Tecnologia, I.P., in the context of the celebration of the program contract foreseen in the numbers 4, 5 and 6 of article 23.º of D.L. no. 57/2016 of 29 August, as amended by Law no. 57/2017 of 19 July and by Research Project UIDB/00183/2020 and Research Project PTDC/FER-FIL/29906/2017.

Dina Mendonça, IFILNOVA/UNL, Portugal

https://doi.org/10.1515/9783110720730-012

state have for our understanding of the structure of the brain in general (Northoff 2012a, 2012b). After delineating these background considerations, the chapter describes the renewed focus on the role of emotions in Kantian ethics, in order to propose how the Kantian view of emotions includes a mediate control over the emotional landscape, in which one of the activities of the brain can be seen as integrating experience and adjusting the subject's general emotional structure to better deal with future experiences. Furthermore, this process can take place during the brain's resting state as a type of calibration. This hypothesis must, of course, be empirically tested, and the chapter ends by pointing out that, for the time being, it is only possible to reinforce the need for future empirical tests with an emphasis on the importance of sleep for an healthy brain, given that it may be in this way that the activity of the brain's resting state enables a sort of calibration of the predictive processing that occurs during the brain's vigilant state.

1 Kant in Recent Neuroscience and Cognitive Science

The links between Kant's work and recent developments in neuroscience and cognitive science have been identified by several researchers (Fazepour and Thompson 2015), with some even going so far as to suggest that "recent cognitive science is outlining a 'Kantian brain'." (Swanson 2016, p. 2) Thus, for example, predictive processing, though labeled as a novel and revolutionary approach which aims to propose a novel theory that takes the brain to be a mostly predictive organ that predicts incoming sensory input (Clark 2015c, p.15), actually shares many insights with the philosophy of Immanuel Kant regarding the structure of the mind and the way that it processes information from the outside world. It is also possible to say that Kant was the first to suggest the top-down approach, one frequently argued for in present cognitive science (Kitcher 1996).

Several other authors have also showed how the predictive mind hypothesis can be understood as having its roots in Kant (Swanson 2016). Andy Clark, one of the major representatives of a philosophical approach to the predictive mind hypothesis, has pointed out how predictive processing evokes Kantian concepts (2013, p. 16), and Gladziejewski has discussed the way that the view of perception proposed by predictive processing is Kantian in spirit (Gladziejewski 2016, p. 16). This is unsurprising, given the fact that Kant's project aimed to be an "elaboration of the Humean problem in its greatest possible amplification"

(Kant, Prol 4: 261) and, analogously, the predictive processing paradigm "has been framed as an answer to Hume's challenge in that it aims to offer an account for how casual structure is extracted from statistical regularities that occur in sensory stimulation (Hohwy 2012; Dennett 2013; Flores 2015)" (Swanson 2016, p. 3).

Accordingly, Swanson, in "Predictive Processing Paradigm has Roots in Kant" (2016) identifies a connection between predictive processing and the Kantian legacy in a more detailed way through a close examination of the commonalities between predictive processing (PP) and Kant's philosophy. He argues that many of the core proposals of predictive processing can be readily identified in Kant, such that it is possible to identify Kantian concepts with analogues in PP (Swanson 2016, p. 1) The first of these is the emphasis on "top-down" generation of percepts, a difference that opposes predictive processing to both classical and traditional approaches to perception and cognition. Much of the literature on predictive processing characterizes other approaches as taking perception and cognition as passive processes, in which the external stimuli of sense data is gathered and accumulated so as to format the information of the mind. PP rejects this picture of perception, which can be described as a "bottom up" process of perception, and argues that, "PP turns a traditional picture of perception on its head" (Clark 2015a, p. 51). This reversal shares many similarities with the Kantian Copernican Revolution, and especially with Kant's rejection of the view that cognition conforms to objects, arguing instead that the "objects must conform to our cognition" (KrV B: xvi).

Another connection between PP and the Kantian project can be seen in the role of 'hyperpriors' in PP, similar to Kant's idea of 'forms of appearance' (Swanson 2016, p. 4). In order to predict, the brain must part from a foundation, meaning that predictive processing requires some constraints to narrow down possibilities. However, while these constraints work as priors that enable the selection of a hypothesis, it has also been discovered that "for complex representational abilities found in human cognition—from children to scientists—a *hierarchical system* of priors is required" (Swanson 2016, p. 5). This means that some priors are more abstract, and prior to others, such that "a multilayered, bidirectional, recursive process of hypothesis generation is a requirement addressed by hierarchical predictive coding models of brain function, and hyperpriors are crucial for such models" (Swanson 2016, p. 5). It is precisely in the discussion on the importance of hyperpriors that Clark references Kant's distinction between the matter of a sensation and its form, such that "special and temporal properties are endogenous features of cognition that impose formal constraints on the possibility of any experience of outer objects (Kant, KrV B: 33–73; Hatfield 2006)" (Swanson 2016, p. 5). In a similar way in which priors require hyperpriors for prediction in PP, the recent trend in neuroscience also proposes that perception only captures appearances, and not 'things in themselves', given that the formal aspects of the cognitive and perceptual systems do not capture objective features of external reality (Swanson 2016, p. 6). Nevertheless, it must be acknowledged that Kant did not assume the evolutionary understanding of priors recognized by predictive processing (Swanson 2016, p. 6). Furthermore, for Kant, these conditions of perception were seen as necessary and unchangeable, while for predictive processing, some priors are the result of experience, even if "many priors could be innate and biologically hard-wired" (Swanson 2016, p. 6).

The third key idea common to both predictive processing and Kant's theoretical framework is the overlap between the general function of generative models of predictive processing and Kant's concept of 'schema' (Swanson 2016, p. 4). The notion of generative models provides an answer to the puzzle of how organisms are able to identify singular objects from manifold perceptual information. The idea is that external stimuli is processed through a comparison with general models, rather than a comparison with previously encountered perceptual landscapes, and in this way, a model is selected to best suit the experience and provide meaning to the patterns observed. In this manner, the "generative model approach describes object recognition as a coordinated balance of both 'top-down' and 'bottom-up' flow of neural signals" (Swanson 2016, p. 7). This, in turn, instantiates a specific generative model that captures what is presented, and that requires several layers of neural hierarchy in which the system learns to generate images instead of merely classifying them (Clark 2015b, p. 27). Swanson argues that Kant's schematism (Kant KrV A: 137) anticipates the strategy described by predictive processing in two major ways: firstly, by positing that there is a generative top-down process akin to imagination aside from the obvious sensory input flow, and secondly, by showing how the mind identifies perceptual objects by comparing them with "the endogenous abstract rules it would use to generate the sensory patterns in imagination" (Swanson 2016, p. 7) instead of comparing them to other previously encountered images.

Fourth aspect that predictive processing shares with Kant the idea of the process of analysis-by-synthesis (Swanson 2016, p. 1). Predictive processing argues that there is an analysis-by-synthesis, in which sensations are analyzed by comparison with internal processes able to synthesize similar patterns. This is similar to Kant's proposal that analysis proceeds by synthesis, and that synthesis is required for analysis. Ultimately, this means that analysis and synthesis must be understood by looking into the "primary target of any investigation about the fundamental workings of cognition" (Swanson 2016, p. 9). Finally, Swanson holds that both predictive processing researchers and Kant agree in arguing for the crucial role of imagination in perception, due to the fact that both consider it to be the engine that allows for generative models to be created and thus concur on its crucial role in facilitating perception (Swanson 2016, p. 9).

Overall, the description of predictive processing shows that recent developments in neuroscience and cognitive science offer "strong support for a view of the mind much closer to that which Kant envisaged" (Swanson 2016, p. 11). Thus, it is not surprising to find Georg Northoff suggesting that Kant's ideas can provide novel insights regarding the mechanisms of the brain, such that neural processing can be linked to consciousness and the self (2012a). Northoff begins by showing that, in opposition to both Descartes and Hume, Kant viewed consciousness, and the self, as the outcome of an intrinsic and an extrinsic view of the mind, such that they were the result of "hybrid processes that result from an interaction between the mind's intrinsic features and the world's extrinsic stimuli" (Northoff 2012a, p. 356). It is the intrinsic features of the mind, such as the unity of consciousness, and the categories, that structure and organize the extrinsic stimuli of the world. This means that consciousness and self are grounded on the interaction "between the mind's intrinsic features and the environment's extrinsic stimuli" (Northoff 2012a, p. 356). The Kantian proposal, argues Northoff, is in line with the discovery of high resting-state activity in certain areas of the brain, and more specifically the default-mode network (DMN) which has led to the proposal of an intrinsic view of the brain's neural activity (Northoff 2012a, p. 356). A precise and complete picture of the activity that goes on during the brain's resting state, which could provide an understanding of how this activity may provide a foundation for consciousness and the self, is yet to be developed, and thus much remains unclear. However, Northoff holds that Kant's view of the intrinsic features of the mind can be understood as those features that offer order and regularity to the extrinsic stimuli, and that these, in turn, can be identified with the brain's resting state (Northoff 2012a, p. 357). This connection deserves to be further explored.

In this way, it is possible to learn about the brain by exploring Kant's conception of the mind. Northoff specifically shows that the Kantian concept of 'I think' enables the development of neuroscientific research by providing a link between resting state activity with the central feature of 'I think' in neuronal terms, thus moving research beyond the conception of stimulus induced activity linked to consciousness (Northoff 2012a, p. 358). More specifically, it shows how the resting state can be considered a "necessary, non-sufficient condition, a neural predisposition of consciousness" (Northoff 2012a, p. 358). That is, it proposes that the resting state can be an important way to better understand the self, because the structure of the resting state may make visible the structure of the brain's interaction with external stimuli. As Northoff writes,

[t]he resting state's self-specific organization may be imposed upon the stimulus during subsequent rest-stimulus interaction. Depending on the degree of match between stimulus and resting state, the latter's self-specific organization is assigned to the stimulus in different degrees. In other words, the better rest and stimulus match, the higher the degree to which the resting state's self-specific organization is imposed upon the stimulus; the higher the latter's degree of self-specificity; and the lower degree of activity of change (i.e., deviation from the resting state). (Northoff 2012a, p. 358)

Ultimately, the structure of the resting state can be taken as the general structure of the self. Furthermore, the degree of self-specificity imposed on a stimulus can provide clues regarding the overall structure of the brain, because the "resting state activity may be organized and structured in a self-specific way" (Northoff 2012a, p. 358).

Hopefully the ground for taking Kant's psychology more seriously than it has been to this point is secure enough to suggest that a reconsideration of the role of emotions in Kant's philosophy also necessitates a reconsideration of what more there is to be learned from Kant (Borges 2004).

2 Kant and Emotions

The general view of Kant's interpretation of emotions' role in ethics is that they have essentially no role to play in morality. As Cohen writes: "Kant's ethics is traditionally portrayed as unequivocal on one issue: affective states, including feelings, emotions, and inclinations, are intrinsically at odds with morality" (Cohen 2017, p. 172). However, the idea that Kant wanted emotions completely banished from the ethical sphere is now seen as a superficial and overly simplistic interpretation of Kant's ethics, and recent work on Kant has uncovered a new dimension of the role of emotions in Kant's ethical work, such that several authors have argued for a very different understanding of emotions' place in Kant's philosophy (Baron 1995; Herman 1993; Sherman 1997; Guyer 1993, 2000; Wood 1999; Sorensen 2002; Cohen 2014, 2017).

Part of this reinterpretation implies understanding how Kant viewed the emotional landscape. Although Kant did not have a theory of emotion *per se*, his work delineates a taxonomy of emotions that recognizes wide variety of phenomena encapsulated within the emotional realm. Once we have described the Kantian taxonomy, it will be easier to point out how some emotional entities are suitable for moral consideration, while others are not. In "Kant's Taxonomy of the Emotions", Sorensen shows how Kant understands emotions as part of a rich taxonomy of desires and feelings, some of which are incompatible with moral reasoning (for example, passions), and others of which are compatible with it under certain conditions. For example, some feelings may sometimes be compatible with moral reasoning, and even some consequences of desires, such as 'moral feeling', as well as certain inclinations and affects, may also be compatible with moral action (Sorensen 2002, p. 128). While Kant's taxonomy of the emotional landscape is different from the distinctions currently in use in theories of emotion, it is important to note the progress this represents in comparison with the theories of emotion used by his predecessors (Deimling 2014, p. 109). First, no one used emotion in exactly the same way we do today (Dixon 2003), and many of the Kantian distinctions do, in fact, embrace states that would be captured by the concept of emotion in its current usage (Deimling 2014, p. 109). One important aspect to highlight is Kant's recognition that not everything that belongs to the emotional landscape can be accurately described under one single category.

Scholars have indicated that, in general, inclinations cannot serve as the foundation of morality within Kant's framework, for multiple reasons. First, inclinations are unreliable guides, stemming from the fact that one may be inclined to do what is not right in general or in specific conditions and moments. Second, inclinations are the product of nature and not of freedom and, finally, they exist without the need for a genuine commitment to morality (Sorensen 2002, p. 4). However, "to deny *inclination* these moral roles is not to deny all emotions a moral role" (Sorensen 2002, p. 112)—Sorensen argues that there are several other occasions on which Kant defends positions in which emotions are a crucial part of the moral endeavor. For instance, Kant suggests that the feeling of sympathy is part of the moral ideal, when he writes in the *Metaphysics of Morals* that, "while it is not in itself a duty to share the sufferings (as well the joys) of others, it is a duty to sympathize actively in their fate" (MM 6: 456– 457). Consequently, when inclinations foster the feeling of sympathy in specific contexts, it is important to recognize this and allow emotions to fulfil their role within morality, because otherwise reason alone may be blind to the need for sympathy, and furthermore, "reason may see that to do one's duty, one needs a strong (if brief) emotional agitation" (Sorensen 2002, p. 124). As Sorensen explains,

> Reason not only produces feelings and desires, but sometimes *must* produce *strong, reflection-inhibition* emotions in order for the agent to do his or her duty. If "enthusiasm" is a common, possible worrisome natural by-product of practical reason, "fortitude" is an affect that is *necessary* for the performance of some moral duties. This is a striking position given the image of Kant many readers take from the *Groundwork* and the second *Critique*. Perhaps all affects do "momentary damage to freedom and self-mastery" (A 7:267); the interesting point is that for Kant, it can be one's moral *duty* to briefly damage this very freedom and self-mastery. (Sorensen 2002, p. 121)

In other words, while an affect may appear suddenly and momentarily, passions are incompatible with moral reason because they are habitual, concealed, and integrated in the very will of the subject, thus making them difficult to identify and switch on or off at the will of the agent (Sorensen 2002, p. 120).

Overall, the more recent interpretation of Kant's work indicates that an accurate description of the Kantian taxonomy of emotions helps us to acknowledge the positive role of emotions in morality, as well as the negative role already historically recognized for deontological ethics (Greenspan 1995).[1] Since feelings impact morality and human agency as the condition for moral feeling, it is important to recognize the many positive roles of emotions in ethics (Sorensen 2002, p. 127) while also taking into account the need for a degree of control and mastery over the emotional realm. One way to better grasp this is to recognize that Kant's reticence with regard to affective states stems from their immediacy, as well as our lack of control over them (Deimling 2014, p. 116). Furthermore, since we are passive, it is only possible to exercise control over emotions in a mediated form. This awareness of the passive character of emotional states does not imply that they are completely beyond our control, and therefore, there is a "scope for responsibility, even if taking control does not amount to an automatic or immediate reversal of one's emotional dispositions" (Sherman 2014, p. 17). For this reason, Kant gives several examples that demonstrate how feelings can be influenced. One can influence their emotions, for instance, by manipulating bodily states (Deimling 2014, p. 117), or through a focus on and selection of what one takes into account in their reasoning (Deimling 2014, p. 118–119), or perhaps by reflecting and discussing specific moral emotions (Deimling 2014, p. 120). Another way to understand this mediated control is by recognizing the contrast between a duty to have a feeling and a duty to cultivate it (Deimling 2014, p. 120). Moreover, "the cultivation of certain feelings is one of our moral duties" (Cohen 2017, p. 172), because it is the cultivation of duty that demands the pursuit of one's own perfection. Alix Cohen describes how, according to Kant, this duty is twofold, because "it prescribes the cultivation of both our natural and our moral perfection. The former is expressed in the maxim 'Cultivate your powers of mind and body so that they are fit to realise any ends you might encounter'" (Cohen 2017, p. 174). Within this general dictum, there is also the goal of cultivating the ability to experience feelings, and to feel pleasure and pain, as they are necessary for human experience. Sorensen states how "Kant points out that certain specifically moral feelings like 'respect' de-

1 Thanks to Professor António Marques for the suggestion that one can look at the positive versus the negative role of emotions for deontological ethics.

pend on a deeper susceptibility to pleasure and pain: '*Sensible feeling*, which underlies all our inclinations, in indeed the *condition* of that feeling we call respect' (KpV 5: 75; emphasis mine)" (Sorensen 2002, p. 114), highlighting that a duty to foster sensibility and the ability to feel and manage pain and pleasure are crucial to morality.

Thus, this sense of the duty to cultivate feeling requires recognizing an important distinction that needs to be made concerning the description of persons as moving towards perfection and excellence. Kant phrased the distinction in terms of the difference between character and temperament, showing that "each temperament has particular natural tendencies, and in particular tendencies that favor certain moods, emotions, and inclinations" (Cohen 2017, p. 175), and that different temperaments require different types of approaches to the cultivation of character. The distinction between temperament and character is not to be taken as two synonymous ways of referring to a person, but rather as a recognition that, because the human emotional landscape is intrinsically relational, it is also reasonable to expect different outcomes from the person-environment relation. Furthermore, "one would expect different feelings to reflect different kinds of person–environment relationships" (Northoff 2008, p. 508), even though the goal of character aims to be convergent, and yet that all different temperaments must strive for similar excellence of character.

In his *Anthropology*, Kant distinguishes between four temperaments: the choleric, the phlegmatic, the melancholic, and the sanguine. Whilst it is unnecessary to discuss these temperaments in detail, crucial to the purpose of the present chapter is the acknowledgement that each temperament has particular natural tendencies, and that these particular tendencies require different ways to model, control and guide emotions for the cultivation of character. As Cohen rightly describes,

> [a] melancholic who develops his sympathetic feelings, or a choleric who learns to control his emotions, is not a morally improved agent; his moral character is not better than if he had not cultivated these capacities. Rather, first, he is a more efficient moral agent in the sense that he will be better armed to carry out his purposes; and second, one could say that this agent will be more confident (though never certain) that he is as committed as possible to the realization of duty; or at least that he will be more warranted in feeling confident than agents who do not cultivate these capacities. (Cohen 2017, p. 176)

Consequently, the cultivation of duty will demand different education and care depending on one's temperament. In our current vocabulary, this might be best described as a distinction between character and personality in that the

> cultivation of a noble character may, for example, be conducted in many different person-
> alities, and different personalities will experience different emotions and different meta-
> emotions to cultivate virtues such that they can choose to act virtuously in experience.
> (Mendonça 2018, p. 49)

The mediate control described above reinforces the importance of freedom and its mystery, and consequently implies that while people's actions are inevitably affected by their feelings, emotions and sentiments, they are also free to either choose to act on them or not. This suggests that, though emotional elements are part of the conditions of choice, they do not fully determine decisions, and although people may not fully understand the emotional component, their actions remain free regardless of the impact of the emotions. As Cohen describes, "when I act, I can be affected by my affective states whilst being ultimately free to choose against them. Insofar as I have to assume that these elements affect me but do not determine my choice, I have to presuppose that I could always have acted otherwise, despite the fact that it is necessarily incomprehensible to me" (Cohen 2017, p. 179). It is important to recognize that mediate control does not necessarily mean full awareness of all the intricacies of the process of decision making. While Kant stresses that the fact that emotions are part of the conditions for action does not eliminate the possibility of freedom, he also suggests that certain feelings may help promote moral actions. Feelings such as the feeling of respect, sympathy, and love all spur action towards the moral order. Deimling points out how Kant "stresses that there are certain feelings that typically aid our efforts to act morally: the feeling of respect, a feeling aris-ing directly from our exercise of practical reason, and other feelings that can be put in the service of practical reason, such as sympathy, love and self-respect" (Deimling 2014, p. 120), and thus that the very same emotional realm that can threaten rational choice can also enable it. In this way, the ability to "cultivate the feeling of respect by turning our attention to the moral law and to our ability to act in accordance with it" (Deimling 2014, p. 120) is a part of the emotional structure that aids morality.

In addition, the description of mediated control also suggests a new regard for the way that different temperaments or personalities can cultivate the sense of duty to improve moral character. Namely, it is possible to conceive of the rest-ing state identified by Northoff as having a Kantian aspect in the way that it plays an important role in calibrating mediated control. That is, rather than ask-ing, as Northoff does, "[h]ow does the intrinsic resting state activity of the brain interact with the extrinsic stimuli from the outside world?" (Northoff 2012a, p. 356); it is possible to ask a different question: "How do emotions impact the intrinsic resting state activity of the brain and what further consequences might this have for the interaction with extrinsic stimuli from the outside world?"

3 A Novel Kantian Hypothesis: Resting as Calibration for Emotional Mediate Control

The deeper understanding of the role of emotions in Kant's work of recent decades, in combination with the way that Kant's perspective on the mind enables further developments in neuroscience and cognitive science in general, provides the opportunity to offer a new conception of emotional regulation, in which the resting state plays a significant role in emotional experience. We suggest that, in the resting state, emotions are further evaluated by meta-emotional processes, while the brain simultaneously introduces extra information from external stimuli and integrates its central features. Thus, the resting state may be one of the moments in which emotions are integrated into the overall predictive structure of the brain, and in this way may be a crucial moment for integration of extrinsic stimuli from the outside world within the processes of the mind.

The Kantian view implies both a recognition of the role of the body and an understanding that to act freely means to act in a situated manner. As Cohen describes:

> In other words, for Kant, from the practical standpoint, the exercise of our rational and moral capacities is experienced 'as empirically embodied' (i.e., as taking place together with the experience of nature's push) rather than happening in some timeless inaccessible world. Since we must see ourselves as empirical beings who act freely, our emotional capacities can be morally relevant without threatening either our autonomy or our capacity for agency. (Cohen 2017, p. 180)

This means that mediate control implies strategies for influencing the emotional state, such that a person can enable themselves to modify how their affects, emotions, inclinations and passions may impact them, and in this way shape the emotional reaction to promote moral actions. This, in turn, implies that "natural emotions can be cultivated, and it is suggested that there is a measure of responsibility in their cultivation" (Sherman 2014, p. 18).

Importantly, it is not merely the expression of an emotional state that is at stake, but the role of the environment in constituting the emotional experience. This is because the body is in direct contact with the environment, and consequently, what happens in the body represents, to some degree, what is happening in the agent's environment. In this way, the environment has a direct impact on the constitution of emotions, such that "emotional feelings should be constituted directly by the respective person's relation to the environment rather than indirectly via bodily representations" (Northoff 2008, p. 502). Consequently, the changes that may occur in the body depend on the impact of the affective states, and more specifically, on the particular situation and context within which the agent is situated. Ultimately, there will be a wide variety of degrees of emotional experience, ranging from an intense experience of fear to an almost imperceptible anxiety, and the "different kinds of affective states in Kant's taxonomy are associated with more or less dramatic bodily responses. An affect, for example, will be typically associated with a more dramatic response than a feeling simpliciter" (Deimling 2014, p. 113). Moreover, incorporating these experiences and affects does not need to occur in the precise moment of action, nor in a state of vigilance, but rather can happen in the resting state, if it is conceived of dynamically in congruence with the Kantian view of the mind. The connection described above suggests that, similar to the way that various instruments require calibration, it may also be the case that the brain requires a similar process to enable it to incorporate relevant information experienced in the vigilant state within its neural structure, so as to attune the dynamic interconnectedness that enables the improvement of predictive processes.

Exploring the metaphor of calibration more deeply may help to better understand the role of the brain's resting state and the potentially decisive role that variation in the experience may play. Calibration defines the way tools record measurements, and consequently controls for mistakes and uncertainties in the mechanism's functioning in a way that is acceptable and, ideally, optimized. It is a process of adjustment designed to meet certain standards, and it can be especially necessary when certain changes to the instruments occur. For instance, it is advised to calibrate a scanner when pairing it with a new printer to better coordinate its output. Calibration is also needed whenever an instrument has been exposed to a shock or physical damage that compromises its functioning, or when observations provided by a specific tool appear to be less accurate when compared to previously set parameters. Consequently, calibration may be required to maintain confidence in the reliability, accuracy and repeatability of measurements provided by instruments and tools in general. We suggest that the brain is an organ that requires a similar type of procedure, and that the resting state provides such an opportunity for calibration.

4 Concluding Remarks

So far, this chapter has focused mainly on indicating the rationality of suggesting the need for emotional regulation in ethics as a form of mediate control. However, this reflection affords the possibility that this regulation can be similarly achieved by the way that emotions play out in aesthetic contexts, because of the pertinent links between aesthetic experiences and resting state. This provides a way to connect Kantian scholarship of aesthetics and ethics, and show that the link to recent cognitive science and neurophilosophy can be extended further. In addition, the connection of mediate control and regulation of emotions is in line with research that shows that sleep has been shown to influence emotional reactivity, recognition, and expression, and "also play an influential role in modulating conditioned fear" (Goldstein and Walker 2014). Importantly, it provides the opportunity for future research possibilities by suggesting that if the resting state calibrates the structure of the mind to process external stimuli, then it is unsurprising that sleep, and dreaming, are fundamental for the healthy functioning of the brain. Of course, it may also be the case that resting without sleeping, or mere isolation and inactivity, may provide the same opportunity for calibration that we propose occurs in the resting and sleeping state. Only further research and empirical testing can fully develop the connections that arise when scholars take up Kant in light of recent developments in cognitive science.

Bibliography

Baron, Marcia (1985): 'The Ethics of Duty/Ethics of Virtue Debate and Its Relevance to Educational Theory". In: *Educational Theory* 35, pp. 135–49.

Borges, Maria (2004): "What Can Kant Teach Us about Emotions?" In: *The Journal of Philosophy* 101. No. 3, pp. 140–158.

Brook, Andrew (2007): "Kant and Cognitive Science". In: Andrew Brook (Ed.): *The Prehistory of Cognitive Science*. New York: Palgrave, pp. 117–136.

Clark, Andy (2013): "Whatever Next? Predictive Brains, Situated Agents and the Future of Cognitive Science". In: *Behavioral and Brain Sciences* 36, pp. 181–204. DOI: 10.1017/S0140525X12000477, accessed on 16 March, 2021.

Clark, Andy (2015a): *Surfing Uncertainty: Prediction, Action and the Embodied Mind*. New York: Oxford University Press.

Clark, Andy (2015b): "Perception as Prediction". In: Dustin Stokes, Mohan Matthen and Stephen Biggs (Eds.): *Perception and Its Modalities*. New York: Oxford University Press, pp. 23–43.

Clark, Andy (2015c): "Radical Predictive Processing". In: *Southern Journal of Philosophy* 53. No. 1, pp. 3–27.

Cohen, Alix (Ed.) (2014): *Kant on Emotion and Value*. New York: Palgrave Macmillan.

Cohen, Alix (Ed.) (2017): "Kant on the Moral Cultivation of Feelings". In: Alix Cohen and Robert Stern (Eds.): *Thinking About the Emotions: A Philosophical History*. Oxford: Oxford University Press, pp. 172–183.

Deimling, Wiebke (2014): "Kant's Pragmatic Concept of Emotions". In: Alix Cohen (Ed.): *Kant on Emotion and Value*. Hampshire: Palgrave McMillan, pp. 108–125.

Dennett, Daniel C. (2013): "Expecting Ourselves to Expect: the Bayesian Brain as a Projector". In: *Behavioral and Brain Sciences* 36, pp. 209–210.

Dixon, Thomas (2003): *From Passions to Emotions. The Creation of a Secular Psychological Category*. Cambridge: Cambridge University Press.

Fazelpour, Sina, and Thompson, Evan (2015): "The Kantian Brain: Brain Dynamics From a Neurophenomenological Perspective". In: *Current Opinion in Neurobiology* 31, pp. 223–229.

Flores, Krivo (2015): "Hume in the Light of Bayes: Towards a Unified Cognitive Science of Human Nature". In: *Res Cogitans* 6, pp. 2–13.

Gadziejewski, Pawel (2016): "Predictive Coding and Representationalism". In: *Synthese* 193, pp. 559–582

Goldstein, Andrea and Walker, Matthew (2014): "The Role of Sleep in Emotional Brain Function". In: *Annual Review Clinical Psych*ology 10, pp. 679–708.

Greenspan, Patricia (1995): *Practical Guilt: Moral Dilemmas, Emotions, and Social Norms*. New York: Oxford University Press.

Guyer, Paul (1993): *Kant and the Experience of Freedom: Essays in Aesthetics and Morality*. Cambridge: Cambridge University Press.

Guyer, Paul (2000): *Kant on Freedom, Law, and Happiness*. Cambridge: Cambridge University Press.

Herman, Barbara (1993): *The Practice of Moral Judgment*. Cambridge: Harvard University Press.

Hohwy, Jakob (2012): "Attention and Conscious Perception in the Hypothesis Testing Brain". In: *Frontiers in Psychology* 3:96. DOI: 10.3389/fpsyg.2012.00096, accessed 30 April, 2021.

Kant, Immanuel ([1783] 2004): *Prolegomena to Any Future Metaphysics: That Will Be Able to Come Forward as Science*. Gary Hatfield (Ed.). Cambridge: Cambridge University Press.

Kant, Immanuel ([1992] 2016): *The Cambridge Edition of the Works of Immanuel Kant*. Paul Guyer and Allen W. Wood (Eds.). Cambridge: Cambridge University Press.

Kitcher, Patricia (1996): *Introduction to Critique of Pure Reason, Pluhar Translation*. Indianapolis: Hackett Publishing Company, Inc.

Mendonça, Dina (2018): "Situations, Emotions and Character Within a Situated Approach to Emotions". In: Sara Graça da Silva (Ed.): *New Interdisciplinary Landscapes in Morality and Emotion*. New York: Routledge, pp. 41–51.

Northoff, Georg (2008): "Are Our Emotional Feelings Relational? A Neurophilosophical Investigation of the James–Lange Theory". In: *Phenomenology and the Cognitive Sciences* 7, pp. 501–527.

Northoff, Georg (2012a): "Immanuel Kant's Mind and the Brain's Resting State". In: *Trends in Cognitive Science* (July) 16. No. 7, pp. 356–359.

Northoff, Georg (2012b): "From Emotions to Consciousness – A Neuro-phenomenal and Neuro-relational Approach". *Frontiers in Psychology* (August) 3. DOI: 10.3389/fpsyg.2012.00303, accessed on 16 March, 2021.

Sherman, Nancy (1997): *Making a Necessity of Virtue: Aristotle and Kant on Virtue.* Cambridge: Cambridge University Press.

Sherman, Nancy (2014): "The Place of Emotions in Kantian Morality". In: Alix Cohen (Ed.): *Kant on Emotion and Value.* Hampshire: Palgrave McMillan, pp. 11–32.

Sorensen, Kelly (2002): "Kant's Taxonomy of the Emotions". In: *Kantian Review* 6, pp. 109–128.

Swanson, Link Ray (2016): "The Predictive Processing Paradigm Has Roots in Kant". In: *Frontiers in Systems Neuroscience* (October). DOI: 10.3389/fnsys.2016.00079, accessed on 30 April, 2021.

Wood, Allen (1999): *Kant's Ethical Thought.* Cambridge: Cambridge University Press.

Josefa Ros Velasco
Kantian *Lange Weile* Within the Contemporary Psychology of Boredom

Abstract: The phenomenon of boredom is the subject of much current research. Its analysis, however, is no longer solely the purview of the philosophers, writers, and theologians of past centuries, but of scientists. Currently, specialists responsible for investigating the eternal question of boredom are often contemporary psychologists and psychiatrists, cognitive neuroscientists, and experts in fMRI technologies. How does the Kantian anthropology of boredom fit into this new research panorama? In this chapter, I introduce both the study of boredom within the contemporary psychological and psychiatric mainstream, as well as within the Kantian anthropology of boredom, to show that Kantian statements support, on the one hand, the view of boredom understood as a mental pathology and, on the other, the association of boredom with the socio-economic structures of modernity.

Keywords: anthropology, boredom, cognitive neuroscience, culture, fMRI, psychology, psychiatry, suicide

1 Again, Boredom

The phenomenon of boredom is, today, omnipresent. But while everyone loves to discuss boredom, nobody enjoys experiencing it. Furthermore, while the questions surrounding boredom seem to grow by the day, answers seem increasingly more difficult to come by. Of course, the issue of boredom is not new but, in fact, ancient, much more so than we dare to admit. Previous approaches to boredom, however, are often forgotten, or outright disregarded by contemporary researchers. One such forgotten theory is that of the German philosopher Immanuel Kant, whom I will attempt to rescue from oblivion in this chapter. What is the Kantian

Acknowledgement: This work was funded by the Real Colegio Complutense at Harvard program of Postdoctoral Fellowships and the Department of Romance Languages and Literatures at Harvard University. I want to thank the editors of this book, especially to Prof. Dr. Nuria Sánchez Madrid.

Josefa Ros Velasco, Harvard University/Complutense University of Madrid, Spain

https://doi.org/10.1515/9783110720730-013

approach to boredom's place within the contemporary framework of the study of boredom?

While many people are currently studying boredom—the number of titles on boredom published each year is staggering—(Ros Velasco 2017a), almost none of this research discusses the philosophical literature on boredom, not even that of a thinker as renowned as Kant. Moreover, there are no works focusing on Kantian philosophy of boredom, at least in the English and Spanish languages, and only two articles in German address the matter (Große 2008; Barbarić 2001).

I began working on the Kantian philosophy of boredom some years ago—the truth is, only eight years ago. When your career as a researcher has just begun, however, and there is so much new knowledge filling your mind, time itself seems longer—something Kant knew very well, as I will explain later. Looking back, I realize that back then I hardly understood the Kantian approach, and disseminated my mistaken interpretation without noticing.

My first contact with this aspect of his philosophy took place in 2012, when I was invited to contribute to the *I Congreso de la Sociedad de Estudios Kantianos en Lengua Española* [*I Meeting of the Kantian Studies Society in Spanish Language*]. Reviewing what I wrote for that conference, I think that, while my reading was quite immature, I did not wholly misunderstand Kantian points. It was during my second approach to the Kantian philosophy of boredom, in the second SEKLE meeting (2014), that I accidentally confused the words of Kant and those of the German philosopher Hans Blumenberg taken from his posthumous book *Beschreibung des Menschen* [*Description of Man*] (2006). At the time, I was writing my Ph.D. dissertation on Blumenberg's thoughts on boredom (Ros Velasco 2017b), and I was absorbed by his work. Thus, I was correct in many points concerning the Kantian approach to boredom, but wrong on the most important one: it was Blumenberg, and not Kant, who wrote, in *Description of Man*, that boredom was a pain that motivated men to continuous action—that is to say, that boredom was a "positive pain", in Kantian terms. However, this was not Kant's view—at least he never said as much in his *Anthropology*. On the contrary—as we will see in this chapter—boredom was the result of an inability to feel "positive pain", according to Kant. To make matters worse, I hadn't realized this misunderstanding until just today, while reviewing Kant's *Anthropology* in preparation for writing my contribution to this volume on Kant and emotions.

Because of my misunderstanding, I was planning to write this chapter on how Kant offered an ideal critique of the contemporary understanding of boredom as a mental disorder, due to the fact that he had stated that boredom was a driving force motivating human beings to action—that boredom was a "positive pain". Again, this is Blumenberg's point (Ros Velasco 2017b; 2019), which I mistakenly thought was inherited from Kant. Nothing could be more untrue—I now see that the Kantian approach to boredom, indeed, contributed to the current understanding of boredom as a pathology. This, however, does not exactly support the idea that boredom is a disorder as such—at least on the basis of the assumptions of the mental health field—since Kant considered that the roots of boredom were not neurological but cultural. This, then, is my second attempt to contribute to a proper understanding of the Kantian philosophy of boredom.

In keeping with the discussion above, in this chapter I will introduce the framework of the study of boredom within the contemporary psychological and psychiatric mainstream. I will also analyze the Kantian anthropology of boredom—amending my previous misunderstandings—to show that Kantian statements support, on the one hand, the present understanding of boredom as a sort of pathology and, on the other hand, that rather than attributing such a disorder to neurological conditions, Kant considered boredom a consequence of the socio-economic structures of modernity. As a conclusion, I will explain why contemporary researchers must continue to utilize the work of thinkers and philosophers like Kant to improve their understanding of boredom and avoid reductionism on this critical issue. For now, though, let me briefly put Kant aside.

2 Neuroscience and Boredom

The phenomenon of boredom was commonly addressed as a socio-cultural condition by philosophers, theologians, and sociologists of the past. Almost nothing on boredom as a medical condition, however, was published for many years, apart from those studies in which boredom was combined with another well-known affect, melancholy, during the Renaissance and the early modern times and, going back further still, studies that posited a link between boredom and depression (Ros Velasco 2017b). From the eighteenth century to the twentieth, what proliferated most were the literary works of those who, in the act of writing, found the remedy against the boredom they often called ennui, spleen, and even disease—metaphorically speaking. However, by the end of the nineteenth century, boredom became a matter of serious discussion among mental health professionals, who started carrying out their investigations by the hundreds.

Perhaps one of the first works on boredom from disciplines such as psychology and psychiatry was *De l'ennui, taedium vitae* (1850), by physician Brière de Boismont. Soon after, the first industrial psychological tests of efficiency in the workplace took place, conducted by the psychologist Hugo Münsterberg (1913). Little by little, investigators started to focus on the affective and cognitive components of boredom. One of the leading representatives of this movement was Émile Tardieu, who published *L'ennui: Étude Psychologique* [*Boredom: A Psychological Study*] (1913), in which he described boredom as psychological pain. Over the same period, Theodor Lipps suggested one of the first psychodynamic definitions of boredom in his work *Leitfaden der Psychologie* [*Guide of Psychology*] (1909). Lipps went a step further and stated that boredom was a psychological pain caused by a conflict between the individual need for mental activity and the lack thereof it, or the individual inability to stimulate oneself.

This was a turning point in the understanding of boredom: One can experience a lack of stimulation not as a result of a tedious circumstance, but because of some mental or personality-related pathology. Moreover, Lipps introduced, in a pioneering move, the idea that boredom may be connected to a lack of attention. Some years later, the psychoanalyst Otto Fenichel lent continuity to these ideas in his essay "On the psychology of boredom" (1953). According to him, boredom was experienced because of a contrast between an individuals' mental engagement and their simultaneous inhibition.

During the first half of the twentieth century, these approaches to boredom as a psychopathological personality-related phenomenon culminated in self-help books aimed at orientating bored people towards releases for their need for mental activity and ways to correct their inability for self-stimulation. Nevertheless, because of the limitations of this approach, some psychiatrists opted to examine the brain. The psychiatrist Joseph Barmack, for example, started experimenting to see the effect of environmental conditions and temperature on a bored subject. He also began supplying benzedrine sulfate and ephedrine hydrochloride to the workers suffering from boredom (1938; 1939). In extreme cases, specialists like Edmund Bergler went so far as to say that boredom was a psychotic disorder with significant neurotic implications, whose cure required genetic intervention, as seen in his paper "On the disease-entity boredom ("alyosis") and its psychopathology" (1945).

From the second half of the twentieth century to its end, the interest of mental health professionals in the phenomenon of boredom blossomed. Thus, by 1996, the understanding of boredom as a psychopathological personality trait was so extended that the concept of boredom was granted a place in Campbell's *Dictionary of Psychiatry*. Nowadays, boredom is simply another encyclopedia entry in volumes of psychology and applied psychology (often found near the sections on depression and ADHD) and is of established relevance for neurologists and specialists in fMRI technologies.

At present, these specialists are the principal researchers studying boredom. Neurologists have inherited the earlier psychodynamic approaches to boredom, and thus continue to understand boredom as a symptom of the inability of an individual to find stimuli in the environment—a phenomenon which has been termed 'endogenous boredom'. Some neurological disorders connected with boredom are now regarded as well-established, including the pathology of chronic boredom (Eastwood et al. 2012; Van Tilburg and Igou 2011a, b; Martin et al. 2006).

In normal circumstances, following the psychodynamic explanation and the flow theory of Csíkszentmihályi in *Beyond Boredom and Anxiety* (1975), people suffer from boredom when environmental stimuli are either repetitive and monotonous (substimulation), or excessive (overstimulation), and thus do not meet their psychic needs. What follows, then, is a lack of mutual adaptation that makes the subject react to the environment. London et al.'s (1972) experiments and Berlyne's (1960) research have demonstrated, by measuring individual physiological changes, that when people are bored, their level of cortical excitement decreases, and the Reticular Activating System (RAS) releases to promote an autonomic activation that pushes the bored subject to look for something capable of normalizing the cortical excitement levels. That is to say, when the pattern of external stimulation is insubstantial and boredom appears, internal excitement increases to compensate for the environment's deficiency, resulting in the subject seeking different actions or stimuli.

In some instances of pathological boredom, however, we can observe individuals in which such an autonomic activation does not take place. In other words, their RAS does not act as expected and, consequently, the subject does not turn to the exploration of novel stimuli to deal with boredom. This kind of boredom arises, rather, from the brain of the subject, just as any other mental pathology or disorder, going so far as to become a real—not metaphorical—chronic disease with severe psychosocial consequences (Eastwood et al. 2012).

Such a paralysis is, at the same time, correlated with other pathologies, such as the inability to clarify one's own desires, the distorted perception of time, the excess or lack of self-awareness, attention deficit disorder, depression and anxiety, or many of them simultaneously (Eastwood et al. 2012; Van Tilburg and Igou 2011a, b; Martin et al. 2006; Sommers and Vodanovich 2000; Vodanovich and Watt 1999; Seib and Vodanovich 1998).

In this sense, specialists hold that if pathological boredom, and its associated disorders, are not intervened but, on the contrary, are experienced for prolonged amounts of time, this can lead to a number of deviant behaviors. Boredom has been suggested as contributing to depression, anxiety, hostile and aggressive behavior, sleep disorders, drugs, sex and gambling addictions, reckless driving, states of despair and loneliness, criminal actions, deviant behavior in school, suicidal tendencies, low self-esteem, lack of social affiliation, and eating disorders, among many other problems (see Vodanovich and Watt 1999; Martin et al. 2006; Van Tilburg and Igou 2011a, b). For this reason, the study of bore-dom is consistently motivated by the need to learn more about the phenomenon so as to predict harmful or deviant behavior—what matters to researchers on boredom are its negative consequences.

This is also the reason behind the increase in research on boredom—the need for more precise diagnoses and the search for essential treatments. A large part of the extant literature on boredom is devoted to this purpose. Special-ists in psychoanalysis and existential philosophy have learned to manage bore-dom and teach others how to cope with its symptoms (Goffman 1959). Some oth-ers explore the effects of dopamine (Branković 2015) and suggest the methylxanthines—a group of agents present in caffeine, theophylline, and theo-bromine—as a drug capable of reversing decreases in performance as a result of boredom and fatigue (Bennet and Morris 2007; Hancock and Mckim, 2013). The current era, more than any other, is witnessing a proliferation of many antidotes to the evil of boredom, whether through the implementation of confrontation or avoidance strategies (Nett et al. 2010).

In sum, we can confidently state that, since the beginning of the last century, the study of boredom has been mainly carried out from within the mental health field and specifically by specialists in neurology (Ros Velasco 2017a, b; 2018). It is this research background, then, which has spread the idea that boredom is a matter of individual conditions, appearing inside the subject as a mental health issue and involving serious psychosocial consequences (Bergler 1945; Eastwood et al. 2012). Recently, boredom has become a matter of special scientific and clin-ical interest, and has been analyzed in the context of its neurological and cogni-tive conditions (Danckert and Allman 2005; Eastwood et al. 2012). Currently, through the use of fMRI technologies, researchers continue to investigate the neurological basis of boredom (Danckert 2018; Danckert and Merrifield 2018).

3 Kantian Philosophy—Anthropology of Boredom

Many authors also claim that boredom is a modern phenomenon, resulting from the various social, cultural, and economic changes that have taken place since the late Middle Ages—secularization, capitalism, rationalization, and alphabeti-zation, as well as changes in entertainment and social protocols, to name a few. While I do not hold this view (although I do agree that boredom is, almost al-ways, a consequence of a particular cultural environment rather than an individ-ual problem), Kant certainly does.

As mentioned earlier, Kant wrote explicitly on boredom in his work *Anthro-pologie in pragmatischer Hinsicht* (Anth 07: 117–332) [*Anthropology from a Prag-*

matic Point of View] (Kant 2007, pp. 227– 429). Following Foucault's study—*Gén-èse et structure de la Anthropologie de Kant* [*Introduction to Kant's* Anthropology] (2008)—it is also possible to find Kantian remarks on boredom in *die drei Kritik-en* (KrV 3: 1– 552; KpV 5: 1– 163; KU 5: 165– 485) as well as in a manuscript by Christoph Mrongovius, dated in 1785 (V-Anth/Mron 25/2: 1205– 1429). This is be-cause Kant's anthropology was taught for 25 years as part of his lectures during the winter semester, beginning in 1772 to 1773. Kant was working on his *Anthro-pology* for almost three decades, and this work was published just as he decided on leaving the teaching profession—for this reason, some of the content of his *Anthropology* overlaps with other works. His brief discourse on boredom, howev-er, is only located in his *Anthropologie in pragmatischer Hinsicht*; more specifical-ly in the first part, entitled "Anthropologische Didaktik" ["Anthropological Di-dactic"] (Anth 7: 125– 229 [Kant 2007, pp. 238– 382]), second book "Das Gefühl der Lust und Unlust" ["The Feeling of Pleasure and Displeasure"] (Kant 2007, pp. 230– 250 [333– 352]), section "Von der langen Weile und dem Kurzweil" ["On Boredom and Amusement"] (Kant 2007, pp. 233– 239, §§ 61– 66, pp. 336– 341). I will focus on this section of the Kantian anthropological and philosoph-ical corpus—while also examining §60 on gratification [*Vergnügen*].

Kant approaches boredom as part of his study of the sensuous displeasures [*sinnliche Unlust*] that human beings suffer as a result of either sensation [*Sinn*] or imagination [*Einbildungskraft*]. Sensuous displeasures result in pain. It is pre-cisely such pain, however, that motivates people to change, moving their lives forward in order to abandon the painful situation to find—in this forward move-ment—sensuous pleasure and gratification: "What directly (through sense) urges me to *leave* my state (to go out of it) is *disagreeable* to me—it causes me pain" (Anth 7: 231. 1–3 [Kant 2007, p. 334]). In this sense, Kant states that pain "*must always precede every enjoyment*; pain is always first" (Anth 7: 231. 25– 26 [Kant 2007, p. 334]). According to Kant, people are willing to do anything to rid themselves of their displeasure, even if they do not know what will come in its absence. This sequence of cause and effect, displeasure and pleasure, pain and gratification, is what rules our lives: "the antagonism of both" (Anth 7: 231. 24 [Kant 2007, p. 334]). That is to say, there is always pain between gratifica-tion, because pain is the incentive to activity and it is in activity that we feel we are alive: "without pain lifelessness would set in" (Anth 7: 231. 37 [Kant 2007, p. 334]). In Kant's view, we must consider such a pain a 'positive pain' ['positiver Schmerz'], a 'bitter joy' ['bitteren Freude'], a sort of 'sweet sorrow' ['süsser Schmerz'].

Inertia occurs when people find themselves in "a continuous promotion of the vital force, which cannot be raised above a certain degree anyway" (Anth 7: 231. 26– 28 [Kant 2007, p. 334])—the one who has everything and has experienced all manner of luxuries and comforts cannot find any gratification to come. Kant also calls this sensation "quick death" (Anth 7: 231. 28 [Kant 2007, p. 334]), "*void* of sensation" (Anth 7: 233. 1 [Kant 2007, p. 335]), *horror vacui* (Anth 7: 233. 18 – 19 [Kant 2007, p. 337]): "To be (absolutely) contented in life would be idle rest and the standstill of all incentives, or the dulling of sensations and the activity connected with them" (Anth 7: 235. 8 – 10 [Kant 2007, p. 338]). This is boredom, *lange Weile* (Anth 7: 233. 1 [Kant 2007, p. 335]), a negative pain:

> Even if no positive pain stimulates us to activity, if necessary a negative one, *boredom*, will often affect us [...]. For boredom is perceived as a *void* of sensation by the human being who is used to an alternation of sensations in himself. (Anth 7: 232 – 233. 35 – 2 [Kant 2007, p. 335])

Boredom, "negative pain", is the result of a specific social, cultural, and economic environment—that of the Enlightenment—in which people are unable to find gratification anywhere. The enlightened "has tried every form of enjoyment, and no enjoyment is new to him any longer" (Anth 7: 233. 15 – 16 [Kant 2007, p. 337]). The sequence of positive pain and gratification is broken, precisely because of human beings' need to pass beyond the present state so as to achieve a better one, and in this way, to feel one's life. In such a case, the only thing remaining is negative pain: boredom.

Boredom makes us feel dread and self-disgust at our own existence, given that a boring life is the signal of an empty life, and one that feels as if it is missing something. Kant highlights the fact that lost time makes us feel our life passes very fast: our time is empty of experiences, even though we experience it as quite long as a result of our boredom. On the contrary, having a pleasant experience involves going through it in detail and stopping at critical moments. While we tend to think intuitively that when we are bored, time passes very slowly (in contrast with when we are feeling entertained), memories of boredom are in fact much more quickly remembered, and yet seem to be shorter because of their insubstantiality. This is precisely the reason why I mentioned that, from my current vantage point, my last eight years feel like such a long time—they were full of work.

Those who fall prey to boredom are willing to "do something harmful to [themselves] rather than nothing at all" (Anth 7: 233. 4 – 5 [Kant 2007, p. 335]). Kant even talks about suicide in the case that people struggle to shake off their boredom unsuccessfully. For Kant, people cannot allow boredom to prevail over intellectual life because, after inactivity, only death follows. In this sense—and since we cannot count on a permanent state of well-being which would be antithetical to our nature—our only option is to fill our time as much as possible through work (Anth 7: 232. 24–28 [Kant 2007, p. 335]):

> Why is work the best way of enjoying one's life? Because it is an arduous occupation (disagreeable in itself and pleasing only through success), and also because rest becomes a tangible pleasure, joy, through the mere disappearance of the toil of work. Without work, rest would be unenjoyable.

To summarize, Kant encourages us to keep working so as to maintain a positive pain towards gratification, and as a way to avoid falling prey to continuous boredom that is characteristic of a society in which we can easily have all kinds of luxuries. In the absence of work, boredom will maintain its grip on our lives until death. While this may sound morose, my misunderstanding of Kant's thesis was actually quite gratifying. It consisted basically of Blumenberg's claim that boredom is, in fact, something like the ultimate positive pain, perhaps the most important emotion, capable of awakening people from their lethargy. In this way, boredom would have been the driving force in our sequence of cause and effect, and even selected for in the course of evolution, because of its usefulness in avoiding inertia. While I may be wrong again, this time I have not seen such a notion in Kant's anthropology or philosophy of boredom, but rather have observed more of a resemblance with Schopenhauer's thesis on boredom in his work *Die Welt als Wille und Vorstellung* [*The World as Will and Representation*] (2016)—Große's chapter (2008) makes sense here.

Instead of using Kant's words to claim, against those who want to *cure* boredom, that we should accept boredom because it is not only inherent but also beneficial to our very evolution (as Blumenberg says), I now see Kant as one of the predecessors of the current understanding of boredom as a deviation or disease. As part of my current research on boredom, I am conducting a multidisciplinary investigation on the evolution of the understanding of boredom as a mental pathology by reviewing different narratives from history. Among those considered responsible for contributing to such an understanding are those who link boredom to depression and to deviant behaviors like suicide. In all likelihood, Kant is not far off this path. However, Kant would disagree with contemporary specialists on boredom in that he would place the burden of suffering from boredom on the environment rather than on the individual. As I will later discuss, this is something psychologists, psychiatrists, and neurologists should take into account so as not to over-diagnose boredom-related diseases. They should pay attention primarily to the role of our society, culture, institutions, and structures in the development of boredom, and, for this, they should turn their attention to Kant.

4 Kant, Again

Now that not only mental health disciplines, but also specialists, have raised boredom to the status of a disorder, we should begin discussing boredom using a clinical approach. This is a tall order. Mental health professionals are not simple phenomenologists: their studies encompass not only theory but also therapy. There are substantial limitations to diagnosing and treating boredom at present, as almost nothing is known about its cognitive and neural implications. Many researchers are attempting to locate the neurological basis of boredom and are tentatively suggesting that the insula plays a vital role (Weissman et al. 2006; Danckert and Merrifield 2018). However, at present, boredom's neurological effects, its treatment through the use of drugs, and their potential side effects, remain almost unknown.

It is not surprising that bringing boredom into the clinical realm arouses special concern and criticism. Many authors, including Blumenberg, point out that the *Diagnostic and Statistical Manual of Mental Disorders* (DSM) promotes a medicalization of life by expanding the number of pathologies and transforming everyday moods into diseases. Allen Frances (2014) himself, the editor of the fifth edition of the DSM, denounces mental health professionals unable to look beyond their narrow specialties, who turn daily annoyances into diseases by overstating the importance of their fieldwork, while also admitting that there is a lack of agreement on what boredom actually is, not to mention its cognitive implications and neurological bases. (Danckert and Allman 2005; Eastwood et al. 2012; Merrifield 2014)

If one thing is clear nowadays, it is that we know almost nothing about boredom, which makes it easier to make a mistake in the clinical setting, while also prompting criticism from those who do not trust the mental health approach to boredom. Undoubtedly, more research is needed in this regard. The mental health researchers themselves are consistent in decrying the paucity of the existing literature on boredom and a perceived lack of interest among scholars. Experts point out both problems as the reasons behind the lack of understanding of boredom. Throughout my research on boredom, I have consistently seen several academic papers on this topic allude to a shortage of literature and that decry the dearth of research interest as responsible for the lack of understanding of the subject. As a result, researchers agree that the study of boredom is in its infancy and has not been paid the attention it deserves (Ros Velasco 2017a). For this reason, the scientific study of boredom seems to remain a relatively obscure niche, and boredom itself is still poorly understood, as John Eastwood et al. (2012) state.

As I have previously demonstrated (2017a), the emotion of boredom has aroused the interest of researchers for centuries, since the very beginning of our history. However, against all odds, mental health specialists working on boredom continue to complain about the scarcity of knowledge on the subject because of a lack of literature on boredom. The reason why we cannot yet get a firm grasp on boredom is that specialists on boredom do not yet work in a multi-disciplinary fashion—that is to say, they are not taking into account the precedents, the background, or even the history of boredom, and the path along which it came to be considered a disease.

After the efforts of authors like Reinhard Kuhn (1976) or Peter Toohey (1988; 1990) to demonstrate that boredom has been part of daily life since ancient times, we must admit that we are studying an old, even ancient emotion. Boredom has been considered the punishment of humanity throughout history. The ancients understood it as a shameful emotion; in the Middle Ages, it became a sin; and in modernity it was seen as the correlate of rationalized time, pre-planned entertainment, and existential feelings of angst and bewilderment. The phenomenon of boredom was commonly addressed in the socio-cultural context by philosophers, theologists, and sociologists in the past, including Kant. However, contemporary researchers on boredom seem to neglect the history of boredom.

Thus, rather than continually expanding the knowledge on boredom already hard-won by philosophers and sociologists, the segregation of disciplines means that the study of this phenomenon starts almost from scratch. Apart from being running the risk of diagnosing and medicalizing a phantom disease, (Ros Velasco 2018), and despite its apparent limitations, this narrow way of analyzing this issue often results in the contributions of even renowned philosophers like Kant to the study of boredom being consigned to oblivion.

It is an established fact that there is a lack of transversalism. Boredom is not one of those realities that can be approached from one sole perspective or discipline. We cannot emphasize enough the role of the humanities—and particularly of philosophy—in helping resolve the puzzle of boredom. The outstanding national and international specialists in the study of boredom must begin discussing the importance of updating the paradigm of the study of boredom to combine formal and empirical science. Of course, that is my principal reason in writing this chapter: to reintroduce and grant visibility to the Kantian approach to boredom. This will inevitably take time. For now, I am happy if I was able to clarify my previous misunderstandings, and perhaps make the reader rethink the Kantian philosophy of boredom and its place within a contemporary, empirical understanding of this elusive phenomenon—especially if I managed not to bore the reader in my attempt.

Bibliography

Barbarić, Damir (2001): "Die Langeweile: ein Schlüssel zur Anthropologie Kants? [Boredom: A Key within Kantian Anthropology?]". In: Volker Gerhardt, Rolf-Peter Horstmann and Ralph Schumacher (Eds.): *Kant und die Berliner Aufklärung: Sektionen IV* [Kant and the Englightenment of Berlin], Vol. 2. Berlin, Boston: De Gruyter, pp. 323–330.

Barmack, Joseph E. (1938): "The Effect of Benzedrine Sulfate upon the Report of Boredom and Other Factors". In: *Journal of Psychology* 5, pp. 125–133.

Barmack, Joseph E. (1939): "Studies on the Psychophysiology of Boredom: Part I. The Effects of 15mgs of Benzedrine Sulfate and 5mgs of Ephedrine Hydrochloride on Blood Pressure, Report on Boredom, and Other Factors". In: *Journal of Experimental Psychology* 25, pp. 494–505.

Bennett, Peter N. and Brown, Morris J. (2007): "Drug Abuse". In: *Clinical Pharmacology*. Oxford: Elsevier Health Sciences, pp. 142–174.

Bergler, Edmund (1945): "On the Disease-entity Boredom ("alyosis") and Its Psychopathology". In: *Psychiatric Quarterly* 19. No. 1, pp. 38–51.

Berlyne, Daniel E. (1960): *Conflict, Arousal and Curiosity*. New York: McGraw-Hill.

Blumenberg, Hans (2006): *Beschreibung des Menschen* [Description of Man]. Frankfurt am Main: Suhrkamp.

Branković, Saša (2015): "Boredom, Dopamine, and the Thrill of Psychosis: Psychiatry in a New Key". In: *Psychiatria Danubina* 27. No. 2, pp. 126–137.

Brière de Boismont, Alexandre-Jacques-François (1850): *De l'ennui: taedium vitae* [On Boredom: *taedium vitae*]. Paris: L. Martinet.

Csikszentmihalyi, Mihály (1975): *Beyond Boredom and Anxiety*. San Francisco: Jossey Bass.

Danckert, James (2018): "Understanding Engagement: Mind-wandering, Boredom and Attention". In: *Experimental Brain Research* 236, pp. 2447–2449. DOI: 10.1007/s00221–017–4914–7}, accessed on 16 March, 2021.

Danckert, James and Allman, Ava-Ann (2005): "Time Flies When You're Having Fun: Temporal Estimation and the Experience of Boredom". In: *Brain and Cognition* 59. No. 3, pp. 236–245. DOI: 10.1016/j.bandc.2005.07.002}, accessed on 16 March, 2021.

Danckert, James and Merrifield, Colleen (2018): "Boredom, Sustained Attention, and the Default Mode Network". In: *Experimental Brain Research* 236, pp. 2507–2518. DOI: 10.1007/s00221–016–4617–5, accessed on 16 March, 2021.

Eastwood, John D., Frischen, Alexandra, Fenske, Mark J. and Smilek, Daniel (2012): "The Unengaged Mind: Defining Boredom in Terms of Attention". In: *Perspectives on Psychological Science* 7. No. 5, pp. 482–495. DOI: https://doi.org/10.1177/1745691612456044, accessed on 16 March, 2021.

Fenichel, Otto (1953): "On the Psychology of Boredom". In: *The Collected Papers of Otto Fenichel*, Vol. 1. New York: W. W. Norton., pp. 292–302.

Foucault, Michel (2008): *Introduction to Kant's Anthropology*. Cambridge: MIT Press.

Frances, Allen (2014): *Saving Normal: An Insider's Revolt against Out-of-Control Psychiatric Diagnosis, DSM-5, Big Pharma, and the Medicalization of Ordinary Life*. New York: Harper Collins.

Goffman, Ervin (1959): *The Presentation of Self in Everyday Life*. London: The Penguin Press.

Große, Jürgen (2008): "Anthropologie der Langeweile zwischen Kant und Schopenhauer [Anthropology of Boredom Between Kant and Schopenhauer]". In: *Philosophie der Langeweile* [Philosophy of Boredom]. Stuttgart: JB Metzler, pp. 51–86.

Hancock, Stephanie and McKim, William (2013): "Caffeine and the Methylxanthines". In: *Drugs and Behavior: An Introduction to Behavioral Pharmacology*. New Jersey: Pearson, pp. 209–246.

Kant, Immanuel (1900ff.): *Kant's Gesammelte Schriften* "Akademieausgabe", 1–22, Königlich Preußische Akademie der Wissenschaften (Ed.), 23, Deutsche Akademie der Wissenschaften zu Berlin: Akademie der Wissenschaften zu Göttingen, 24–29.

Kant, Immanuel (2007): "Anthropology from a Pragmatic Point of View". In: Günter Zöller and Robert B. Louden (Eds.): *Anthropology, History, and Education*. Cambridge: Cambridge University Press, pp. 227–429.

Kuhn, Reinhard C. (1976): *The Demon of Noontide: Ennui in Western Literature*. Princeton: Princeton University Press.

Lipps, Theodor (1909): *Leitfaden der Psychologie* [Guide of Psychology]. Leipzig: Wilhelm Engelmann.

London, Harvey, Schubert, Daniel S. P. and Daniel Washburn (1972): "Increase of Autonomic Arousal by Boredom". In: *Journal of Abnormal Psychology* 80. No. 1, pp. 29–36. DOI: http://dx.doi.org/10.1037/h0033311, accessed on 16 March, 2021.

Martin, Marion, Sadlo, Gaynor and Stew, Graham (2006): "The Phenomenon of Boredom". In: *Qualitative Research in Psychology* 3, pp. 193–211. DOI: http://dx.doi.org/10.1191/1478088706qrp066oa, accessed on 16 March, 2021.

Merrifield, Colleen (2014): "Toward a Model of Boredom: Investigating the Psychophysiological, Cognitive, and Neural Correlates of Boredom". Doctoral Dissertation. University of Waterloo, Waterloo.

Mrongovius, Christoph C. (2013): "Anthropology Mrongovius". In: Allen W. Wood and Robert B. Louden (Eds.): *Lectures on Anthropology*. Cambridge: Cambridge University Press, pp. 335–510.

Munsterberg, Hugo (1913): *Psychology and Industrial Efficiency*. Boston: Houghton-Mifflin.

Nett, Ulrike E., Goetz, Thomas and Daniels, Lia M. (2010): "What to Do When Feeling Bored? Students' Strategies for Coping With Boredom". In: *Learning and Individual Differences* 20. No. 6, pp. 626–638. DOI: https://dx.doi.org/10.1016/j.lindif.2010.09.004, accessed on 16 March, 2021.

Ros Velasco, Josefa (2017a): "Boredom: A Comprehensive Study of the State of Affairs". In: *Thémata*, 56, pp. 171–198. DOI: 10.12795/themata.2017.i56.08, accessed on 16 March, 2021.

Ros Velasco, Josefa (2017b): "El aburrimiento como presión selectiva en Hans Blumenberg" [Boredom as Selective Pressure in Hans Blumenberg]. Doctoral Dissertation. Universidad Complutense de Madrid, Madrid. https://eprints.ucm.es/46061/, accessed on 16 March, 2021.

Ros Velasco, Josefa (2018): "Boredom: humanising or dehumanising treatment". In: João G. Pereira, Jorge Gonçalves and Valeria Bizzari (Eds.): *The Neurobiology-Psychotherapy-Pharmacology: Intervention Triangle: The Need for Common Sense in 21st Century Mental Health*. Wilmington: Vernon, pp. 251–266.

Ros Velasco, Josefa (2019): "Hans Blumenberg Philosophical Anthropology of Boredom". In: Josefa Ros Velasco, Alberto Fragio and Martina Philippi (Eds.): *Metaphorologie*,

Anthropologie, Phänomenologie. Neue Forschungen zum Nachlass Hans Blumenbergs [Metaphorology, Anthropology, Phenomenology. New Research on Hans Blumenberg's Nachlass] (forthcoming). Freiburg: Karl Alber Verlag.

Schopenhauer, Arthur (2016): *The World as Will and Representation*. New York: Routledge.

Seib, Hope M. and Vodanovich, Stephen J. (1998): "Cognitive Correlates of Boredom Proneness: The Role of Private Self-consciousness and Absorption". In: *The Journal of Psychology* 132. No. 6, pp. 642–652. DOI: https://doi.org/10.1080/00223989809599295, accessed on 16 March, 2021.

Sommers, Jennifer and Vodanovich, Stephen J. (2000): "Boredom Proneness: Its Relationship to Psychological- and Physical-Health Symptoms". In: *Journal of Clinical Psychology* 56. No. 1, pp. 149–155. DOI: https://doi.org/10.1002/(SICI)1097–4679(200001)56:1<149::AID-JCLP14>3.0.CO;2-Y, accessed on 16 March, 2021.

Tardieu, Emile (1913): *L'ennui: Étude psychologique* [Boredom: A Psychological Study]. Paris: Libraire Félix Alcan.

Toohey, Peter (1988): "Some Ancient Notions of Boredom". In: *Illinois Classical Studies* 13. No. 1, pp. 151–164.

Toohey, Peter (1990): "Acedia in Late Classical Antiquity". In: *Illinois Classical Studies* 15. No. 2, pp. 339–352.

Van Tilburg, Wijnand A. P. and Igou, Eric R. (2011a): "On Boredom: Lack of Challenge and Meaning as Distinct Boredom Experiences". In: *Motivation and Emotion* 36. No. 2, pp. 181–194. DOI: https://doi.org/10.1007/s11031–011–9234–9, accessed on 16 March, 2021.

Van Tilburg, Wijnand A. P. and Igou, Eric R. (2011b): "On Boredom and Social Identity: A Programmatic Meaning-Regulation Approach". In: *Personality and Social Psychology Bulletin* 37. No. 12, pp. 1679–1691. DOI: 10.1177/0146167211418530, accessed on 16 March, 2021.

Vodanovich, Stephen J. and Watt, John D. (1999): "The Relationship Between Time Structure and Boredom Proneness: An Investigation Within Two Cultures". In: *The Journal of Social Psychology* 139. No. 2, pp. 143–152. DOI: https://doi.org/10.1080/00224549909598368, accessed on 16 March, 2021.

Weissman, Daniel H. et al. (2006): "The Neural Bases of Momentary Lapses in Attention". In: *Nature Neuroscience* 9, pp. 971–978. DOI: 10.1038/nn1727, accessed on 16 March, 2021.

Index of Names

Index of Subjects

www.ingramcontent.com/pod-product-compliance
Lightning Source LLC
Chambersburg PA
CBHW020156090426
42734CB00008B/840